THORNTON
WHO'D 'AVE THOUGHT IT?

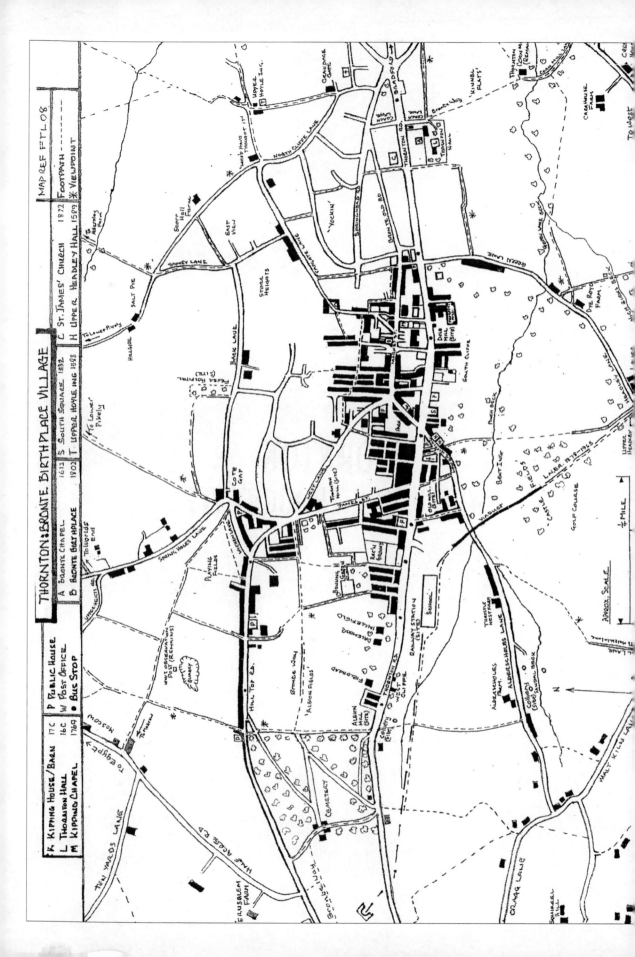

THORNTON: BRONTË BIRTHPLACE VILLAGE

MAP REF FTL08

K	KIPPING HOUSE/BARN	17C	P PUBLIC HOUSE
L	THORNTON HALL	16C	W POST OFFICE
M	KIPPING CHAPEL	1769	● BUS STOP

A	BRONTË CHAPEL	1612	S SOUTH SQUARE	1832	L ST. JAMES' CHURCH	1872	— — FOOTPATH
B	BRONTË BIRTHPLACE	1902	T UPPER HOYLE ING	1698	H UPPER HEADLEY HALL	1589	✳ VIEWPOINT

APPROX. SCALE

¼ MILE

THORNTON
WHO'D 'AVE THOUGHT IT?

THORNTON ANTIQUARIAN SOCIETY

BANK HOUSE BOOKS

First published in the United Kingdom in 2009 by

Bank House Books, PO Box 3, New Romney, TN29 9WJ UK

www.bankhousebooks.com

British Library Cataloguing in Publication Data
A catalogue record for this book is available from the British Library

ISBN 9781904408567

Typesetting and origination by Bank House Books

Printed by Lightning Source

CONTENTS

ACKNOWLEDGEMENTS

Jean K. Brown began collecting these news items ten years ago, for personal pleasure, making use of the microfilm facility at Bradford Central Library. Latterly she has selected them online. Time and patience and an interest in gossip, tragedy, nonsense and scandal have provided the stories trawled primarily from nineteenth-century newspapers.

Thornton Antiquarian Society has provided sponsorship, so that the fruits of Jean's labours can be shared with a wider audience. It is hoped that many people will enjoy these stories, while future generations will use the book as a source of reference when studying Thornton life from 1751 to 1938.

Many thanks are due to Michael Smith who provided the photographs and to Frank Leonard who drew the maps; to Alison Noble for her patience in translating our efforts (both words and pictures) on to computer; and finally Terry Miller for presiding over the book project and, with some good advice from Reuben Davison along the way, presenting it for publication.

ACKNOWLEDGMENTS

INTRODUCTION
A Short History of Thornton

Thornton was known as Torenton in the Domesday Book of the year 1068, because of the many native hawthorn trees in the area.

As late as the early nineteenth century it was still only a hamlet of twenty-three dwellings around Main Street,which became Market Street. Together with the surrounding hamlets the total population was estimated at 1500. These other hamlets, School Green, Headley, West Scholes and Close Head, eventually became part of Thornton for electoral and administrative purposes.

In about 1850 the Industrial Revolution came to Thornton in the shape of textile mills. Migrant workers, together with people already living in the area, provided the workforce. Many streets of stone terraced houses were built as offshoots of Market Street and the newly established Thornton Road. Local quarries supplied the stone and many more migrants came to build the properties. Soon Thornton had a thriving industrial scene, and shops appeared, along Market Street and Thornton Road, to supply the needs of the increased population, which by 1850 had reached approximately 5000.

Mention should be made of the most famous of Thornton's sons and daughters, the Brontë family, born in a house on Market Street in the 1810s.

The railway arrived in Thornton in the 1870s to improve transportation of both goods and people to Bradford, and west towards the Pennines and Lancashire. The impressive viaduct across the Pinch Beck valley became a significant landmark in the village.

Religious activity of many kinds provided much of the social life in Thornton, evidenced by the many chapels and churches that were built by the communities.

The two world wars took their toll of Thornton menfolk, and the cenotaph in Thornton cemetery bears witness to their sacrifice.

After the Second World War in 1945 a new industrial revolution quietly began to take place, but this time with an adverse effect on Thornton. Coal and stone, traditionally supplied by the Thornton area, were replaced by new materials and methods of heating. Other countries began making textiles at lower cost, through the use of new technology, and took away the markets previously supplied by the local mills.

Thornton is now mainly a dormitory township with a few shops and small businesses in the service industries. Most people travel outside the area to work, and shop in the big supermarkets well established in the Bradford area. Pride is still taken, however, in living in Thornton, and when the opportunity arises to enhance the area's appearance Thorntonians become involved and wholeheartedly support the efforts that are made to make the village a nice place to live in and to visit. Particular mention should be made of 'Thornton in Bloom', which has quite an impact on the neighbourhood.

Chapter One
1751–1829

Horse kills man – Brontës depart for Haworth – Kipping mansion to be let – Thornton turnpike road opens – Angel of mercy drowns

Leeds Mercury, 5 February 1751

TO BE SOLD. At the House of Jonas Robinson in Thornton, within the parish of Bradford, on Thursday the 7th day of February next, in the afternoon, A FREEHOLD ESTATE, in Thornton aforesaid, in the occupation of Caleb Ackroyd and Abraham Brooksbank, consisting of a Messuage with a Barn, Stable, and other Outhouses and Conveniences thereto belonging, in good repair; together with about 21 acres of land, Tythe free, lying contiguous to the said Messuage. Particulars whereof may be had of Thomas Vicars, of Rawden, the Owner.

Leeds Mercury, 1 October 1782

A few days ago was married, Mr. Michael Horsfall, grocer and linen draper at Thornton, to Miss Cousen, daughter of Mr. James Cousen of Bradford.

Leeds Mercury, 11 December 1787

To be LETT

And entered into at OLD CANDLEMAS *and* MAY-DAY next

A FARM, at LEVENTHORPE MILL, in Thornton, about two Miles from Bradford, consisting of a Messuage, Barn, and upwards of 60 Days Work of Land, now in the Possession of Mr. Thomas Leach.

For Further Particulars inquire of Mr. John Smith, of Wilsden, or Mr. Lister, of Manningham
The present Tenant, or Mr. William Fox, the Miller, will shew the Premises.

Leeds Mercury, 4 February 1797

Whereas there has been MISSING about Three Weeks, a Man of the following Description, viz. about Five Feet High, Sixty Years of Age, very active and nimble, ruddy Complexion, a little bald on the Top of the Head, and has lost his Teeth, which causes him to lisp in his Speech. Had on a drab coloured Cloth Coat, green Shag Waistcoat and black stuff Breeches. He left Thornton, near Bradford, the Place of his Residence, on Monday the Eighth of January last, on an Errand to Leeds, where he is supposed to have stopped all that Night, and which Place he appears to have left on the Tuesday, but has not since been heard of. Whoever will give Information so as to lead to a Discovery of the said Person, to Mrs. Rushworth at the Slip-Inn Yard, Leeds; Mr. John Blackburn, Clothier, Hunsworth-Lane near Bradford; or Mrs. Deborah Wheater, Thornton, near Bradford, shall be well rewarded for their Trouble, and have all reasonable Expences allowed them.

At Bradford parish church Richard Wheater of Manningham had married Deborah Dewhirst on 1 January 1751. They moved to Thornton where on 1 December 1774 Richard Wheater assigned his apprentice, Thomas Hudson, to John Rawnsley of Bradford by indenture. Round About Bradford by William Cudworth, written in 1876, said: 'In 1800 two principal employers were Jonathan Wright and Wheater. Gross production of each was only 4 or 5 pieces which Jonathan shouldered down to Bradford but Wheater took in front of him on horseback.' At Toad Lane, or Chapel Lane, Unitarian chapel in Bradford the registers for 1797 contain the entry: 'Richard Wheater, Thornton, was buried 4th March Æ 67. N.B. Early in the month of January he walked to Leeds for the Purpose of paying the Land Tax, of wch he had been the Collector, and fm that day (after having executed his Business) disappeared. Seven weeks & some days after, Persons employed to take Sand out of the River Aire Below the Bridge at Leeds found the Body (nearly sunk) in a Sand Bed. Coroners Inquest Verdict - Accidental Death by Causes Unknown.)'

Leeds Mercury, 6 January 1798

NOTICE TO CREDITORS, January 1st, 1798, Whereas Thomas Horsfall of Lower-Headley within Thornton in the Parish of Bradford and County of York, Carrier, hath by Indenture dated the Eighth Day of December last past assigned over all his Estate and Effects unto JOHN HIRST of Denholme within Thornton aforesaid, Yeoman, IN TRUST for the Benefit as well of him the said John Hirst as of all other the Creditors of him the said Thomas Horsfall who in respect of the Full of their respective Debts shall on or before the Second Day of February next ensuing the Day of the Date of the said Assignment comply with the Terms and Conditions therein contained. NOTICE is therefore hereby given that such Assignment is left at the House of Richard Withrop at Thornton aforesaid for the Inspection of the said Creditors and for their Acceptance of the Provision thereby made; and their Attendance with the said Assignment will be given at Halifax on the Twenty-seventh Day of this Instant January at Mr. Hardcastle's at the Gaol; and at Bradford on Thursday the First Day of February next at Mr. Wilson's, the Shoulder of Mutton in Kirkgate, between the Hours of Two and Four o'Clock in the Afternoon of each Day. And that all Persons indebted to the said Thomas Horsfall neglecting to pay the said John Hirst their respective Debts will forthwith be sued for the recovery of the same.

Leeds Mercury, 5 March 1808

On Saturday last, as John Walker, of Thornton near Halifax, was walking over the fields he was met by a cow that gored him so dreadfully as to occasion his death.

Leeds Mercury, 4 February 1809

THORNTON. TO be SOLD by AUCTION. At the house of Mr. John Robinson, the Black Horse Inn, at Thornton, on Monday the 20th of February Inst., between Six and Nine o'Clock in the Evening, (subject to Conditions to be then and there produced). A Desirable FREEHOLD ESTATE, consisting of Two New-erected Cottages or Dwelling-Houses, and Eight Closes of Land, containing by estimation Twelve Acres, (be the same more or less), situate in Thornton, in the parish of Bradford, in the county of York, and now in the possession of the said John Robinson, and his Undertenants. This Estate adjoins the Highway leading from Thornton to Denholme-Gate, and will be sold in five separate lots, being eligibly situated for building ground, and is supposed also to contain a valuable bed of stone. Also, Two Closes of Land, situate at a place called Morton-End, near Denholme-Gate, containing eight acres (more or less) and now occupied by the said John Robinson. All the land is in a good state of cultivation and well watered. The Tenant will shew the premises, and for further particulars apply to Mr. Abraham Riley, of Swain Royd, in Allerton; Mr. Joseph Hinchliffe, of Quarry Gap; or at the office of Mr. John Brogden, in Kirkgate, Bradford.

Leeds Mercury, 23 May 1812

A person of the name of Robert Drake who resided at Thornton near Bradford and who travelled with the stallion 'Ruler' died at Huddersfield on Wednesday morning in consequence of a stroke the horse had given him on the lower part of his belly. A Coroner's inquest sat on the body on Tuesday and returned a verdict:- died of such wounds etc, and fined the owner of the horse in a penalty of 40s.

Leeds Mercury, 16 July 1814

The Rev. Thomas Atkinson, B.A., of Thornton; son of the late Rev. Miles Atkinson, of this town, was admitted M.A. at the late Commencement at Cambridge.

Leeds Mercury, 20 August 1814

TO BE SOLD BY AUCTION, By Mr. CRAVEN, At the Talbot Inn, at Bradford, on Tuesday and Wednesday, the 20th and 21st of September, 1814, in Lots, and according to Conditions. DIVERS LAND and TENEMENTS, situate in the Parishes of Bradford and Calverley, at Crosley-Hall, Leventhorpe, Birkheads, Ling Bob, Nooks, Pikeley-Green, Sydall, and in Allerton, Wilsden, Thornton, and Bolton. The Sale to begin each Day at Eleven o'Clock in the Forenoon. Plans of the Lots and Printed Particulars are left with Mr. Craven, the Auctioneer, at Bradford.

Leeds Mercury, 18 October 1817

Died on Thursday the 28th Ult., in Thornton Workhouse near Bradford, aged 69, John Drake. The following awful visitation ensued:- Cornelius, his brother, having given directions for the grave and funeral, prayed that he might die and be interred at the same time. His prayer was heard; for he expired on the Saturday, aged 68. These two old bachelors had always lived together.

Leeds Mercury, 3 April 1819

STONE-QUARRY TO LET, Situate at Thornton-Heights, nearly Five Miles from Bradford and Bingley. CONSISTING chiefly of choice SLATE and FLAGS, fit for Facing and Scouring. The Quarry is completely opened, with good Hill-room, and a short easy descending Road on the Highway. A Quantity of Stone is now bared and quite ready for getting. The Thickness of Baring about Three to Five Yards;

the Stone about Four Yards.

For further Particulars apply to Mr. John S. Firth, Thornton, aforesaid; By whom GIST HORSES and CATTLE will be taken in from Monday, 17th May, for 21 Weeks, at the following Prices:-

£ s d

Horses, 3 Years old, 5 5 0

Do. 2 do. 4 4 0

Do. 1 do. 3 3 0

Heifers, 2 do. 2 12 6

Calves, 1 do. 1 16 0

Cows, from 3½ Years to 6, according to size 4 4 0

And who has also TWO small adjoining FARMS to LET, of about Twenty-Six Days' Work of Land each, with good new roomy Houses and Barns upon them, in Thirteen Closes, all in Grass, very well fenced and watered. *(One concern.)*

Leeds Mercury, 19 June 1819

The Rev. P. Brontë, curate of Thornton, has been presented by the Rev. Henry Heap, vicar of Bradford, to the valuable perpetual curacy of Haworth, in the parish of Bradford, vacant by the death of the Rev. James Charnock.

Leeds Mercury, 30 October 1819

The Rev. Samuel Redhead of Horton has been licensed by his Grace the Archbishop of York to the Perpetual Curacy of Haworth, upon the nomination of the Rev. Henry Heap, vicar of Bradford.

Leeds Mercury, 26 February 1820

The Rev. Patrick Brontë, of Thornton, has been nominated to the Perpetual Curacy of Haworth, in the parish of Bradford, and has been licensed to the same by his Grace the Archbishop of York.

Leeds Mercury, 8 November 1823

KIPPING, TO BE LET, for a Term of Years, and entered into, the Land at Candlemas, and Buildings on May-day next, the MANSION HOUSE of KIPPING, with the Stables, Barns, and other Outhouses, and the FARM, containing about Twenty-three Acres of LAND, in a high state of cultivation, all situated in the parish of Bradford, and county of York, and at present occupied by Mrs. Firth. The House is pleasantly situated, well finished, and commodious, has attached to it a good Garden, with a southern aspect, and would be very suitable for a private Gentleman, on accounts of its retirement; or a principal Manufacturer in the worsted trade, owing to its situation, being only six miles from Halifax, and four from Bradford, and having many facilities in the way of Mercantile pursuits and concerns.

The Land and Buildings are capable of being divided, if required. For particulars, inquire of Matthew Thompson, Esq., Manningham Lodge, near Bradford; or Mr. Drake, of Wilcock, near Thornton. The servants on the place will show the premises. Oct. 26, 1823.

Leeds Mercury, 7 May 1827

The electric fluid emitted in the thunderstorm of Saturday last struck the steeple at Bramham and damaged the bell stays, bearing away the wood with great violence. At Thornton near Bradford both sides of a barn in the occupation of Mr. Joseph Foster were thrown down, leaving the gable ends standing. Though the roof fell in, a boy and a horse in part of the building escaped unhurt.

Leeds Mercury, 7 July 1827

DEATH OF A CLIMBING BOY. The following are brief particulars of an inquest, held before Mr. Stocks at Thornton on Wednesday the 4th instant on the body of a boy named Jonathan Banks in the service of James Holgate of Leeds, chimney sweeper. So considerable a body of evidence was produced that it was found necessary to adjourn the inquest until the following day, when the inquiry was resumed and did not terminate until a late hour in the evening. The deceased was employed to sweep the chimney of Joseph Knowles of Thornton, woolcomber, about ten o'clock in the forenoon of Tuesday last, and went up very cheerfully, but from some cause or other (he himself alleged from having lost his brush) he durst not come down. Finding this, Holgate twice sent up another boy, whom he told he would be down soon enough, and then got higher up, to prevent the boy taking hold of him. He was not fast, but merely stupid. This so enraged Holgate that he swore he would cut him to pieces and that, when he got down, he would give him his dinner; he also used several other similar expressions. Holgate then lighted a fire to bring him down, which had not the desired effect, and he at length sent up another boy with a rope which he fastened on the leg of the deceased, and with which Holgate pulled him down about two yards then fastened the rope to the bars of the grate to prevent his ascending again. Shortly after this, Holgate went up to the deceased himself and stayed with him about five minutes and,

Bronte Birthplace, Market Street

when he came down he said he had nipped him and felt his feet and thought he was dying. He then shortly after went up again and untied the rope, and on his return said he was dead enough. The chimney was then pulled down and the deceased taken out quite dead. That part of the chimney in which he was found was only one foot by ten inches. When taken out it was three o'clock in the afternoon. The body, chest and head of the deceased were opened by Dr. Outhwaite and Messrs. Sharp & Trotter of Bradford, Surgeons, who found considerable fullness of blood in the vessels of the head, in all probability arising from suffocation, and on the head and body of the deceased several bruises, but none of which bruises were, in the opinion of the medical gentlemen, quite sufficient to cause death. The Jury returned a Verdict of Manslaughter against Holgate and he was committed, on the Coroner's warrant, to York Castle.

Leeds Mercury, 28 July 1827

The new turnpike road from Bradford to Thornton will be opened this day, from the former place to Fairweather Green; and the whole line as far as Kipping is expected to be ready for travelling upon in the course of five or six weeks.

Leeds Mercury, 4 August 1827

YORKSHIRE ASSIZES, YORK CASTLE. Before Mr. Justice Bayley and Mr. Baron Hullock. Friday August 3rd. MANSLAUGHTER.

JAMES HOLGATE (aged 23), a chimney sweeper, was indicted for killing Jonathan Banks, a boy in his employ, at Thornton near Bradford on the 3rd July last.

MR. BAINES stated the facts of the case and called the following witnesses.

JOSEPH KNOWLES, a woolcomber at Thornton; prisoner came with two boys to sweep his chimney at ten in the morning of 3rd July last. Deceased was sent up the chimney; there was a little fire then in the range but an iron bake-stone was put over it. Witness came into the room in consequence of a great smoke in the house, and, on his remonstrance, prisoner put the fire out. Prisoner then sent up the other boy, Brayshaw, to fasten a rope to the leg of the deceased; this being done, the prisoner pulled the boy down with force about two yards; the boy cried out 'Don't pull' and the prisoner said he would not pull if the boy came down. The prisoner then went up the chimney himself, and after remaining two minutes he came down and said he did not know whether the boy was dead or not. He went up again, and said 'He's dead enough.' The boy was then taken out and he was dead.

BETTY KNOWLES, wife of the last witness, saw the deceased sent up the chimney; there was then only a handful of fire in the grate, which they had covered with an iron bake-stone. When the boy had been long enough to sweep the chimney prisoner had called several times to him, and threatened him if he did not come down.

The other boy was then sent up, and said deceased said he would come down soon. After waiting a quarter of an hour longer prisoner said he would smoke the lad down and he threw a quantity of soot on the fire; the smoke filled the house. Soon after, prisoner threatened to send Brayshaw up to tie a rope round his leg; witness tried to dissuade him and, as she could not, she left the house and saw no more. (Cross-examined by Mr. Greenwood.) It was three hours from the time the deceased went up to the time of throwing the soot on the fire. He was altogether up five hours.

JOHN BRAYSHAW, apprentice to Holgate, came to the house after the boy had been up a long time; Holgate sent witness up the chimney to fetch him down; the deceased got higher up the chimney, and would not for a long time answer but at last said he would come down soon. Witness again descended and went to sweep another chimney; he returned in about an hour and found the boy still in the chimney. Witness went up to him, and found him in the same place; the deceased said he had lost his brush but would come down soon. Witness again descended and went to sweep another chimney; he was fetched again and sent up with a rope to tie round the deceased; he tied it, and then they pulled him down about two yards; the boy cried, and the witness descended. His master then went up and stayed five minutes; he said when he came down that he had nipped the boy's foot and thought he was dying; he ascended a second time and said the boy was dead. (Cross-examined by Mr. Marshall.) His master had done everything to persuade him to come down before he used force; the deceased was a very stupid boy and was in the habit of staying an extremely long time in chimneys. Never heard of a rope being sent up in such a case before. Holgate never behaved ill to them; he was the kindest journeyman witness ever went out with.

JOHN POLLARD, shoemaker at Thornton, went into the house when the rope had been sent up the chimney; prisoner pulled the rope violently and with jerking; witness told him he would either kill or lame the boy. Witness left the house, but came in again and helped to take out the boy's body; the body was quite fast in the chimney.

Mr. WILLIAM SHARP, surgeon, of Bradford, was called in to examine the body on the 5th of July at the adjourned inquest; found on the boy's legs several slight injuries, but on the left a very considerable exceration which might have been produced by a tight ligature; there was a bruise on the forehead and on the back part of the head; there were no other bruises on the body. The veins of the brain were very much gorged with dark-coloured blood, and on the right side of the chest there was an ounce of extravasated blood; on the left side the lungs adhered to the ribs, which must have been the effect of a former disease. In his opinion the boy's death arose from suffocation. (Cross-examined.) If he was wedged in the chimney that would suffocate him as much as if he were drowned; thinks this must be the cause of his death.

9

The *JUDGE* said he thought the suffocating had arisen more from the boy's having forced himself into a bad position in the chimney than from any external violence.

The *PRISONER* said he had never desired to injure the boy or anybody else; he had done all he could to make him come down quickly before tying the rope.

The *JUDGE* summed up the evidence, and the *JURY* returned a Verdict of Not Guilty, but said they thought the prisoner very reprehensible in his conduct.

The *JUDGE* said he thought so too. The trial terminated at a quarter to eight o'clock.

Leeds Mercury, 31 May 1828

On Tuesday afternoon, two girls from Thornton, near Bradford, were returning from a visit to see some of their relations in the vicinity of Haworth, when they met an aged female, at the rivulet which runs near Denholme, and which was much swollen by the heavy rains. They had just crossed the temporary bridge, which consists of a plank, and one of them was assisting the old woman over the bridge, when they both fell into the water, and the poor girl was drowned. The old woman was washed down the stream, some distance, but she preserved her own life by taking hold of a branch of a tree, and in that way escaped out of the water.

Leeds Mercury, 21 February 1829

DISINTERESTED BENEVOLENCE. On Friday last, Mr. Wilson, of Bradford, a benevolent gentleman, belonging to the Society of Friends, visited Thornton and Allerton, and diffused joy and gratitude amongst the poor of those places, by distributing to them his usual gifts of coverlets, blankets, cotton, serge, harding, and other useful and necessary articles, suited to the wants of the destitute, at this time of year.

Chapter Two
1831–1836

Mystery of headless chickens – Dissenters dispute church dues – Mechanics' Institute established – Beer sold on Sunday– Thornton road a disgrace

Leeds Mercury, 2 July 1831
THORNTON NEAR BRADFORD, BY Mr. G.T. Lister at the house of Mr. John Blamires, the Traveller's Inn at Queen's Head in Northowram, on Monday 4th July next at 6 o'clock in the evening (subject to such Conditions as will then and there be produced)
All that Valuable FREEHOLD ESTATE situate in Thornton in the parish of Bradford in the county of York called Moor Royd Gate, consisting of a good Farm House with a barn, stable, cow-house, yard, garden and outbuildings thereto belonging and also 10 closes of excellent Land situate near to the said Farm House and lying in a Ring Fence, and containing with the site of the said buildings 32 Days' Work or thereabouts, lately the property and in the possession of Mr. Jonas Foster, Coal Merchant, deceased. The estate is situated near the Denholme-Gate and Brighouse Turnpike Road and about 4 miles distant from the towns of Halifax and Bradford. The property is plentifully supplied with Water, a powerful stream flows through the Land and renders it an eligible situation for the erection of a Worsted Mill or Factory. The Land Tax is redeemed and immediate Possession may be

11

had if required. For further Particulars application may be made to Mr. John Foster* of Queen's Head in Clayton; Mr. Jonathan Foster of West Scholes; or Mr. James Pearson of Close Head and Mrs. Stephen Drake of Wilcock in Thornton or at the Offices of Messrs. Lamberts & Hudson, Solicitors, in Bradford.

*John Foster, born in Thornton and founder of Black Dyke Mills in Queensbury.

Leeds Mercury, 17 September 1831
Sale advertisement, first part concerning a nursery at Beverley in East Yorkshire, but continuing:

PLANTING GROUND IN THORNTON NEAR BRADFORD
Also an ALLOTMENT or PARCEL of GROUND containing 60 acres or thereabouts, heretofore Parcel of the Commons, Moors and Waste Grounds, within the Township of Thornton near Bradford in the West Riding of Yorkshire. This Allotment is Leasehold, for the Remainder of a Term of 99 Years, commencing on the 1st January 1813, at a mere nominal Rent for many of the First Years; and the Lessee has the Liberty of cutting down and taking away any Tree during any Part of the Term (except the last Nineteen Years) which he may plant thereon. Application to Mr. Bentley, Solicitor, Bradford, as to the Ground at Thornton.

Leeds Mercury, 17 August 1833
On Saturday last, as Jonas Wilson, of Thornton, was returning from Bradford, whither he had been for provisions for the tide, which was on the following day, he was struck with apoplexy, and died by the road side. An inquest has been held on the body and a verdict returned – 'Died by the visitation of God.'

Leeds Mercury, 26 October 1833
CHURCH RATES AT THORNTON. The parochial chapel, at Thornton, in the parish of Bradford, and diocese of York, is of ancient standing, and the usual way of supporting the place has been by rates collected in the Chapelry, from the township of Thornton-cum-Denholme, Allerton-cum-Wilsden, and Clayton. About ten years ago, when the rage for building new churches prevailed, the Commissioners for building new churches, contrary to the wish of a great majority of the inhabitants of Allerton and Wilsden, determined to build a large and elegant church in Wilsden, to be a district church for Allerton and Wilsden. When it was completed in 1826, the inhabitants of the district, of course, thought that the exchange of two-fifths of a chapel for a large new church was quite as much as they could expect, and of course deputed the Churchwarden with others to go and

settle their accounts with Thornton. However, as might be expected, the Thornton people did not like to lose their friends, and therefore repeatedly demanded the rate as usual, but without effect, until a while ago, when a summons was resorted to. At the meeting before the Magistrates the two wardens for Allerton and Wilsden said they disputed the validity of the rate, and the case was dismissed.

Soon after this it was referred to the Consistory Court of York, and was decided there on 25th July last, before the Worshipful Granville Harcourt, M.A. 'The judge said, that the case was very properly and very creditably brought before him. It certainly did appear very hard that Wilsden and Allerton should have to contribute to the repairs not only of the church at Wilsden and the parish church, but also to the chapel of Thornton. He did not consider that the chapel of Thornton ought to be considered as a parish church, and the only ground for his giving judgement as he was about to do was, that the case was not at all provided for in the new building acts. The inhabitants of Wilsden and Allerton were at present bound to repair the chapel of Thornton from immemorial usage. They were liable under the common law, and whatever might be the intention of the framers of those acts, there was nothing in them to render them exempt. It was not clear to him that even at the end of 20 years they would be exempt. He hoped that not many months would elapse before this and similar cases were provided for, but he must take the law as he found it, and he therefore adjudged that the building of the chapel at Wilsden did not exonerate the townships of Wilsden and Allerton from their liability to the repair of the chapel of Thornton. The plaintiffs obtained judgement with costs.'

Now as this is the law that two small townships must support the grandchild, and help to support the mother and grandmother, what are they to do? Well, they have determined to be careful, and allow them what nature requires, but no more.

On the 4th of October a meeting was called to lay the rate, and pass the accounts of the last year. As might be expected, great numbers assembled, and the Rev. Mr. Bishop not being present, the meeting called Mr. CHRISTOPHER ANDERSON to the chair. After comparing the rate laid and the sums expended, it was found that a cost estimated at £3 10s, for the orderly man, and the repairing of a stable at £3 6s 6d not having been provided and done, they were, with some other small items, struck off; and the accounts were passed. The Churchwardens then proposed items for a rate of upwards of £40. An amendment was moved by Mr. G. Hanson, who remarked that as the Churchwardens said the church was in good repair, he would move as an amendment, 'that for wine, and other necessary things, £5 10s 6d be allowed for the next year.' This was carried by one hundred to one; and the meeting closed well satisfied.

However, it is seldom that all men are pleased at such meetings. Soon after, a notice was again issued, calling the inhabitants together on the Wednesday, the 23rd, – and although the morning was wet, and many had to walk two to three miles, a great number were there in time. At this meeting, the Rev. Wm. BISHOP, the incumbent, presided, and of course he pleaded hard for the usages of the church, and was very free to tell the Dissenters, that if they had the same right, he would not deprive them of a farthing if it was in his power. In answer to which he was told that the Dissenters had no intention of keeping back any thing that the law gave to the church. On the Churchwardens being asked if they considered the former meeting legal, they said they did; it was then proposed and carried without opposition, 'that the business of that meeting be confirmed.'

Mr. HANSON inquired what was their reason for collecting the rate-payers again? The worthy Chairman referred to the law respecting clerks and their support, and wanted a rate for that, as he said ancient usage had gained him a salary, and he should have it.

On inquiry as to the choice of the clerk, the Chairman said it was with him. The answer was, that he ought then to pay him; and the poor clerk was requested by the Dissenters to call upon them for relief, if neither the Minister who chose him, nor the people who were served by him, would do what was necessary. The poor man, in a fit of grief, said he never had had any thing yet, but he would have.

Mr. HANSON now proposed, as an amendment, 'that the further consideration of the propriety of laying a church rate for the Chapelry of Thornton be adjourned till the 22nd day of October 1834.'

This the Chairman at first refused to put to the meeting. However, when he was told that neither he or some other Chairman must, he consented: and also, when the motion had been passed, signed the proceedings in the book, and closed the meeting by giving out – 'Praise God from whom all blessings flow,' &c. After this the old 100th psalm was sung, and forty-nine out of every fifty left the place pleased.

Bradford Observer, 13 February 1834
LOWER HEADLEY FARM in Thornton in the parish of Bradford
TO BE LET
A FARM called Lower Headley, situate in Thornton, consisting of a FARM HOUSE, TWO BARNS, seven COTTAGE HOUSES, and Forty Acres of good Meadow, Arable and Pasture LAND. Mr. Jonas Greenwood, the present Tenant, will show the Premises, and further Particulars may be known on Application to George Priestley, Esq., White Windows; or Mr. Samuel Washington, Land Agent, Crow Nest, near Halifax. February 10th, 1834.

Leeds Mercury, 22 February 1834
A watchman of one of the mills on the Thornton New-road came the other day suddenly upon some young men who very precipitately took to their heels at his appearance, leaving behind them four hens which had been relieved of their heads. The fowls, which no doubt had been stolen, have not been owned.

Bradford Observer, 14 August 1834

THORNTON MECHANICS' INSTITUTE. We are informed that the Mechanics' Institute which has just been established at Thornton, near this town, has every appearance of prosperity. Upwards of seventy members have been already admitted and a great number of books have been purchased in order to form a library; and what is of still greater importance, a grammar class has been formed, which will be conducted by Mr. William Harrop, whose qualifications for this undertaking cannot be disputed.

Bradford Observer, 6 January 1835

SERIOUS ACCIDENT. On Tuesday last as Mr. Jonathan Ackroyd, of Thornton, carrier, was returning home from Halifax, riding in his cart, the horse was going at a rapid speed down a steep place near Queen's Head, the cart was upset, and the unfortunate man was killed on the spot.

Bradford Observer, 4 June 1835

THORNTON. On Monday evening last a meeting was held at the Church Chapel, Thornton, for the purpose of laying a rate for the purchasing of a large quantity of land as additional burial ground. It may not be generally known that the inhabitants of Wilsden and Allerton are compelled not only to pay the church rates for the support of the parish church of this town and Wilsden but also to Thornton Chapel. We presume that few persons can be found who will deny that this is above all other things unreasonable. The inhabitants groan under their burden, and well they may, when it is remembered that more than nine-tenths of them are dissenters, and consequently have their own places of worship to uphold besides what they are forced to pay to all these churches.

Bradford Observer, 9 July 1835

THORNTON MECHANICS' INSTITUTE. On Friday the 3rd inst. this Society held its first annual meeting; the Rev. J. Gregory, President of the Institution, in the chair. After giving a very clear exposition of the nature, objects and beneficial tendencies of such Institutions towards the diffusion of useful knowledge and the improvement of the mind, the Chairman called upon the Secretary and Librarian for their Reports, which were highly interesting and encouraging, both as respects the usefulness of the past and the prospects of the future. It appeared from the Secretary's Report that twenty-six lectures on scientific, geographical, literary and other subjects had been delivered during the year, all of which, except three on chemistry and electricity and one on the manners and customs of Jews, have been given by members of the Institute. The Librarian's Report stated that reading prevails to a considerable extent, seven hundred and fifty deliveries of books having been made during the year; that there is a valuable and select, though not extensive, collection of books in the library; and that much good has not only been already done, but that there are more flattering prospects for the future. Many of the members expressed in animated terms their gratitude for the pleasure and improvement they had derived from the Institute since its commencement; and such a general feeling pervaded the members to do each other good, that there is the most encouraging prospect of a continuance of that unanimity which has hitherto conduced so highly to the prosperity of the Thornton Mechanics' Institution.

Bradford Observer, 23 July 1835

ACCIDENT. On Saturday last as some mowers were at work in a field belonging to Mr. Thomas Leach of Worlden Lodge near Thornton one of his boys came in contact with a scythe which nearly cut off one of his feet. We are glad to hear, however, that the boy is doing well, and is likely to recover without having the limb amputated, which was at first expected.

Bradford Observer, 7 January 1836

ORDER OF FORESTERS. Friday last, being New-Year's-day, was a grand day with the Foresters. Court 149 held their anniversary at the house of Mr. William Baxter, King's Arms Inn, where an excellent dinner was furnished by the worthy host. On the same day, the Foresters at Thornton walked in procession from the New Inn, Thornton, to the Bay Horse, Thornton Heights, where a new Court was opened. A new Court was also opened at the Wheatsheaf, Bowling, under the designation of 'Hope to do better.'

Bradford Observer, 17 March 1836

A swindler of plausible address, who calls himself George Thompson, is going about the county with a begging letter, purporting to be signed by Hudson & Craven of Thornton, near Bradford, representing that he is in great distress, from having lost several horses; he has with him a book containing the names of several respectable gentlemen, of Leeds and the neighbourhood, who are set down as having contributed handsome sums, most of which are fictitious. The public will do well to be on their guard.

Bradford Observer, 17 March 1836

IN THE MATTER OF DAN MITCHELL, an Insolvent. THE CREDITORS of DAN MITCHELL, late of Clayton, in the parish of Bradford, in the County of York, weaver, Insolvent Debtor, lately discharged from the Gaol of York Castle, in the County of York, are requested to meet the Assignees of his Estate and Effects at the house of Mr. Jonas Robinson, the New Inn, in Thornton, in the parish of Bradford, in the said County of York, on Saturday, the Second day of April next, at the hour of Eleven o'clock in the Forenoon precisely, in order to assent to the said Assignees selling and disposing of the Real and Personal Estates of the said Insolvent by public auction, in such manner and at such places as shall be approved of by the major part in

Mechanics' Institute and Cinema.

value of the Creditors who shall then be present, pursuant to the Act of Parliament in that behalf. By Order, WILLIAM HUDSON, Bradford.

Bradford Observer, 7 April 1836

THORNTON ORATORIO. We seldom remember attending a musical performance of this nature where we have received so much real pleasure as from this Oratorio. It certainly must have been a rich treat for all lovers of 'the concord of sweet sounds.' This praise extends to the general character of the performance, though we must award the palm of vocal excellence to the female portion of the singers. Part I, commenced with Haydn's magnificent 'In the beginning;' followed by the chorus, 'And the Spirit of God,' to which the band did complete justice, with a slight exception or two. 'Now Vanish,' sung by Mr. Parker, went beautifully and was well supported by the grand chorus 'Despairing, cursin', rage.' But the favourite air 'With verdure clad,' sung by Miss Sykes, in our opinion, was most to be praised. There was some very excellent vocal music towards the close of this part, in which the superior tone and expression of Mr. Parker's singing was distinguishable. Part II opened with the Coronation Anthem, a composition we never much admired, though from the superior instrumental accompaniment we tolerated it with better humour than usual. After this we were glad to relax for Miss Sykes's liquid execution and brilliant tones in Mozart's 'Lamb of God.' The

17

splendid chorus 'From the Censor,' was executed in better style than we remember to have heard by a similar orchestra. At the close of Miss Sykes's beautiful song from Turk, 'Shepherds, view the sight inspiring,' the excitement of a portion of the admiring audience was beginning to be audibly expressed, but the respectful example of the more sensible part, silenced the incipient acclamations. A similar occurrence took place at the conclusion of Mr. Parker's song, 'O Lord, my God,' which received a more direct suppression, by a person out of the chorus openly desiring them to desist. 'He gave them Hailstones,' was the best chorus of the selection, and was performed both vocally and instrumentally, in the true spirit of the composition. On the whole the Oratorio was well directed, and gave, we believe, full satisfaction.

CONCERT. This entertainment, instead of commencing at seven o'clock, as announced in the bills, did not begin until nine. We suppose this was owing principally to a deficiency of books, and in a *great measure* to the *indisposition* of an eminent performer on the violin. As to the Concert itself we scarcely know how to express ourselves. There was evidently much hurry and confusion, though we are of the opinion that much blame was attributable to the sober source above alluded to. After the Overture from Mozart came the Glee 'Now Tramp,' a quartet, sung by Miss Sykes, Messrs. Mercer, Parker, and Armitage. Next succeeded the Grand March, with Band accompaniment, on the trumpet, by Master Phillips, which, next to Mr. Oddy's Flute Obligato, was the finest thing of the evening. The 'Soldier's Song,' by Mr. Parker, did that gentleman infinite credit, though, if we might venture a word of advice, we would recommend him to avoid degenerating into a sort of nasal twang which occasionally disfigures his otherwise excellent singing. 'Lo! Hear the gentle Lark,' by Miss Sykes, was encored, but she escaped a repetition. Mr. Cadmore's Concerto in the minor, was got over in a charming manner, considering that gentleman's indisposition. A song by Mr. Armitage closed the first part. The overture from Cherubini introduced the Second Part; and Miss Sykes' beautiful singing was again the theme of general admiration in 'Bid me discourse.' The trumpet Waltz, performed by its youthful composer, went splendidly; as also the 'Soldier Tired,' in which Master Phillips' trumpet accompaniment was in fine adaptation to the singer's tones. The effect of some of the evening's singing was rather lessened, inasmuch as certain of the vocalists, by way of being delicate, completely escaped being heard. The Concert was well attended, but scarcely in proportion to the Oratorio; and we hope, after the payment of the expenses, a handsome surplus will be left for the benefit of the schools.

Bradford Observer, 26 May 1836

DISSOLUTION OF PARTNERSHIP. NOTICE IS HEREBY GIVEN, that the Partnership concern heretobefore existing between us, the undersigned, JOSEPH FAIRBANK and JOHN WOOD, as Worsted Spinners, formerly carried on at Lenthorpe Mill, Thornton, in the parish of Bradford, in the County of York, under the Style or Firm of 'JOSEPH FAIRBANK and COMPANY,' but lately carried on at Harper Gate Mill, in the Lordship and Liberty of Tong, in the parish of Birstall, in the said County of York, under the style or in the Name of 'JOSEPH FAIRBANK,' hath this day been Dissolved by mutual consent. The Debts and Credits of the said Partnership will be respectively paid and received by the said Joseph Fairbank, who is now carrying on Business in the said last Premises on his own account only, as witness our hands this Twentieth Day of May, One Thousand Eight Hundred and Thirty-six. JOSEPH FAIRBANK JOHN WOOD. Witness, JOHN REID WAGSTAFF, of Bradford, Attorney-at Law.

Bradford Observer, 26 May 1836

Bradford Petty Sessions (in list with other offenders from places around Bradford): Joseph Briggs, inn-keeper, Thornton, was fined £2 and 14s costs, for keeping his house open during the hours of divine service, and Jonas Holling, beer seller, of the same place, was fined £2, and 14s costs, for keeping his house open for the sale of beer at a later hour than is allowed by law, and an order of the Magistrates.

Bradford Observer, 30 June 1836

THORNTON. TO BE SOLD BY AUCTION. At the House of Mr. DAVID BROOKSBANK, the Black Bull Inn, in Denholme, in the township of Thornton, on Monday the 4th Day of July, 1836, at Seven o'clock in the Evening. SIX COTTAGES or DWELLING-HOUSES, situated at Lodge Gate, in the Township of Thornton, Five of which are in the several occupations of William Sugden, William Walker, Thomas Sugden, Timothy Whittaker, and Mary Brooksbank, and one is at present untenanted. The Tenants will show the Premises, and for further Particulars apply to Mr. MICHAEL PEARSON, of Thornton, or to Mr. MOULDEN, Attorney-at-Law, Bradford. Bradford, 6th June, 1836.

Bradford Observer, 15 September 1836

Early in the morning of Sunday last, a loving couple from Thornton having agreed to conform to the law of marriage, set out for the parish church in 'our good town.' On reaching the first open public house, the fair bride described herself as feeling unwell, and requested a bed. None, however, being procured at the said hostelry, it was determined to proceed to the church as speedily as possible, and for this purpose a coach was procured to convey the fair bride; before she could leave the inn yard, however, an *accoucher* was needed, who safely delivered the unmarried fair of a first-born son, in the chaise. The mother and child were at once conveyed into the Commercial Inn, where, it is needless to say, they received every attention from Mrs. Crook, the worthy hostess. On Tuesday, the mother was sufficiently well to proceed with her intended to church, and was indissolubly united in the silken cords of matrimony.

Bradford parish church registers for Tuesday 13 September 1836 show only one marriage, number 289. It was between Jonathan Dawson, woolcomber, bachelor, and Mary Spencer, minor, spinster, both of Bradford parish, by banns and with consent of the bride's father. R. Milnes, curate, officiated. Groom and bride and witness Mary Dawson all made their marks, but second witness James Hainsworth signed his name.

Bradford Observer, 15 September 1836

Bradford Petty Sessions (in list with other offenders from places around Bradford): George Suthers and Thomas Barker were charged with Sabbath-breaking at Thornton; severally fined 3s 4d and 8s 4d costs. Mark Hodgson, charged with being drunk at Thornton; fined 5s and 4s costs.

Bradford Observer, 17 November 1836

SACRILEGE. During the night of Sunday last, the Church chapel at Thornton was entered, and a silver communion cup, two surplices, and a number of books were stolen. The thieves yet remain uncaptured.

Bradford Observer, 8 December 1836

THORNTON ROAD. A correspondent has called our attention to the present disgraceful state of the road between this town and Thornton. The distance thither is only four miles, and although in that short space there are two toll bars to pass, the road is almost impassable; and to those obliged to travel in the dark, decidedly dangerous.

Chapter Three
1837-1839

Highwaymen on Thornton Roads – Horses drown in flood – Rise in illegitimate births – Hill-Top cottages for sale – Six policemen for Thornton

Bradford Observer, 2 February 1837
DISSOLUTION OF PARTNERSHIP

Notice is hereby given that the partnership lately subsisting between us, John Jowett and Joshua Jowett, at Thornton in the parish of Bradford in the county of York in the Trade or Business of Stuff Makers under the Firm of 'J. & J. Jowett' was this day dissolved by mutual consent. ALL DEBTS owing to and from the said Firm will be received and paid by the said John Jowett. As witness our hand this first day of February 1837. John Jowett, Joshua Jowett. Witness to the signatures, William George, Solicitor, Bradford.

Bradford Observer, 16 March 1837

DENHOLME GATE. Ale and Porter Brewery. Jonathan Knowles returns thanks to his Friends and the Public for the Patronage he has already received, and begs to inform them that he has COMMENCED BREWING IN HIS NEW AND MORE EXTENSIVE PREMISES, and respectfully solicits a Continuance of their Favours. To be sold by private contract, FOUR SMALL WORKING STONES AND BREWING PAN. Apply at the Brewery (one concern), Denholme Gate. 13th March, 1837.

Leeds Mercury, 8 April 1837

THORNTON, near BRADFORD. – (Duty Free.) By Order of the Assignees of Cockcroft and Whitaker, Bankrupts, by Mr. THOMAS DAVIS, at the House of Mr. Joseph Greenwood, Innkeeper, near Thornton, in the Parish of Bradford, in the County of York, *on Wednesday, the Nineteenth Day of April next,* at Six o'Clock in the Evening, subject to such Conditions as will be then and there produced: ALL those SEVEN COTTAGES, situate at BACK HEIGHT, in Thornton aforesaid, late in the several Tenures or Occupations of George Spenceley, Isaac Wright, James Robinson, Betty Pearson, Joshua Drake, Samuel Jagger, and William Crabtree, their Assigns or Undertenants, but now in the Occupation of Mr. Joseph Greenwood and his Undertenants. And also ALL that Valuable Close of LAND, called the UPPER CLOSE, adjoining to the said Cottages, and containing, by Admeasurement, One Acre or thereabouts, be the same more or less, also in the Occupation of the said Joseph Greenwood. Further Particulars may be known on Application to Mr. JOSEPH GREENWOOD, Innkeeper, Thornton; Mr. RILEY MANKS, Southowram; Mr. JOHN HOLT, the Woolpack Inn, in Halifax; Messrs. STOCKS & MACAULEY, Solicitors, Halifax; and Messrs. PARKER & ADAM, Solicitors, Halifax.
Halifax, March 27, 1837.

Bradford Observer, 15 June 1837

ELEGANT HOUSEHOLD FURNITURE FARMING STOCK & STOCK IN TRADE
THORNTON, NEAR BRADFORD. TO BE SOLD BY AUCTION, BY MR. T. INGHAM. By order of the Trustees of Mr. Moses Sharp, Worsted Manufacturer,
at Thornton aforesaid. On Monday, the 26th day of June, 1837, and the following days until the whole be disposed of. All the very valuable HOUSEHOLD FURNITURE, comprising splendid mahogany four-post bedsteads richly carved, with moreen, chintz, and other hangings, feather beds, bolsters and pillows, counterpanes, with bed linen; hair and other mattresses; mahogany square and circular fronted chests of drawers, with cupboards; wash stands and dressing tables, with towel horses to match; sets of mahogany chairs with hair seating; sofas;

Brussels, Scotch, and Wilton carpets, with hearth rugs, staircase ditto and rods; mahogany sideboard; mahogany dining, loo, card, Pembroke, and other tables; clock in mahogany case; excellent chimney, pier, and dressing glasses; brass and steel fenders with fire-irons, valuable chimney ornaments, japanned tea trays and waiters, fire screens, wine and spirit decanters, glass and china, window drapery, cornices and holders, passage oil cloth, barometer, oil paintings and prints by celebrated artists, brass kettle and stand, brass pans, kitchen chairs and tables, block tin dish covers, large dresser, dinner and tea services, iron pans, and all the valuable kitchen requisites; also one excellent square Piano Forte, six and a half octaves; likewise all the STOCK in TRADE, comprising upwards of 200 pairs of slays and healds of different sets and breadths, yarn and warp bins, piece tables, weighing machine, counting house desk and buffets, scale beam, ends and 3½ cwt. Of weights, cart covers, several sets of sizing frames with rollers and sticks, steam piping, large set pan, sizing rings; also all the live and dead FARMING STOCK, comprising one milch cow, one aged draught horse, one bay horse fit for saddle or harness with good action, one grey pony, eleven sheep, thirteen lambs, one wagon, one cart, one carriage or van, one phaeton, double and singles sets of harness, two saddles, horse gearing, plough, harrows, rakes, forks, &c, &c. Catalogues are in course of preparation, and may be had, with particulars of lots for each day's Sale, price three-pence each, at the Printer's, and at the principal Inns in Bingley, Keighley, Halifax, Thornton, and Wilsden, and of T. INGHAM, Auctioneer, Market-street, Bradford.

Bradford Observer, 13 July 1837
The Rev. Henry Heap, B.D., Vicar of Bradford, has given consent to the Rev. Wm. Bishop to solemnize marriages in the Episcopal Chapel at Thornton.

Leeds Mercury, 29 July 1837
PLEASANT COUNTRY RESIDENCE, STONE QUARRIES, &c, at THORNTON, near BRADFORD, To be LET, with immediate possession, all that excellent MESSUAGE or DWELLING-HOUSE called 'Kipping' with the Warehouses, Cottages, Outbuildings, Gardens, and Land, late in the Occupation of Mr. Moses Sharp, and his Undertenants.
Also, a most valuable STONE QUARRY, at Bell Dean, and another at

Storr Height, late in the Occupation of Messrs. Cockcroft and Whitaker. Apply to Mr. G.T. LISTER, Land Agent, Albion Court, Bradford. Bradford, July 27th, 1837.

Bradford Observer, 21 September 1837

THORNTON. A correspondent has sent us an account of a Radical meeting in the township on Monday last which we should very willingly insert if our space would admit.

Leeds Mercury, 7 October 1837

Married on Wednesday at the Kipping Independent Chapel, Thornton, by the Rev. James Gregory, Mr. Brook Wilkinson to Miss Ann Green, being the first marriage at this chapel under the new act.

Bradford Observer, 12 October 1837

THORNTON ROAD. A correspondent complains of what he describes 'the disgraceful and highly dangerous' state of Thornton Road; and he further states, that for the greater part of the distance between this town and Thornton, at about the space of five or six yards, great stones, weighing half a hundred-weight, lie promiscuously in the horse track, apparently (though of course not intentionally) with a view to endanger the lives of Her Majesty's subjects journeying hitherward.

Bradford Observer, 16 November 1837

HIGHWAY ROBBERY. On Thursday, Mr. Birch of Thornton was returning from market when three men rushed upon him near Whitley-lane Bar, and took from him his pocket-book, which contained a £5 note and some silver.

Bradford Observer, 28 December 1837

THORNTON. Two very valuable horses, belonging to Mr. Isaac Wood, farmer, of Headley near Thornton, were drowned in a brook which runs between Thornton and Headley. The horses, which were yoked together, were endeavouring to ford the rivulet, which, at that time, was very high, owing to the heavy rain which had fallen during the day. Two men, who were with the horses, were thrown into the water, but happily they escaped with their lives. On the same day, as the horses and cart belonging to Mr. James Holdsworth of Clayton (who is accustomed to work for weavers) were endeavouring to ford the brook, at Brookhouse in Ovenden, they were, together with the driver, overpowered by the waters; the cart, together with moreen warp and weft, with which it was very heavily loaded, were taken down with the torrent, but happily the man and horse escaped with their lives, owing to the assistance given to them by their neighbours.

Bradford Observer, 1 February 1838

THORNTON. Registration of Births, Deaths, and Marriages, in the District of Thornton and Clayton, for the half year ending 31st December 1837:- Births, 206, of which 105 are females and 101 males; majority of females 4. Of the above, 12 are illegitimate, or 1 in 17. Parents who could not sign the register book of birth, 158; those who have, 48; majority of those who cannot write, 110. Deaths, 116, of which 58 are male and the same number female. Persons who could not sign the register book of deaths, 72; those who have, 44; majority of those who cannot write, 28. Out of the above deaths, 3 died within an hour of the birth; 2 within a day; 4 within a week; and 2 within a month. Under 1 year old, 22; and between that age and 10 years old, 18. Above 80 years of age, 4 have died; above 70 years of age, 8; above 60 years of age, 8; above 50 years of age, 6; above 40 years of age, 3; above 30 years of age, 9; above 20 years of age, 16; above 10 years of age, 11. Total 116, of which 2 died of asthma; abscess, 2; breaking of a blood vessel, 1; consumption, 29; continued fever, 10; child-bed, 3; dropsy, 5; dysentery, 8; fits, 15; fever in the brain, 1; inflammation, 14; paralysis, 2; smallpox, 1; scarlet fever, 2; spasms at the stomach, 1; St. Anthony's fire, 1; water in the brain, 2; old age, 11; accidentally burnt, 2; and 4 of what is incident to young children, such as teething &c. Marriages, 4 – two of which have been solemnized at the Kipping Independent Chapel, and two at the Episcopal Chapel, Thornton.

Leeds Mercury, 31 March 1838

THORNTON. On the 23rd instant Mr. David Wright and Mr. Jonas Pearson were elected Overseers of the poor of the above township; Mr. Isaac Wood and Mr. Richard Smith, assessors; and Mr. Jonathan Craven and Mr. Jonathan Foster, collectors of the assessed taxes for the same period. Mr. Isaac Wood, of Kipping, and Mr. James Pearson, of Leventhorpe Mill, are the guardians of the poor for this township; and Mr. Jonas Wilkinson, of Clayton Heights, for Clayton.

Bradford Observer, 3 May 1838

CAUTION TO BEER SHOP KEEPERS. Jonas Holdsworth of Thornton was charged by Thomas Barker of Thornton with having company in his house at half past ten at night on Saturday the 14th day of April last. He was convicted on the charge and fined £2, costs 17s 6d, and to have his licence suspended. John Butterfield, beer-shop keeper, also of Thornton, was charged by Thomas Barker with allowing company to be drinking in his house at half past ten on Saturday night last. In this case Mr. Barker failed to establish his charge and it was accordingly dismissed.

Northern Star & Leeds General Advertiser, 26 May 1838

BRADFORD. CAROL AGREEMENT. A number of practitioners in sacred music were to have met on Friday evening, the 18th instant, at the New Dolphin

Inn, Ford, near Queenshead, for the purpose of performing a number of select pieces from 'Judas Maccabeus' and the 'Creation.' One of the parties, from some cause not yet explained, gave notice to some of his friends that he could not attend; but this was only done the night before the meeting; and as a number of other friends had also been invited to attend, a meeting took place accordingly. The disappointment would have been very great, had it not been for some friends who came from Thornton, who, having ascertained the cause, immediately adjourned the meeting to a friend's house, at Queenshead, and, in a few minutes, had a grand 'set to.' A young boy, about thirteen years of age, displayed a masterly hand on the violin; and Miss Helliwell also surpassed in her songs, which she sung in a marvellous manner – such as the following: 'Come smiling,' &c.; which elicited great applause from the audience. The choruses which were sung were a selection from 'Judas Maccabeus;' and were performed in a masterly style by those persons present, and thought not to have been surpassed by any previous performers. Great thanks are due to the Thornton friends for their exertions on this occasion.

Northern Star & Leeds General Advertiser, 12 June 1838

BRADFORD. CHURCH RATES. A church rate meeting of the township of Thornton, Clayton, Denholme, Allerton, and Wilsden, lately holden in St. James's church, Thornton, was adjourned for 12 months. A subscription was made to pay the beadle for cleaning out the church after the meeting.

Bradford Observer, 12 July 1838

THORNTON NEAR BRADFORD. TO BE SOLD BY AUCTION by Mr. G. T. LISTER. At the house of Mr. Jonas Robinson, the New Inn, in Thornton, on Friday the 27th day of this instant July, at six o'clock in the evening. ALL THOSE ELEVEN FREEHOLD COTTAGES, with good frontsteads, situated at Hill-Top, or MOUNT PLEASANT, in the occupation of Widow Duckett, and others. These cottages were erected about Ten Years ago. They are built in the most substantial manner, and are in good repair, and fitted up with Ovens, Ranges, and Boilers, and well supplied with good Water. They are also respectably tenanted, and produce on a moderate letting a clear yearly rental of £40 and upward. Mr. Thomas Driver of Thornton, Joiner and Appraiser, will show the premises, and further particulars may be had of him or of Mr. William White junior, All-Alone, Idle, near Bradford, or at the office of Messrs. Bentley, Bentley & Thompson, Solicitors, Bradford.

Northern Star & Leeds General Advertiser, 4 August 1838

BRADFORD. ACCIDENT – CHILD KILLED. Yesterday week as a little girl, about four years of age, was playing in an empty cart at Stream Head, near Thornton, she fell from the shelvings into the body of the cart, when her head stuck fast in a hole at the bottom, in which position she was found dead.

Northern Star & Leeds General Advertiser, 22 September 1838

BRADFORD. On Monday last, an inquest was held at the house of Mr. J. York, Wells Head Inn, Thornton, on view of the body of Samuel Wademan, labourer, whose death was caused by a large quantity of scale falling upon him. Verdict, 'Accidental death.'

Bradford Observer, 4 October 1838

THORNTON. Last Friday an inquest was held before G. Dyson, Esq., coroner, at Mr. Joseph Greenwood's, of Rock and Heifer Inn, in this township, on view of the body of a little boy, about four years old, son of Henry Speight, delver. The accident arose from the boy lighting a match at the fire in the morning while undressed and in the momentary absence of the father who had just gone out to fetch some water. Verdict, *accidental death*.

Bradford Observer, 4 October 1838

Mr. Robert Leach, manufacturer, Thornton, was the first witness examined on Friday evening. He said I am a manufacturer and employ about 250 hand-loom weavers on my own account. They are employed on weaving figured merinos, or as they are usually called, fancy goods; they are chiefly woven by men; I have no power looms; I pay 12*s* 6*d* for eleven score hanks, 50 set.

(Question): When you deliver out, when do you expect to receive a piece back?

After being fairly set to work we expect a piece a week. To start a new engine it occupies half a week, but that is for once only – at the commencement of a weaver working upon these particular kind of goods. I consider one piece a week a fair week's work. Inferior hands could not do a piece a week. It requires a tolerable good workman to average a piece a week on figures. The power-loom has been applied extensively to figures. I believe the power-loom manufacturers would eventually be able to drive us out of the market. I believe there are advantages connected with the power-loom, for it is certain that there are many manufacturers beginning to work figures by power. I have been connected with the manufacturing business all my life; from the year 1820 I have taken an active part in the business along with my father. In 1836 we paid at the rate of 2*s* a score; in that year the first important reduction took place. In November or December of that year a reduction of 5*s* a piece took place. In the February following, there was a further reduction of 4*s*. In August 1836, an advance of 1s occurred, but I ought to state that this period we took off 12 hanks, being from 15 to 14 score 8. I attribute the advance to a temporary demand for that fabric; that advance continued until December of the same year, when a decline of 2*s* for the 14 score 8 took effect. The decline has been gradual since that time. We thought at the time that the decline was on account of the competition of the power-loom, and the falling off of the demand also. The goods I manufacture require good and ingenious workmen.

(Question): Then the wages of hand-loom weavers generally would be considerably below what you have stated as the earnings of your weavers?

Generally so. The average work of our weavers may be taken at one piece in 9 days, or two in three weeks. It is far beyond an average to say one a week. A superior workman, or a bad engine, will make a great difference. We endeavour invariably to give out good warps; at times we may be deceived; but it is our interest to give out the best.

(Question): Are there many manufacturers of figured goods in this town and neighbourhood?

Many, Sir.

(Question): Is there not some material difference in the amount of wages paid by different manufacturers?

It has been so stated; but I am not aware that there is material difference; there may be sixpence a piece, but I do not know of it as a fact.

(Question): Is the embezzlement of weft by the weavers a thing you have reason to complain of; is it a thing the weavers are generally chargeable with?

No, it is not by any means general. I have nothing of the kind to complain of myself. I am not aware of any loss sustained from that cause at present.

(Question): You expect, of course, to have the whole of the weft put in, which you must deliver out with a piece?

I do expect the whole to be put in; but if a few hanks be returned and the piece be good, we make no reduction; if the piece be bad, a reduction is just.

(Question): Would you discharge a weaver who had not put

in all the weft given out, if you thought the piece too thin?

I should not always discharge a weaver for leaving out a little weft, unless I should have reason to suppose that it was from some unjust cause.

(Question): An undue degree of strictness would offer a temptation for embezzlement, would it not?

I always put my own judgement on the piece, and if I find it a good one, and a little left out, so much the better.

(Question): In some cases a weaver will state that he has put in more weft than he actually has?

I think that if a weaver puts his own judgement on the piece it is much better than asking the weaver what the piece has actually in it (hear, hear, from the weavers present). We have never relaxed for 16 or 18 months giving employment; upon figures, full employment. There has, during that time, been considerable fluctuations on other kinds of goods, and a slackness of employment. I do not manufacture any plain goods; I have formerly had management of 800 hand-loom weavers.

Bent Ing Bridge.

Question: Are the hand-loom weavers, as a body, an orderly body of men?

Generally speaking, and from my own experience I would say the hand-loom weavers are an orderly body of men; in so large a body of men there must necessarily be exceptions.

(Question): If the manufacturer took care as to the character of the men they employed would it not have a tendency to raise the moral character of that body?

It certainly would, but they cannot at all times do that; they may be imposed on by representations. The recurrence of a demand for goods would preclude the possibility of discriminating, and other causes might arise to prevent their exercising a choice. The hand-loom weavers have certainly had much to contend with. A depression of trade will be sure to fall upon them. Some few manufacturers would keep their hands on and accumulate goods, but many could not do so for want of capital.

(Question): Can you suggest any thing as a remedy, as a means of improving the condition of the men?

No.

(Question): Have you thought of the suggestion of establishing a Board of Trade?

I think it would do no good.

Mr. Chapman here explained to Mr. Leach the nature of the Board of Trade as expounded, he said, by. Mr. Fielden in the House of Commons, and asked Mr. Leach what was his opinion of the subject. Mr. Leach said, could such a plan be carried into effect it certainly might be effective of good, providing power was included in the arrangement, and for short periods.

(Question): What length of time would you suppose most likely to meet with the approbation of the masters?

Three months is too long a period, much inconvenience might be experienced in that time by a sudden depression of trade. A month, I think, might not be inconvenient. There are certain descriptions of goods on which it would be difficult to fix a rate of wages, there being a difference in goods nominally the same.

(Question): Have you turned your attention to the subject of taxing power-looms?

I see so great a difficulty in placing a tax upon power-looms, that I cannot see how it can be done without taxing every description of machinery, and that would put a stop to improvement at once.

Bradford Observer, 1 November 1838

MANOR COURT. On Friday last at the Court Leet of B. Rawson Esq., Lord of the Manor of Bradford, the following appointments took place. Constables:- Thornton – James Pearson and Jonathan Foster, Chiefs; Thomas Barker, Stephen Bairstow and John Ambler, Deputies; William Robinson, Bye-lawman and Pinder.

Bradford Observer, 15 November 1838

THORNTON. During the last week several depredations have been committed in this and the adjoining town of Allerton. Mr. Thomas Booth, of Allerton Green, has had a lamb stolen; Mr. Benjamin Hindle, near the same place, a sheep stolen; Mr. Miles Gawthorp, of School Green, Thornton, some geese stolen; and on Tuesday night Mr. Jonathan Ackroyd, butcher, Thornton, had a sheep stolen.

Bradford Observer, 22 November 1838

THORNTON WESLEYAN METHODIST CHAPEL. On Sunday last two sermons were preached in the above chapel, by Mr. Braithwaite, of Bradford, and the Rev. Mr. Freeman, after which collections were made towards defraying the expenses of lighting the chapel with gas, that evening being the first time of its being lighted up with gas. The gas is obtained from the works of Mr. Simeon Townend, and the cost about £30 fitting up &c.; towards discharging which upwards of £20 in the above collection and previous contribution is now raised.

Bradford Observer, 10 January 1839

THORNTON. Like most other places the wind on Monday morning has done considerable damage all round this neighbourhood in windows, slates, etc. But the most serious misfortune is the blowing down of the new mill belonging to Messrs. William and Henry Foster, manufacturers, Denholme. This mill had only just got erected, and is now blown down to the first story [*sic*], and the damage estimated at £500 or £600.

Bradford Observer, 20 June 1839

THORNTON WESLEYAN SUNDAY SCHOOL ANNIVERSARY. On Sunday last, after two sermons by the Rev. Mr. Thompson, of Halifax, for the benefit of the above school, the very handsome sum of £240 10s 9d was collected, thus evincing a laudable liberality in support of an institution which is the means of doing much good in the neighbourhood.

Bradford Observer, 20 June 1839

THORNTON. Last Sunday afternoon a novel and interesting scene took place at the Kipping Chapel. The members of the three Independent chapels at Thornton, Wilsden, and Allerton having agreed that they will publicly take the Sacrament together once a year at one of the above chapels in rotation, the first of this series of impressive meetings took place last Sunday afternoon at the Kipping Chapel, when that large and commodious place of worship was well filled, and addresses, suitable to the solemnity of the occasion, were delivered by the pastors of the respective chapels – the Revds. Messrs. Gregory, Savage, and Hutton.

Northern Star & Leeds General Advertiser, 26 October 1839

BRADFORD. FELONY. David Wilson, of Thornton, was committed for trial for obtaining a warp, from Mr. Wright, of that place, under false pretences.

Chapter Four
1840-1842

Thornton spy arrested – Fraudulent spinsters robbed – Drunkard in the stocks – Thornton Grammar appeals for boarders – Doctor dies

Northern Star & Leeds General Advertiser, 8 February 1840

BRADFORD. THE SPY ARRESTED – AND MORE CHARTISTS ARRESTED. . . . Thomas Drake, weaver, of Thornton, whom our readers will recollect, was apprehended in Bradford on the morning of Monday, the 27th ult., but discharged for want of direct evidence, was, along with Squire Normington, of Thornton, delver, taken into custody on Saturday last, and after a private examination, were remanded until Monday, when Mr. Clarkson appeared for them. Two additional witnesses were produced, but their testimony being immaterial, it was rejected; and on the prisoners' attorney applying for their discharge, immediately Normington was ordered to be set at liberty, on two sureties entering into recognizance for his future appearance, if required. Drake still remains in custody, and is to be brought up, along with the other Bradford victims at present in York Castle, on Monday next for final examination.

Bradford Observer, 12 March 1840

HOME NEWS. ASSISTANT OVERSEERS. To-morrow the Board of Guardians will proceed to the election of an assistant overseer for the respective townships of Wilsden, Allerton, and Heaton. The only candidates we have heard named are Mr. David Wright, late of Thornton, and Mr. Samuel Crabtree, late a carrier between Leeds and this town.

Bradford Observer, 30 April 1840
BRADFORD COURT HOUSE

BEERSHOPS. John Johnson, of Thornton, was charged by the constable with having company in his house on Sunday, the 19th instant, at half-past eleven in the forenoon. Mr. Wagstaff appeared for the defence; and in answer to questions put by him the constable said there were two men in the house who were strangers to him. He could not say that they had been travelling. They were not fresh. They were drinking ale, and had a full pint before them. Joshua Smith for the defence said, he went to Thornton, on Sunday the 19th of April, to see a friend who was going off next day for America. They went to Johnson's and had one pint of ale, and only one. The magistrates inquired if that person had gone to America? Smith said he had, and that he went with him to Manchester the next day. The magistrates said, under these circumstances, they would dismiss the case, which was done accordingly.

Leeds Mercury, 23 May 1840

BURGLARY AT THORNTON – THE BITERS BIT. On Monday evening a robbery of a rather novel description was effected at a lonely place called Guy House, at the point where Thornton and Northowram townships meet. In the above house, both of them at a very advanced age, two sisters of the name of Shaw live together. They have been regularly receiving parochial relief – one from Northowram, the other from Thornton – for a great many years, and to all appearances were in very poor and needy circumstances. Contrary to their usual custom, both sisters happened to be from home at the same time, and one or more of the numerous gang of burglars which infest that neighbourhood seized the opportunity of breaking into the cottage, forced open the box which was always kept locked, and were no doubt agreeably surprised to find therein, carefully wrapped up in an old long glove, upwards of £47 in gold and silver! thus exposing the hypocrisy, and leaving in reality, what before they only appeared to be, two very old women in very indigent circumstances. Two men of the names of Barrett and Wilson were taken up on suspicion on Tuesday, examined before the Bradford Magistrates on Wednesday, and were fully committed for trial at the approaching quarter sessions. On the same night, the house of Mr. Blakey Nicholls, of West Scholes Gate, Thornton, shopkeeper, was broken into, and goods of different descriptions to the amount of upwards of £20 were stolen therefrom. Two men have been apprehended for this burglary, owing to some women falling out about their shares of the stolen property.

Bradford Observer, 21 May 1840
BRADFORD COURT HOUSE

CAUTION TO WEAVERS. Thomas Best, of Thornton, was charged by Mr. George Leach with detaining and refusing to deliver up an engine belonging to complainant. George Leach said that Best had an engine belonging to them which they could not get from him. Witness had given him notes to bring in the engine. Had had it six months in his possession since he left off weaving for them. Witness had given him leave to weave a warp with it for Robert Leach, but not for any other person's work. It was two weeks since witness gave him notice to bring it in. The Bench said it was their duty to commit him to prison, and they must do so unless he would agree with Mr. Leach. This he did and had to pay costs of 8s.

Bradford Observer, 28 May 1840
BRADFORD COURT HOUSE

ROBBERY. William Wilson, comber, and Abraham Barratt, collier, both of Thornton, were charged by Susan Bentley, an old woman and a pauper of the town, with having broken into her house, and with having stolen therefrom 35 sovereigns, 16 half crowns, and four pounds in silver, her property. The old woman stated that on Monday last she went to Halifax and locked up her house. On her return she found it had been broken into and the money described, which she had left in a glove, in some, as she thought, safe place, was gone. Grace Robinson said that she saw the prisoners come out of Guy House, the residence of the old woman, and run into a field at a short distance, where one lay down and the other stooped or sat down. She was a very reluctant witness on account of both the young men being neighbours. Several other witnesses were examined, and the case was brought so clearly home that the magistrates refused to admit the prisoners to bail, and they were both committed to take their trial at the ensuing Bradford Sessions.

Bradford Observer, 28 May 1840
BRADFORD COURT HOUSE

VAGRANTS. Benjamin Goldsborough, shoemaker, and Mary Boocock of Leys, prostitute, were charged with stripping the handkerchief off the neck of James Spence, of Thornton, at half-past one on Sunday morning; committed for one month each.

Leeds Mercury, 6 June 1840

INQUESTS BEFORE G. DYSON, ESQ. On Monday, at the Bull's Head, Thornton, on the body of Thomas Fearnside, collier, aged 20, accidentally killed by falling down a coal pit. Verdict – 'Accidental Death.'

Bradford Observer, 24 June 1840
BRADFORD COURT HOUSE

FELONY. James Drake, of Thornton, weaver, was yesterday committed for trial for stealing a quantity of wearing apparel and other articles the property of David Parkinson of Clayton. The prisoner had lived servant with the complainant.

Bradford Observer, 6 August 1840
VALUABLE FREEHOLD ESTATES,

In Thornton in the Parish of Bradford, and at Barcroft, in the Parish of Bingley.

TO BE SOLD BY PRIVATE CONTRACT.

Lot 1. ALL THAT MILL, now used as a WORSTED MILL, situate at Thornton in the Parish of Bradford, late in the occupation of Mr. DAVID WRIGHT, but now in the occupation of Mr. Simeon Townend, as Lessee for Ten Years, with the Steam Engine, Main Shafting, and Gas Apparatus belonging thereto; also the Sizing Rooms, Drying Rooms, Washhouses, and other Outbuildings.

The above Premises are in excellent Condition and are well supplied with good Water, and comprise an area of 1a 0r 33p.

Lot 2. All that Close of MEADOW LAND, at Storr Height in the Township of Thornton aforesaid, late in the occupation of Mr. David Wright, called the Height, and containing by admeasurement 1a 1r 27p. This Close of Land possesses a very valuable Bed of Stone, it is near to the village of Thornton, and is only about four miles from Bradford.

Lot 3. All that Close of MEADOW LAND situate at Salt Pie, or Small Lane End, in Thornton aforesaid, lately in the occupation of Mr. David Wright, called the Three Nooked Field, containing by admeasurement 1a 1r 14p

Lot 4. All that COTTAGE or Dwelling-House situate in Green Lane, in Thornton aforesaid, in the occupation of Thomas Barker.

Lot 5. All that MESSUAGE or FARM HOUSE, situate at or near Harden in the Parish of Bingley, and called Barcroft, with the Barn, Stable, Cowhouse, and other Outbuildings thereto belonging; and also all those Ten several Closes of Arable, Meadow, and Pasture LAND occupied therewith, and called the Dean Ing, the Six Days' Work, Faugh Closes, Short Field, Duckworth Ing, Over Hey, Far Day's Work, Upper Croft, Over Ruff, and Lower Ruff, containing by Estimation 63 Days' Work, and in the occupation of Isaac Doughty; also those SIX COTTAGES adjoining thereto, late in the occupation of Joseph Midgley, John Mitchell, Mary Haigh, Nathan Mitchell, Thomas Bailey, and David Feather.

The premises comprised in this lot are now under lease to Mr. Isaac Doughty for 19 years, 13 of which are unexpired, at the annual rent of £70.

Further Particulars may be had on Application to Messrs. STANSFIELD & CRAVEN,

Solicitors, Halifax, or Messrs. MORRIS & CLEGG, Solicitors, Bradford.

July 1, 1840.

Bradford Observer, 10 September 1840
HOME NEWS

THORNTON – RURAL POLICE. On Tuesday, a public meeting of the ratepayers of this township was held at the Vestry of Thornton Chapel, to take into consideration the propriety of memorializing the magistrates of the West Riding respecting the introduction of the Rural Police Bill into this Riding. A series of resolutions were proposed, and universally carried against the introduction of the measure into this part, and a numerously signed Memorial will be presented to the magistrates, founded on the resolutions passed at the public meeting.

Bradford Observer, 15 October 1840

INFORMATION AGAINST A LICENSED VICTUALLER. Joseph Briggs, of Thornton, was charged by the constables with having company in his house at 11 o'clock in the forenoon of Sunday last, being the hour of divine service. James Hardacre and John Ambler, constables, stated that on going their rounds on Sunday morning, they found the window blind of the defendant's house drawn, and on going in they found a company of seven individuals with ale before them on the table. For the defence Mr. Weir called three witnesses, who swore that they were in the house when the constables entered, and that they left the house with the constables, and drew their attention to the circumstances of the church bells being at that time ringing for morning service. This the constables denied, but on account of the contradictory statements the case was dismissed.

Bradford Observer, 15 October 1840

GAMBLING. Seven boys of the township of Thornton were convicted of gaming on the highway, on the information of the constable, and ½ were fined 3s 4d each with costs 9s 2d½ each.

Bradford Observer, 15 October 1840

THE STOCKS. A circumstance of rare occurrence was carried into effect on Monday week, in this place. Timothy Robertshaw, of Thornton, weaver, but better known as a disturber of the public peace, had several times been convicted of drunkenness and making a disturbance in the streets of this town on Saturday nights, and on each occasion a week had been allowed him to pay fines and costs. On Saturday night he was again up in his gear, but down on his luck, the chance of paying was not given him, but as an incorrigible, he was placed for six hours in the stocks.

Bradford Observer, 26 November 1840
HOME NEWS

FATAL ACCIDENT. Last Thursday evening, as the wagon of Mr. Abraham Hardy, of Thornton, corn-miller, was on his return from Leeds, with a wagon load of corn, a most lamentable accident happened at Kirkstall Bridge. The deceased, who was a very steady man, and much respected, was riding on the wagon shafts, and seeing a coach approaching, jumped down, his foot fell on some dross which made him lose his balance, and the wheel going over his breast caused his death instantaneous.

Bradford Observer, 24 December 1840

THORNTON GRAMMAR SCHOOL MR. BUTLER, Master of the above school, has accommodation for a few Boarders. His terms per annum are:- For Boys under twelve, 25 guineas. For Boys above that age, 30 guineas. These Terms are for Board and Instruction in all that is implied by a 'sound English Education,' as well as in the Latin, French, and Greek languages. Mr. B's residence is healthfully situated. It will be his constant endeavour to render those entrusted to his care, comfortable, clever, and good. School Green, Thornton. December 19, 1840.

Bradford Observer, 31 December 1840
HOME NEWS

INCENDIARISM. At a late hour on Wednesday night, or early on Thursday morning week, an attempt was made to set fire to a barn belonging to Mr. Booth, at Thornton Hall; fortunately, however, notwithstanding three holes were burnt in the door, the fire extended no further, and thus a large quantity of valuable hay was preserved.

Leeds Mercury, 27 March 1841

MEDICAL APPOINTMENTS. Yesterday week, Mr. Thomas Fawthrope, surgeon, of Thornton, was elected surgeon by the Bradford Board of Guardians for the townships of Thornton and Clayton; and Mr. Sister, for the townships of Tong, Drighlington, Hunsworth, and Cleckheaton.

Old Thornton Grammar School, Thornton Road.

Bradford Observer, 28 April 1842

To Schoolmasters. WANTED. A Master for Thornton Free Grammar School, Salary £45 per annum. Apply to Mr. G.T. Lister, Albion Court, Bradford.

Bradford Observer, 29 October 1842

Died on Tuesday last, deeply regretted by a numerous circle of friends and relatives, Mr. John Fawthrop, of Thornton, surgeon and doctor, aged 55.

Chapter Five
1843-1844

Pig and weft theft – Skeleton found in jar – Kipping chapel unsafe, to be rebuilt – Sixty year old visited by God – Illicit still found in cottage

Bradford Observer, 12 January 1843

THORNTON. On Tuesday evening a splendid silver tea-pot was presented to Mr. Nathan Pearson, at the Black Horse Inn, for the upright and efficient manner in which he had discharged the duties of assistant overseer for that township. The gift was presented by Mr. Isaac Wood, as chairman of the meeting.

Bradford Observer, 12 January 1843

A ROBBERY FROM WANT. A farmer's labourer, named Bennet, was charged with having stolen two old horseshoes, the property of Thomas Greg, blacksmith, of Thornton. The prisoner, on Tuesday last, went into the prosecutor's smithy and offered two door hinges for sale as old iron. Prosecutor weighed them, and then said 'Why these will bring very little,' alluding to the weight and their value. The prisoner then pulled two old horseshoes from under his smock, and said 'Then these will.' Prosecutor, recognising them at once as his own property, accused prisoner of stealing them, but he denied it. On a constable being sent for, however, he acknowledged having picked them up as soon as he entered the shop and hid them under his frock. He stated that distress was the cause; he had been pining three days. His last master had sold half his land, and then had no occasion for him and since that time, about a month, he had subsisted on some little money he had to draw of his master or had pined. The magistrates committed him for fourteen days in Wakefield House of Correction.

Bradford Observer, 26 January 1843

THORNTON. Early on Friday morning last, the house of Mr. John Patchett, Green Clough Head, in this township, was entered, and a pig which was in salt, a cheese, and other articles were stolen therefrom. The entrance was effected by the cellar window, out of which place the thieves proceeded forward to the parlour, where, for more safety, the bacon, etc., were placed, and after making fast the parlour door, they decamped with their booty back again through the cellar window. The family had not retired until 2 o'clock on the morning of the robbery. On the following day, the Worsted Inspector and a constable for Keighley, while visiting a man's house of the name of Pollard, who lives not far from Mr. Patchett's, discovered in an out-house adjoining his, about half of the stolen bacon. On his premises the Inspector also found some weft which is supposed to be embezzled, and consequently he will undergo an examination on both charges before the Keighley magistrates.

Bradford Observer, 16 February 1843

THORNTON. On Thursday last, an inquest was held at the house of Mr. Joseph Greenwood, the Rock and Heifer Inn, before G. Dyson, Esq. coroner, on view of the body of a little boy, nearly four years old, son of Isaac Drake, weaver. In the absence of the father, who had gone for some bobbins, and was not more than about five minutes away, the clothes of the child caught fire, and almost immediate death was the result. Verdict: *Accidental Burning.*

Bradford Observer, 9 March 1843

THORNTON. On Sunday last an inquest was held at the house of Mr. W. Riley, the Bull's Head Inn, before G. Dyson, Esq., on view of the body of a little boy, about three years old, son of Christopher Yeoman, labourer. The accident, which has resulted fatally, happened about three weeks ago. The boy happened to be standing near the fire as his mother was taking the porridge off, some of which boiled over on the boy's neck and breast. Verdict, 'Accidentally burnt.'

Bradford Observer, 23 March 1843
NOTICE

I, JESSE DRAKE FAWTHROP, at present, and for five months past residing at School Green, in Thornton, in the Parish of Bradford, in the County of York, and for six months previously residing at Green Gates, in Eccleshill, in the Parish of Bradford aforesaid, and for two years previously residing at School Green aforesaid, and being by profession a Surgeon, do hereby give Notice, that I intend to present a Petition to the Court of Bankruptcy for the Leeds District, praying to be examined touching my Debts, Estate, and Effects, and to be protected from all Process, upon making a full disclosure and surrender of such Estate and

Effects, for payment of my just and lawful Debts; and I hereby further give Notice, that the time when the matter of the said Petition shall be heard is advertised in the *London Gazette* and in the *Bradford Observer* Newspaper, one Month at the least after the Date hereof. As Witness my Hand this 22nd Day of March, in the year of our Lord One Thousand Eight Hundred and Forty Three. JESSE DRAKE FAWTHROP, Signed in the presence of THOMAS ASHWORTH, Attorney at Law, Hustler's Buildings.

Bradford Observer, 30 March 1843

MONUMENT. A chaste tablet of white marble has this week been erected in the church of St. James, Thornton, to the memory of the late Mr. John Fawthrop of that place: The execution of this beautiful tribute to a good and clever man reflects the highest credit on the artist – Mr. J.B. Leyland, of Halifax. The inscription on the tablet is as follows: This Tablet is erected by public subscription to the memory of Mr. John Fawthrop; veterinary surgeon of this place. A man no less remarkable for the extent of his practice, than the uniformity of his success. To the poor he was in the habit of giving his advice and applying medical assistance, on terms which precluded him from attaining that affluence to which his skill and assiduity most justly entitled him. His death, in the full vigour of life, is regarded as a public loss, and his memory will long be held in grateful remembrance. He died October 20th 1842, aged 42 years.

Northern Star & Leeds General Advertiser, 29 April 1843

BRADFORD. DISCOVERY OF HUMAN BONES. On Thursday last, as Mr. Isaac Wood's man, of Kipping, Thornton, was ploughing at the Pikeley Farm, in the township of Allerton, the plough went so deep as to break the top of a large pot jar, into which the man put his hand, and to his astonishment found it contained the remains of a human being. From what has transpired since the discovery there seems little doubt but the remains in question are those of a little boy about eleven years old, who was apprenticed to a coal miner about Dent's Head, and who mysteriously and suddenly disappeared forty-three years ago. The boy had been cruelly used by his master on the night previously to his disappearance, and the probability is that one of his blows proving fatal, he put him into the large pot jar, capable of holding half a pack of flour, so as to escape the justice which his crime deserved. The coal miner always said that the boy had run away, and nothing has been heard of him up to this time. The supposed murderer died nearly twenty years since.

Bradford Observer, 25 May 1843

KIPPING CHAPEL, THORNTON. Rumours being afloat that the state of this building was not so as to be considered safe, the trustees got Mr. Metcalfe, architect, Bradford, and some other experienced persons to examine it. Their decision has confirmed the report of its inefficiency and at a meeting of the trustees on Tuesday, it was determined to pull the present building entirely down, and rebuilt on its present site. The estimated expense is £1,000.

Leeds Mercury, 27 May 1843

KIPPING CHAPEL, Thornton, is about to be pulled down and rebuilt.

Bradford Observer, 20 July 1843

THORNTON. On Monday last, an inquest was held at the White Horse Inn, Well Heads, Thornton before G. Dyson, Esq., coroner, on view of the body of Jeremiah Butterfield, a pensioner, about 60 years of age, who, near his own house, last Friday evening, dropped down and died instantly. Verdict: 'Died by visitation of God.'

Northern Star & Leeds General Advertiser, 18 November 1843

BRADFORD. A youth named Butterfield, was on Thursday brought from Thornton to the Infirmary, having received a severe wound on his left hand, owing to a gun, which had missed fire, having discharged itself when he was in the act of examining the priming.

Bradford Observer, 7 December 1843

ALLERTON – SEIZURE OF MALT, &c, BY THE EXCISE. Last Friday morning, Mr. William Jack, of Thornton, excise man, having had his suspicions raised by something which he had previously seen, entered the dwelling house of a poor man of the name of William Ingham, who lives in Allerton Lane, and on proceeding up stairs found the process of malting in full and complete operation with the exception of the cistern. He immediately procured assistance and removed the malt, along with what was in process, to the premises of Mr. Exley Barker, maltster. Ingham now acknowledges having thus made malt for several years – report says about ten years, but hitherto managed to escape detection – thus paying a compliment to Mr. Jack's superior vigilance and observation.

Bradford Observer, 7 December 1843

THORNTON, NEAR BRADFORD, TO BE SOLD BY PRIVATE CONTRACT, ALL THAT MESSUAGE or TENEMENT, with the Barn and other Outbuildings, and the following CLOSES of LAND, namely, The Croft or Ing, Middle Intack, Great Intack (now in two Closes), New

Kipping Chapel and the Mechanics' Institute.

Field, and Morton Close (now in two), and called Whams Lane and Morton Close, containing together Twelve Acres, Two Roods, and Twenty Two Perches, in the occupation of John Wilkinson. Also, FOUR COTTAGES adjoining the above Premises. The above desirable FREEHOLD PROPERTY is situate at Intack, in Thornton, and will be sold either together or in Lots. The old Inclosed Land contains valuable BEDS OF COAL, now working within Half a Mile. For Price, or any other Information, apply to Mr. THOMAS DIXON, Land Agent, Bradford; or Messrs. HAXBY AND SCHOLES, Solicitors, Wakefield. Bradford, Dec. 4th, 1843.

Bradford Observer, 21 December 1843

MAN MISSING. We hear that a weaver named Thomas Bentham, about sixty years of age, who resided lately at Schole House Green, near Thornton, left the house of his son, in Hodgson Lane, Manningham, on Saturday last, and has never since been heard of. It seems he was in low spirits, and has been so for some time. His afflicted friends are making every search for him, and will be happy if they succeed in finding him.

Bradford Observer, 21 December 1843
VALUABLE FREEHOLD ESTATES,
In the Township of Thornton, Near Bradford.

43

TO BE PEREMPTORILY SOLD BY AUCTION,
BY MR. G.T. LISTER,
At the Albion Hotel, in Bradford, on WEDNESDAY, the 3rd of January, 1844, at
Six o'Clock in the Evening, subject to conditions, and in the following or such
other Lots as may be agreed upon at the time of Sale.

LOT 1. ELEVEN substantially-built COTTAGES, with the Yards and
Conveniences, situated near the Town Street of Thornton, and now or lately in
the Occupations of Nanny Ackroyd, Jonathan Illingworth, Jonathan Leach and
others.

LOT 2. A PLOT of GROUND, in the Village of Thornton, called Upper Shepley,
or Smith's Field, and containing 1 rood and 20 Perches.

LOT 3. An UNDIVIDED MOIETY of the Valuable BEDS of COAL, at
Thornton, now being worked by Mr. Abraham Ackroyd, and lying under the
following Closes of Land, viz., the Broad Dole, the Vascan's Brace, the Ing, the
Clough, the West Field, the Far Ped Hill, the Near Ped Field, the Far Field, the
Middle Field, the Priest Royd, the Greaves Wood, the Grim Croft, the Lane End
Croft, the Upper Dick Field, the Lower Dick Field, the Lane End Ped Hill, and
the Fold, containing 60 Days' Work (more or less), and now or late in the
Occupations of Abraham Ackroyd, David Wright, and James Holdsworth, and
John Ackroyd; and under the Croft, the Garth, the Orchard, the Near Load Hill,
the Far Load Hill, the Fall Bates, the Laugh Hall Croft, the Horse Close, the
Copy and Sweet Lips, the Clews, the Riding, with the Fold and Yard.
Containing about 30 Days' Work, and now or late in the Occupation of Isaac
Wood, his Undertenants or Assigns; and also under the Great Ing, the Croft, the
Wilman Ing, the Dick Field, the Near Lower Sowden, the Far Lower Sowden,
the Upper Sowden, the Near Coat Dole, the Far Coat, the Green, the Calf Croft,
and the Fold, containing together about 32 Days' Work, and now or lately in the
Occupation of Stephen Illingworth.

LOT 4. ONE UNDIVIDED SIXTH PART or SHARE, and all such other PART
or SHARE as may accrue by Benefit of Survivorship, of and in the Monies to
arise from the Valuable FREEHOLD ESTATE of Mr. Thomas Bairstow,
deceased, called Leaventhorpe Mill Estate, situated in the Township of
Thornton, consisting of TWO WATER MILLS (One a Worsted Mill, the other a
Corn Mill), and several MESSUAGES, COTTAGES, BARNS and BUILDINGS,
and about SIXTY-THREE ACRES of Excellent Arable, Meadow, and Pasture
LAND, including some Valuable WOOD LAND. Further Particulars may be
obtained on application at the Office of Mr. TOLSON, Solicitor, Bradford.

Bradford Observer, 28 December 1843

THORNTON – ANNIVERSARY OF THE KIPPING SABBATH SCHOOL. On Tuesday, the Sabbath school connected with the Kipping Chapel, held its anniversary in the School Room. The scholars were regaled with spice cakes and tea, and after their separation, the teachers and other friends of this institution sat down to enjoy the pleasures of the 'cup that cheers but not inebriates;' after which the Rev. J. Gregory took the chair, and the meeting was addressed by the chairman, Mr. Thomas Jowett, the superintendents, and other friends belonging both to their own and the Wesleyan body. The school consists of nearly 400 scholars, and was stated to be in a very prosperous condition. A vote of thanks was passed to the 'Dorcas Society' here, for the very great benefit it rendered the institution in providing clothing, &c, for many of the poorer children. The meeting, in the evening, was very numerously attended – a pleasing excitement seemed to animate the audience – and the announcement of the probability of the early establishment of a day school on the best principle of teaching, in connection with this chapel, seemed to give general satisfaction.

Bradford Observer, 14 March 1844

THORNTON GUARDIANS. Mr. Isaac Wood, Kipping, and Mr. William Wood, Black Carr, are nominated guardians of this township for the ensuing year. There will not be any opposition here.

Kipping Sunday School, Thornton Road.

Bradford Observer, 21 March 1844

On Tuesday, Mr. Joshua Craven was re-elected surveyor of the highways for the township of Thornton, for the ensuing year, and at the same time Mr. Jonas Craven and Mr. Joseph Whitley were re-chosen overseers of the poor for the same period.

Leeds Mercury, 13 April 1844

KIPPING CHAPEL, THORNTON. SPLENDID EXAMPLE OF THE VOLUNTARY PRINCIPLE. On Good Friday, the above commodious and beautiful chapel, the design and execution of which reflect much credit on the ability and taste of the architect, Mr. Metcalfe, Bradford, was opened for divine worship, when two sermons were preached by the Rev. G.B. McDonald, Wesleyan minister, Leeds; and on Easter Sunday, the Rev. R. Vaughan, D.D., Theological Professor of Manchester, preached in the morning and afternoon; and the Rev. R.W. Hamilton, LL.D., of Leeds, in the evening. The cost of the chapel is about £1,200, towards which the Kipping congregation have subscribed £1,040 13s 7d, and the munificent sum of £197 19s 9½d was collected at the opening services; thus the chapel is now entirely free from debt, and a surplus of £38 13s 4½d left towards defraying sundry incidental expenses. This is, indeed, a noble specimen of the working of the voluntary principle, and cannot fail to be a source of pleasure and satisfaction to all concerned in it.

Bradford Observer, 15 August 1844

THORNTON. On Monday last, being Thornton feast, the Temperance Society had made arrangements for their meeting in Kipping School, with a view of counteracting the excesses and evils mainly attendant on such festive occasions. Mr. Jack, the President of the Society, occupied the chair. The principal speakers were Mr. Bowes, master of the Wesleyan day-school there, and Mr. Thompson of Leeds, one of the agents of the British Temperance Society. Mr. Bowes illustrated his subject by some beautiful drawings of the human stomach in health and under alcoholic excitement; but time not allowing sufficient opportunity for properly showing and explaining them, the speaker said he would more fully elucidate them on Wednesday evening. Mr. Thompson is now so well known in this division of the riding that his name is sufficient guarantee that the picture would be touched with a master's hand. The meeting was delighted with his happy and humorous manner, and the impression made on the minds of many of his audience was considerable. On Tuesday evening there was a meeting at Allerton, at which the Rev. T. Hutton presided; the principal speakers being those mentioned above.

Bradford Observer, 15 August 1844

FORESTERS' PROCESSION. On Monday last, there was a splendid and numerous procession of the Courts of Foresters of Thornton, Denholme, Cullingworth, &c. The procession consisted of a very numerous body of horsemen, intermixed with vehicles of various descriptions, and accompanied with four bands of music, flags, banners, &c. After perambulating the township in various directions, the Courts separated to their own respective places, and the evening was spent in the festivities customary on such occasions.

Bradford Observer, 26 December 1844

THORNTON BRITISH SCHOOL. Last Friday evening the first public examination of the scholars of the above school took place in the Kipping School Room. The Rev. J. Gregory presided, and the proceedings were the most interesting and delightful that ever took place on any similar occasion in Thornton. So varied and valuable is the knowledge acquired in these schools, that their practical advantages cannot fail to be appreciated. The school was opened in May last, and is conducted on the principles of the British and Foreign School Society. So great has been the general improvement and progress of the scholars in the various branches of learning that great credit is reflected on Mr. Gobert, the master, and Miss Drake, the mistress, for the pleasing results which were witnessed could only have been produced by continuous labour and attention. If any one department may be mentioned as showing superior progress, that of drawing ought not to be passed over. The splendid and various specimens which were hung around the room astonished all who had the pleasure of seeing them. Unlike the old system of teaching, it could not fail to be observed that the present one aims at expanding and developing the intellectual faculties by such a course of questioning, that the young and tender mind is led into such habits of thoughts as must eventually produce beneficial and important results to the rising generation. The scholars showed great intimacy and proficiency in Geography, English History, Scripture History, Mental Arithmetic, and Grammar. The new chairman examined them in Scripture History in an uncontrolled and promiscuous manner, so as to fairly test their knowledge, and the result was highly satisfactory. In the other branches they were equally open to questions of a miscellaneous character, from Mr. Bower, the Wesleyan schoolmaster here, and other persons, and all tended to show that the information they had acquired was as sterling and sound as it was tried and useful. After the examination, the chairman distributed, with appropriate remarks to each, a number of books, knives, pencil cases, medals, &c, to those who had distinguished themselves; and in the afternoon, through the liberality of Mr. Joseph Craven (who also presented the committee with the prizes), the scholars were all regaled with tea, and spice cakes. The chairman then called on Mr. Kay, the secretary, to read the report, which was highly satisfactory and encouraging, and shewed, as may have been already inferred, that the establishment of this school is likely to be attended with many advantages to the neighbourhood, as a good and sound education is now placed within the reach of all classes. The thanks of the meeting were voted to Mr. Gobert, the master, for his unremitted exertions and attention, to the secretary to the committee and to the chairman for his services during the evening, and the company separated convinced of the capabilities of this newest stem of education to produce many advantageous, practical, results to the rising generation.

Chapter Six
1845-1849

Nine sign the pledge — Brown pony found — Thornton mill owner treats his workers — Sagar's dole money distributed — Working men can read — Reformed convict gives lecture

Bradford Observer, 9 January 1845

FATAL ACCIDENT. On Saturday week, a person of the name of Nathan Horsfall, a native of Thornton, met with an accident while working on a railway which is cutting near Bury, in Lancashire, which has ended fatally. The unfortunate man was immediately conveyed to the Manchester Infirmary, and had his arm amputated on the following day. Hopes were at first entertained of his recovery, but he died last Saturday and his remains have been removed for interment at the Kipping Chapel, Thornton. The deceased was unmarried and about 33 years of age.

Bradford Observer, 30 January 1845

THORNTON TEMPERANCE SOCIETY. On Monday evening, Mrs. Jackson, the celebrated and successful advocate of the principle of total abstinence, gave in the Kipping School-room, Thornton, the first of a series of lectures which she is engaged to deliver this week at Thornton, Wilsden, Allerton, Cullingworth, and Denholme. At the conclusion of the lecture, 9 signed the pledge.

Bradford Observer, 17 April 1845

NOTICE. TAKEN UP, on Friday, the 4th of April, at Denholme Park, A BROWN PONY, about 12 hands high, with a white spot on its back, and a slight wound produced by the saddle. The Owner may have the Pony again, by payment of expenses, on application to JOSEPH ROBINSON, the Pinder of Thornton, and NOTICE is hereby given that, if the Pony be not Claimed, and the expenses paid, in a week from the Date hereof, he will be Sold to defray the same. Thornton, April 16th, 1845.

Bradford Observer, 19 June 1845

A CONSTABLE AT FAULT. On Friday, at the Court House, Thomas Midgley and James Driver, of Thornton, two respectable individuals, were charged with having stolen a quantity of sand, the property of John Gawthorp, plasterer of Thornton. Mr. Gawthorp stated that he had taken the plastering of a mill for Mr. Craven, of Thornton, and on doing so, purchased of him a quantity of sand, then lying by the road side, and which the defendants had since taken away and sold, notwithstanding their knowledge that he had bought it. In answer to Mr. Pollard, it was stated that the sand had been collected from the road at different times previous to his purchasing it; the defendants took it away in a cart in the day time, and without concealment. Mr. Pollard: Who is the constable in this case? Barker (a constable of some standing): I am, sir. You are? What do you mean by bringing men up on such a charge as this? I thought it had been some of the new constables sworn in last time, who had not yet learned their duty, I did not expect to see an old officer like you so acting. Mr. Barker said Mr. Gawthorp came to the Court House for a warrant; the clerks would not make one out, and he came back and said he (Barker) was to take the defendants into custody without a warrant. Mr. Pollard: And did you take the men without a warrant? You know well there is no pretence to charge them with a felony. Mind what you are about, or you'll be getting yourself into a scrape. The defendants were then discharged. In a short time Mr. Gawthorp returned into court, bleeding from the right ear, and begging an information and summons charging Mr. Midgley with having assaulted him. He stated that as soon as he left the court he said a few words to Mr. Midgley, telling him that he knew whose sand it was, and had no right to take it, upon which Mr. M. flew at him and tore his ear. Mr. Pollard: You called him a thief, I suppose? Nay, I don't know that I did. Well, but didn't you call him a thief? I can't say; I am not aware what I said, I was so grieved, you know. The summons was refused. (It appears that when Mr. Gawthorp applied for a warrant against Mr. Midgley and Mr. Driver, Mr. Mossman's clerks informed him that the magistrates would not issue a warrant on the evidence then brought forward; but that he must tell the constable to examine further into the case, and act on his own discretion. If the significant looks and speeches of the two persons charged, when they left the court, mean anything, they mean ulterior measures 'in another place.' The sand being gathered from the Queen's highway was, according to the law laid down at the Court House on Friday, the property of the rate-payers of the township vested in the surveyors, and therefore could not be collected or sold by any other parties but the surveyors, or those authorised by them to do so. What right Messrs. Midgley and Driver had to take it away, and, according to Mr. Gawthorp's averment, to sell it, did not appear.)

Bradford Observer, 24 June 1845

EMBEZZLEMENT. An old man, named Thomas Butterfield, from Thornton, was charged under the Worsted Act with having in his possession three quarts and one pint of Galipoli oil – an ingredient used in the worsted trade, which the officers suspected he had purloined. The defendant has a son living with him, and employed as a woolcomber by Mr. Simeon Townend, of Thornton, the defendant occasionally assisting his son with his work. Foster, inspector, from some information he received, searched the defendant's house on the 17th inst. and found the oil produced in the cellar. The defendant was convicted in the penalty of £20 and in default was committed for a month. Jonas Butterfield, a son of the last defendant, was also convicted in the penalty of £20 for not giving a satisfactory account of his possession of another quantity of Galipoli oil, used in the combing of wool. In these cases Mr. Wagstaff appeared for the Inspector, and Mr. Terry for the defendants; he raised some legal objections, but they were overruled.

Leeds Mercury, 30 August 1845

IMPORTANT TO FACTORY OWNERS. A case came before the Magistrates of Bradford on Wednesday, in which Mr. Simeon Townend, of Thornton, appeared as defendant. The sub-inspector, Capt. Hart, of Halifax, laid an information against the proprietor for not fencing off a certain line of horizontal shafts in the mill at Thornton, whereby a fatal accident occurred to an individual, a whitewasher, who had mounted a ladder (contrary to instructions) during the motion of such shaftings. Capt. Hart and Mr. Baker, both sub-inspectors, admitted that not a single mill in the county, or kingdom, had similar shafts boxed off; being at such a height from the floor, viz. between 7 and 8 feet. Still, the interpretation clauses distinctly state – 'That all shafts, whether upright, horizontal, or oblique, are to be fenced off.' This being, then, a first case, induced the magistrates to convict in the lowest penalty; and the chairman remarked, 'that this reflected no discredit whatever upon Mr. Townend for the manner in which the mill was conducted;' which was also spoken of by Mr. Baker as one of the best regulated he had seen in his survey of eleven years. The consequence of this decision is, that every millowner in the kingdom who does not securely fence off every shaft, whether upright, horizontal, or oblique, is liable to brought up any day, and fined £10 and upwards.

Leeds Mercury, 28 February 1846

THORNTON. It is intended to form a Board of Surveyors for the management of the highways of the township of Thornton, which is an extensive township, having a population of about 7,000.

Bradford Observer, 16 April 1846

ROBBERIES. On Friday morning last, the house of Mr. T. Scott, of Denholme Gate, innkeeper, was broken into by some thieves, who have so far escaped detection. The booty obtained was ten hams, the silver plate, and what money there was in the house, with all of which they got clear off. Four suspicious-looking men, with bundles, were seen passing, between three and four o'clock in the morning, in the direction of Thornton and Clayton. Also, on Saturday night, as the waggoner of Messrs. G. Townend and Brothers, Cullingworth, called to get a glass of ale at Causeway Foot, though he left a boy in the waggon, a bag, containing two hams, was immediately stolen from the waggon, and the thieves got clear off. The waggoner had only just before bought them in the neighbourhood.

Bradford Observer, 30 April 1846

INQUEST. On Saturday night, an inquest was held at the house of Mr. Joseph Briggs, West Scholes Gate, Thornton, before G. Dyson, Esq., coroner, on the body of a little boy, twelve months old, son of Jonas Ingham, woolcomber, Law Hill. The deceased was found dead in bed the previous morning. Verdict accordingly.

Bradford Observer, 30 April 1846

ROBBERIES. On Sunday night, the house of Mr. J. Rollinson, beer seller, School Green, Thornton, was broken into by some thieves who obtained a few pounds in money. The owner heard somebody in the house, and got up, but not having sufficient courage either to fire his gun, which was loaded, or go downstairs to them, he remained an attentive and frightened but silent listener to the proceedings below, so that they got off undetected. On the following night, another beer-house in the same neighbourhood, near to Leventhorp Bar, kept by Widow Laycock, was broken into and nearly all the wearing apparel of the family was stolen therefrom without any noise being made so as to disturb the slumbers of the owners, consequently, the gang escaped this time also.

Leeds Mercury, 7 August 1847

INQUESTS BEFORE GEO. DYSON, ESQ. On Friday, at the Rock and Heifer, Thornton, on the body of James Beanland, aged six years, who died from injuries caused by a fall in Stream Head Pit, there. On Monday, at the Brown Cow, Paddock, Huddersfield, on the body of William Marsland, who was found drowned. Verdicts accordingly.

Bradford Observer, 17 September 1846

SUDDEN DEATH. On Monday morning an inquest was held at Well Heads, Thornton, on view of the body of a woolcomber, aged 25 years, of the name of Jonathan Shackleton. The deceased retired to bed on Saturday night in his usual good health, and his father, who slept with him, awaking at about three o'clock on Sunday morning, he was just expiring. Verdict – 'Died by visitation of God.'

Bradford and Wakefield Observer and Halifax, Huddersfield and Keighley Reporter, 16 December 1847

STEALING A COW. At the Court House, on Monday, a young man named Abraham Bairstow, from Thornton, was brought up on a charge of stealing a cow, the property of Mr. Jesse Wade, farmer and corn miller, residing at Leventhorpe Hall, near this town. The cow was stolen from the mistal at Leventhorpe Hall, during the night of Thursday. She had been seen in the mistal about 10 o'clock the preceding night; and not being able to find the key, the prosecutor's servant, a person named Knapton, left the door unlocked. On going to the mistal at 6 o'clock the following morning, the cow was missing. The prosecutor, some time afterwards, set off to Gargrave, a fair having been held there on Friday last, and two miles beyond Skipton he identified his lost cow amongst a group of cattle, which, the fair having closed, were being driven towards Skipton. The prosecutor had had the cow not more than five weeks, and amongst other peculiarities which made up its identity was that, so familiar in nursery legends, of its being 'a cow with a crumpled horn.' The cow was claimed by the prosecutor as his property, and being seized at Skipton accordingly inquiry began as to the thief. It turns out that on Thursday afternoon the cow appeared under the charge of the prisoner at Gargrave fair, and was exhibited in the neighbourhood of a group of cattle under the charge of one Thomas Carr, cattle dealer, of Blackburn, in Lancashire. Carr asked the price of the beast, and seven guineas was named as his figure. Attempts were made at a bargain, and Carr at last bought it of the prisoner for £5. The beast was subsequently sold by Carr's partner for £6 to one Mr. Morris, of Leeds, and was on its way, under the charge of his ownership, when recognised by its old master. The appearance and dress of the prisoner were described; and he was apprehended at his father's house, at Thornton, on Saturday. The prisoner said nothing in reply to the charge, not putting even a question to the witnesses against him. He was committed for trial at the present York assizes.

Bradford and Wakefield Observer and Halifax, Huddersfield and Keighley Reporter, 23 December 1847

STEALING A COW. At the Court House on Friday, a young man named Richard Ogden, was charged with having, in November last, stolen a cow, the property of Mr. John Hirst, of Clayton, farmer. The cow was found in the possession of a person at Cleckheaton, and had previously passed through several hands by way of sale. The prisoner was remanded till Monday; but on that day he could not be identified as one of several persons of whom the cow was first bought, after being taken from Mr. Hirst, and he was consequently discharged. It was said that the young man, Bairstow, who was last week committed for stealing a cow from Leventhorpe Hall, was one of the party who sold the cow belonging to Mr. Hirst; so that it is probable, if his identity can be proved, that a second indictment will be preferred against him.

Bradford Observer, 4 January 1849

THORNTON. Last Tuesday, Mr. Joshua Craven, manufacturer, Thornton, treated all the workpeople in his employment with a good, substantial dinner, in the top room of his new mill. After dinner, music and other amusements contributed to their enjoyment, and the company separated in the evening highly gratified and delighted with the proceedings and pleasures of the day.

Bradford Observer, 18 January 1849

THORNTON. SAGAR'S CHARITY. On Tuesday last, the annual distribution of the above charity, commonly called 'dole money,' took place at the house of Mr. Isaac Wood, the Victoria Inn, and though employment is much more plentiful, the number of applicants was unusually large.

Bradford Observer, 1 February 1849

THORNTON. During the boisterous winds last week, some one or more persons broke into the shop occupied by Mr. John Pollard, boot and shoe maker, but fortunately the adjoining neighbour, who sleeps over the shop, heard the lock picked, and immediately got up, and the burglars had to make a precipitate retreat, though not without taking goods to the value of several pounds.

Bradford Observer, 22 February 1849

FOOT RACE. On Monday last, a foot race, three-quarters of a mile, for £10 a-side, was run at Four Lane End, Manningham, between Drake, of Thornton, and Garlick, of Lidget Green. The former was the winner.

Bradford Observer, 29 March 1849

FOOT RACE. On Monday last, the race which has been the cause of so much excitement in the neighbourhood of Thornton, Clayton, Horton, &c, took place on the Manchester race course. The contest was between Drake, of Thornton, and Garlick, of Horton – three quarters of a mile for £50. Drake was again the winner.

Bradford Observer, 29 March 1849

GUARDIANS FOR THORNTON. Mr. Jonas Craven, Mr. Matthew Jarratt, Mr. Isaac Wood, Mr. Isaac Baxendale, and Mr. Joseph Leach were, on Monday, nominated for guardians for Thornton for the ensuing year.

Leeds Mercury, 8 June 1849

THORNTON WESLEYAN SUNDAY SCHOOL.- On Sunday last, two impressive sermons were preached in the Wesleyan Methodist chapel, Thornton, near Bradford, by the Rev. John Smithson, Wesleyan minister, from Hinckley, Leicestershire. The chapel was crowded to excess, and many not being able to gain admittance, a sermon was preached in the burial ground, to a large congregation. Mr. Smithson, at the request of his friends, preached the following evening. At the close of the sermons on the Sabbath, collections were made, which amounted to £34 5s 7d – the largest sum ever raised in the chapel on such an occasion.

Bradford Observer, 5 July 1849

THORNTON MECHANICS' INSTITUTE. On Friday evening a lecture was delivered in the above institution by Mr. John Sutcliffe – 'On the advantages of reading.' The lecturer, who is a working man, and a member of the institution, gave general satisfaction and shewed considerable ability for one whose means of acquiring knowledge have been so limited as those of a working man must necessarily be.

Bradford Observer, 6 September 1849

At the West Riding Court, on Monday, a person named David Hainsworth was brought up on a charge of stealing 64 stones of apples, the property of Mr. Isaac Wood, of Thornton, and was committed for trial at the sessions.

Bradford Observer, 13 September 1849

THORNTON. LECTURES BY A RETURNED CONVICT. Last Friday and Monday, Mr. C.A. King, the returned convict, gave two lectures on transportation, &c, in the Kipping School Room, and on both occasions the audience was very numerous. Exceedingly interesting is the manner in which the lectures are given, and the difficulties, dangers, hardships, and miseries which he detailed as occurring in the convict's life, can scarcely fail of being the means of doing much good, especially to youth. The history of his own downward course is well calculated to act as a warning to those who are unconsciously, perhaps, commencing the step to crime. After being led on by the amusements of a concert room at an inn, he spent all his money and formed bad associations – was tempted to join in the committal of a burglary – was taken the next day, tried, convicted, and sentenced to transportation – went on board the hulks – was then sent to Van Diemen's Land – from there, after enduring unheard of hardships, made his escape – got to America, and at last arrived in England – was betrayed and retaken in Manchester by Mr. Green, the present superintendent constable at Dewsbury – tried again at Liverpool Assizes before Mr. Justice Coleridge – was sentenced to transportation for life, the first ten years in chains; but so great an impression did his recital of the miseries he had gone through make, that his address to the judge caused many to become interested in his favour. A petition, signed by upwards of 60,000 persons, was presented to the Queen, praying her Majesty to commute his sentence; she did so, to five years' solitary confinement in a small cell in the Milbank Penitentiary; he there learned to read, write, and think. At the close of his term he received a free pardon, and he is now giving the benefit of experience to the world, in warning the thoughtless to beware of the first step to crime. His first lecture is given in the dress and chains worn by the convicts in Van Diemen's Land, and the second in the mask now worn at Wakefield and other prisons in England. It is desirable that the lectures should be encouraged as extensively as possible by Mechanics' Institutions and other societies, as the lectures cannot fail to be beneficial wherever they are delivered, and especially to the rising generation. – *Correspondent.*

Bradford Observer, 6 December 1849

THORNTON BRANCH BUILDING SOCIETY. On Monday night, a public meeting of the Branch of the South Lancashire Permanent Building Society was held in the Kipping School, Thornton, when a deputation from the head office, Manchester, attended to explain the practical working, and to show the advantages of the society. Mr. Joseph Craven, manufacturer, occupied the chair, and after his opening statement of the nature and objects of the society, the meeting was addressed by the deputation and Mr. Kay, the agent for Thornton and neighbourhood. The society was shown to be in a very sound and

Dole Mill employees, 1897.

prosperous state, and is very rapidly extending. A dividend after the rate of 9 per cent per annum has been declared for the first year out of the realized profits on it. This dividend belongs to depositors only. The explanations and statements of the deputation gave complete satisfaction to the meeting. After the meeting several new shares were entered, and the Thornton Branch now has 43 members and 221 shares.

Bradford Observer, 27 December 1849

ODDFELLOWS AT THORNTON. On Christmas day the Rock of Hope Lodge held its anniversary, at the Black Horse Inn, Thornton, when the members sat down to a good substantial dinner. In the evening the lodge was thrown open for the admission of a few friends invited by the members; Mr. E. Kay presided. A number of appropriate speeches, recitations, songs, &c, were given, and the evening was spent more happily than its predecessors. A party of glee singers added much in the intervals to the pleasure of the evening, and all went off well.

Chapter Seven
1850–1851

Thornton deaths outstrip births – Thornton pit explosion – Cricket:
Thornton beats Rawdon – Great sermon to 1500 at Hoppitt Well –
Farmer's wife dies milking cows

Bradford Observer, 3 January 1850

ANOTHER FESTIVAL AT THORNTON. On New Year's-day Messrs. Joshua Craven and Son, manufacturers, treated all the workpeople in their employment with a good old English dinner, in their new warehouse. There was plenty of every thing calculated to make them all joyous and happy; and, amid the pleasures of music and other entertainments, the remainder of the day was spent in harmony and delight, and will long be remembered by those who had the pleasure to witness and enjoy the encouraging and happy scene.

Bradford Observer, 24 January 1850

HIGHWAY ROBBERY. On Sunday evening, the 6th of January, George Spenceley, of Thornton Heights, was returning from East Bierley Chapel to his home, when at a spot called Beacon Hill, near Clayton Heights, he was attacked by three men. Two of them held him, while the third rifled his pockets. They robbed him of a sovereign, a shilling, a sixpence, a fourpenny piece, and a halfpenny. One of them seized the chain of his watch, but the guard broke, and at that moment one of them, uttering an oath, said to his companions, 'We'll go!' They all then ran off across the fields. In a moment afterwards, three men came up the road, and it was thought by Spenceley that the thieves heard the approach of these men and had consequently run off. On Monday morning last, Superintendent Ingham proceeded with Spenceley to the houses of three notorious and suspicious persons residing in Little Horton – viz. – Daniel Elmsley, James Atkinson, and William

Rotheray, their description tallying with that given by Spenceley. He identified two of them, Atkinson and Elmsley, as of the party who had robbed him, but he would not swear positively to Rotheray. These three persons were taken into custody, and on Monday remanded by the magistrates till Wednesday. Yesterday the prisoners were brought before Joshua Pollard, Esq., Elmsley and Atkinson were identified by the prosecutor, and were committed to York for trial at the assizes. Rotheray was discharged.

Bradford Observer, 7 February 1850

From a list covering the entire Bradford district:

Quarterly Returns of Marriages, Births, and Deaths.

Thornton: Births 96; Deaths 102.

The deaths are about 30 per cent. above the average, owing principally to the prevalence of measles, scarletina, and pneumonia. The measles has been very fatal.

Bradford Observer, 28 February 1850

THORNTON MECHANICS' INSTITUTION. Last Friday evening, the Rev. J. Ward, Wesleyan minister, read a very interesting paper to the members and friends of the above institution, on 'Instinct and Reason.'

Bradford Observer, 28 February 1850

TAXES ON KNOWLEDGE. A petition to the House of Commons, praying for the abolition of the excise duty on paper, the advertisement duty, the stamp upon newspapers, &c, has been signed by members of the Thornton Mechanics' Institution, and will be immediately forwarded for presentation to Richard Cobden, Esq., M.P. for the West Riding.

Bradford Observer, 28 March 1850

THORNTON MECHANICS' INSTITUTION. Last Friday evening a very interesting lecture was delivered by the Rev. Mr. Silson of Swain Royd, Bolton, to the members and friends of the above institution, on 'The Geological Effects of the Deluge.'

Bradford Observer, 28 March 1850

ACCIDENT AT THORNTON. On Monday morning an explosion took place in the new Engine Pit, New Road Side, Thornton, when a collier of the name of Jonas Jennings was seriously buried.

Leeds Mercury, 6 April 1850

TESTIMONIAL OF RESPECT TO THE REV. JAMES GREGORY, THORNTON. On Monday evening last, a very handsome purse, of the most exquisite needlework, containing fifty guineas, was presented by the Sabbath school teachers and friends, to the Rev. James Gregory, minister of Kipping chapel, Thornton, as a token of their high esteem for, and ardent attachment to, their worthy pastor, for his laborious, efficient, and faithful labours amongst them for a period of 16 years. Tea was provided by the teachers and friends in the commodious school rooms. After singing a hymn, and an introductory prayer by the Rev. B. Firth, Independent minister, of Wyke, Mr. Francis Craven, one of the superintendents, was called to the chair, and in a short, but very appropriate speech, explained the object of the meeting, with which he had most cordially united his small quota of influence, and then called upon Henry Harrop, Esq., one of the deacons of the church, to present the testimonial to their much esteemed pastor, which he did in a brief but comprehensive speech, full of excellent sentiment, appreciating, as he said, most of all, the motive by which the young people connected with the school had been actuated, which was of far more value than the purse of gold itself. After the presentation, the Rev. J. Gregory rose to reply, evidently much affected by this pleasing and to him most unexpected effort of the young people with whom he is so happily associated, and in a very impressive speech expressed his deep and heartfelt gratitude for this token of their ardent attachment to him as pastor, esteeming most of all, as the venerable deacon had observed who presented the testimonial, the motive from which the whole had originated. The meeting was afterwards addressed by the superintendents, and several teachers and friends, who had come from a distance to witness the interesting and encouraging scene. Much was said about this being the starting point by all parties concerned, for increased and renewed exertion, both in the church and Sabbath school. The company, after having been highly entertained and delighted with the evening's proceedings, separated about nine o'clock. A few months ago, the female weekly Bible class presented their pastor with a splendidly bound Bagster's Polyglott Bible and a chair for class purposes. In both cases the gifts have been so quietly and unostentatiously bestowed, as greatly to augment their value.

Bradford Observer, 29 August 1850

Died on Saturday last, in her 88th year, Mary wife of Mr. Robert Robinson of Thornton. It is a singular fact that, though the above couple had been married upwards of 60 years, and had a large family, death has never previously entered their dwelling.

Bradford Observer, 23 January 1851

THORNTON. On Wednesday last, Sagar's Charity, or which is better known by the name of 'Dole Money,' was distributed at the house of Mr. Isaac Wood, the Victoria Inn; and though the goodness of the times would warrant the inference that there was less necessity and distress than in former years, the applications were equally numerous with other times.

Bradford Observer, 5 March 1851

THORNTON POST. *To the Editor of the Bradford Observer.* SIR. – The village of Thornton is only four miles from Bradford, and contains a population of several thousand inhabitants, amongst which are some extensive and spirited manufacturers and tradesmen, and yet the only postal arrangements are so defective as to allow only two hours and a half each day for the receipt and despatch of letters. As there is no delivery on the Sabbath, the total weekly average of time will only be about fifteen hours. Letters are despatched from Bradford soon after eight, and reach Thornton about twelve, and the bag closes again at half-past two. We have an excellent and obliging postman; the fault is not with him, but in the circuitous route he is obliged to take, having to go round by Great Horton and Clayton. Surely the inhabitants will not be long ere they bestir themselves in seeking an improvement in this matter. I would suggest that a public meeting should be called, to consider what steps to take in obtaining the necessary alterations. Yours, AN INHABITANT.

Bradford Observer, 20 March 1851

Died on Friday last, aged 55, much respected, Mr. Nathan Pearson, relieving officer, Thornton.

Bradford Observer, 20 March 1851

Married on Tuesday last, at the Kipping Chapel, Thornton, by the Rev. J. Gregory, Mr. Francis Craven, merchant and manufacturer, to Maria, daughter of Mr. Simeon Townend, worsted spinner, all of Thornton.

Bradford Observer, 27 March 1851

THORNTON MECHANICS' INSTITUTE. On Saturday week the members of the above institution held their annual festival in the Kipping New School Room. A brief notice of which appeared in our last publication, but as the Thornton Institution is manifestly effecting no small amount of good, we deem the proceedings worthy of a larger paragraph. On the occasion referred to the Rev. J. Ward, Wesleyan minister, occupied the chair, and spoke upon the value, importance, and advantages of such institutions for the developement [*sic*] of intellect and the general improvement of the mind. Mr. William Kay, president of the institution, in the absence of Mr. Wm. Bell, the secretary, read the report. It showed a large accession of members during the year, the number now being 228; also a considerable increase in the library and in periodicals. During the year, Mr. Joseph Craven, Kipping Lane, has presented to the institution the Penny Cyclopædia, complete, and the library now contains 310 volumes. There have been 2136 exchanges of books, and the periodicals and newspapers are much read in the room. The classes for elementary instruction are numerously and regularly attended on the Monday and Wednesday evenings. Various instructive lectures have been delivered during the year by the Revs. Messrs. Jowett, Glyde, Gregory, Bilson, Ward, Fraser; and also by Messrs. J. Craven, Geo. Townend, and S.

Top Coal Pit, Thornton Road.

Holdsworth. The meeting was subsequently addressed by the Rev. J. Gregory, the Rev. Mr. Morton, late a missionary, the Rev. J.P. Chown, of Bradford, J.V. Godwin, Esq., of Bradford, Mr. James Leach, Mr. Jas. Crabtree, and other members of the institution. Everything went off well, the only regret being that the meeting was not more numerously attended. A party of singers enlivened the proceedings by their valuable services. The usual thanks were then tendered to the ladies and to the rev. chairman, after which the meeting broke up with feelings of great pleasure and satisfaction.

Bradford Observer, 3 April 1851

OVERSEERS OF THE POOR. In the Court of the West Riding magistrates, on Thursday, the constables of the various townships within the district returned the list of persons who had been nominated as overseers of the poor for the ensuing year, when the following gentlemen were appointed by the magistrates: THORNTON – Henry Harrop and Joshua Craven. [Overseers for numerous other townships are also listed.]

Bradford Observer, 24 April 1851

In the Matter of the Petition of RICHARD FEARNSIDE, residing at Thornton Heights, in the Township of Thornton, in the Parish of Bradford, in the County of York, Shopkeeper and Woolcomber, *Notice is hereby given*, that Charles Heneage Elsley, Esq., the Judge of the County Court of Yorkshire, at Bradford, acting in the matter of this petition, will proceed to make a final order thereon, at the said Court, Darley Street, Bradford, on the 20th day of May, 1851, at Eleven o' Clock in the Forenoon precisely, unless cause be then and there shown to the contrary. CHARLES CLOUGH, Clerk of the Court.

Bradford Observer, 8 May 1851

THORNTON WESLEYAN CHAPEL. The above chapel has been greatly enlarged and beautified, and at the re-opening services, after sermons by the Revds. Dr. Newton, Dr. Beaumont, Mr. McDonald, Mr. Felvus, Mr. Sugden, and others, the collections amounted to the very handsome and liberal sum of upwards of £150.

Bradford Observer, 22 May 1851

THORNTON. Last Friday, a meeting was held in the vestry of Thornton Church, for the purpose of taking into consideration the propriety of putting into force in this township the Small Tenements Rating Act. The proposition was affirmed by a considerable majority, so that in the next poor and highway rate, all houses under the yearly rateable value of £6 will have the assessment laid on the owners instead of the occupiers.

Bradford Observer, 29 May 1851

THORNTON MECHANICS' INSTITUTE. On Saturday last, a news-room in connection with the above institution was opened in the Kipping Old School. A number of papers and periodicals were ordered to commence with, including the Leeds Mercury, Leeds Times, Bradford Observer, Manchester Examiner and Times, The Illustrated London News, &c. Also, the British Quarterly Review, the Eclectic, and a variety of other periodicals and serial publications.

Bradford Observer, 29 May 1851

THORNTON V. RAWDEN CRICKET. On Saturday last, a friendly game at cricket was played on the Thornton Ground between the above two clubs, when, after a severe contest, Thornton proved victorious.

Bradford Observer, 29 May 1851

KNOR AND SPELL. On Saturday last, the long-pending match at the above game was played, at Swillhill, between Sutcliffe of Ovenden, and 'Jack o' Bents,' of Sowerby. The match was 30 rises each, when Sutcliffe, the winner, averaged upwards of 10 scores each rise. There were thousands of spectators, and much interest and betting on the game.

Bradford Observer, 3 July 1851

OPEN AIR PREACHING. An interesting spectacle occurred at Hoppit Well, a sequestered spot between Thornton and Denholme, on Sunday last. At this place is a Sunday School sustained by the congregation of Kipping Chapel, and some alterations in the school-room being required, it was determined to have public services in the open air. The novelty of the arrangement, and we hope we may add, the interest felt in the enterprise, attracted a large concourse of people, who, to the number of 1,500, worshipped God in that wild moorland beneath the open canopy of the sky. The afternoon sermon was preached by Mr. Wood, British school master, Thornton; and the evening by the Rev. E. Heron, of Denholme. A sum amounting to nearly £15 was raised on the occasion for the benefit of the school.

Bradford Observer, 28 August 1851

THORNTON MECHANICS' INSTITUTE: PRESENTATION. Last week the members and friends of the above institution had a tea party in the Kipping School, after which the Rev. J. Wood, Wesleyan minister, who is about to move to Burlington, gave his farewell address to the Institute, of which he has been a very zealous advocate and supporter. At the conclusion of the address Mr. James Leach, on behalf of the Institute, presented the rev. gentleman with a splendid silver inkstand for the very valuable services he had rendered during his residence at Thornton. The presentation was made in a neat and appropriate speech, and the meeting, over which Mr. Joseph Craven presided, was afterwards addressed by the Rev. J. Gregory, Mr. Geo. Townend, and several other members of the Institute.

Bradford Observer, 4 September 1851

THORNTON CHURCH. On Sunday last the Rev. G. Thomas, the Incumbent of this church, preached his farewell sermon to a numerous congregation. The rev. gentleman's discourse was remarkable as well for its sound Evangelical doctrine as for its firm attachment to the tenets of his church, and it is but justice to say that these two points have been consistently maintained by the Rev. gentleman during the entire course of his ministry in this neighbourhood. – *Correspondent.*

Bradford Observer, 11 September 1851

CRICKET: THORNTON *V.* OVENDEN. On Saturday last a match between the above parties was played on the Ovenden ground, when the former were victorious, with seven wickets to fall.

Bradford Observer, 25 September 1851

THORNTON. SUDDEN DEATH. On Saturday an inquest was held on view of the body of Jane, wife of Mr. James Thompson, farmer, Cockin-lane, Clayton. Last Thursday afternoon, the deceased, who was 44 years of age, went into the mistal in her usual good health to milk the cows, and while doing so was seized with a fit, and died instantaneously. Verdict accordingly.

Bradford Observer, 25 September 1851

BACK HEIGHT, IN THORNTON, TO BE SOLD BY AUCTION, by Mr. TIMOTHY INGHAM, at the House of Mr. Joseph Greenwood, the Rock and Heifer Inn, at Back Height, in Thornton, in the county of York, *on Friday, the 10th day of October*, 1851, at Six o'clock in the Evening precisely, subject to Conditions. ALL those SEVEN COTTAGES or Dwelling-houses, situate at Back Height, in Thornton aforesaid, and now in the tenure or occupation of the said Joseph Greenwood or his tenants; and also all that Close or Parcel of LAND or Ground, also situate at Back Height, in Thornton abovesaid, immediately adjoining upon the said Cottages or Dwelling-houses, containing by admeasurement, including the sites of the said Cottages or Dwelling-houses, One Acre or thereabouts, and now also in the tenure or occupation of the said Joseph Greenwood. Mr. GREENWOOD will, on application, show the Estate; and for further particulars, apply to Messrs. C. and W. CARR, Solicitors, Gomersal, near Leeds.

Leeds Mercury, 4 October 1851

FATAL ACCIDENT. On Monday, an inquest was held at the New Inn, Thornton, before George Dyson, Esq., on view of the body of Wm. Jonas Ambler, of that place, who accidentally met with his death by a slip of earth falling in him while cutting a drain. The deceased, who had been many years chapel-keeper, &c, at the Kipping chapel, was extensively known and much respected, and was in the 60th year of his age.

Bradford Observer, 18 December 1851

Births: On the 15th inst., the wife of Francis Craven, Esq., of Kipping House, Thornton, of a daughter.

Bradford Observer, 18 December 1851

Marriages: On Tuesday last, at Kipping Chapel, Thornton, by the Rev. J. Gregory, Joseph Craven, Esq., merchant and manufacturer, to Anne, eldest daughter of Simeon Townend, Esq., worsted spinner, all of Thornton.

Chapter Eight
1852–1853

Ladies' seminary to open in Thornton – Wesleyan reformers move – Big property sales – Toddler dies when dress catches fire – Everything happens to Amos on Christmas Day

Bradford Observer, 8 January 1852

LADIES' SEMINARY, THORNTON, Near Bradford. Conducted by the MISSES LONGFIELD. The system of tuition comprises the branches of a useful English Education, with Music, Drawing, and Flower Painting. Languages taught by masters. The situation is highly salubrious, and strict attention is paid to the health and comfort of the pupils.

Terms and references furnished on application. The School will be Re-opened on Monday, January 19th.

Bradford Observer, 8 January 1852

THORNTON. On Monday last an inquest was held at the house of Mr. Joseph Greenwood, the Rock and Heifer Inn, on view of the body of Timothy Robertshaw, a woolcomber, aged 46 years, who met with his death on New Year's Day, near Denholme Gate Inn, by injuries received from accidentally falling. Verdict accordingly.

Bradford Observer, 22 January 1852

THORNTON MECHANICS' INSTITUTE. LECTURE ON ELECTRICITY. Last Friday evening, Mr. William Harrop, of Cullingworth, delivered a valuable and interesting lecture on Electricity to the members and friends of the above institution, in the Kipping School-Room. The audience was very numerous, the experiments were very successful, and the illustrations of the principles of the science so clear, that the lecturer was frequently applauded. A vote of thanks was passed to the lecturer for his valuable services, and the company retired both profited and pleased.

Bradford Observer, 25 March 1852

THORNTON MECHANICS' INSTITUTE. The annual *soirée* of the Thornton Mechanics' Institute was held in that village on Monday evening, when about 900 of the members and friends of the institution partook of tea in the old school-room connected with Kipping Chapel. After tea, an adjournment took place to the larger and in some respects more commodious new school-room, which was well filled. Mr. Kay, the president of the institution, occupied the chair. The occasional performance of pieces of music by Mr. Radcliffe and a portion of the choir of Kipping Chapel served very agreeably to diversify the proceedings of the evening.

The PRESIDENT had to regret and to apologise for the absence of several friends of the institution. The Rev. Mr. Woodward, the incumbent of Thornton, had been unexpectedly called from home, or he would without doubt have been present. Letters of apology for unavoidable absence had also been received from the Hon. and Rev. the Dean of Ripon; Edward Baines, Esq., of Leeds; and the Rev. J.P. Chown, of Bradford. The Dean of Ripon had received her Majesty's commands to attend in London, and preach at the Chapel Royal, but had promised to make a note of the invitation, and hoped at some future time to be able to pay them a visit. Mr. Kay expressed great pleasure at being able to meet with them after having, on the two former occasions, been deprived of the opportunity of doing so. He offered some brief but appropriate remarks as to the objects and advantages of Mechanics' Institutions, and urged their claims upon the support of all classes of the community.

Mr. W. Kay, the secretary, read the fourth annual report. It appeared that at the last annual meeting the number of members on the books was greater than at present, and the institution was apparently in a more flourishing condition, but this difference was easily and satisfactorily accounted for. Previous to that time the committee, with a view to extending the usefulness of the institution as much as possible, passed a rule making young persons of the age of 13 eligible to become members. This so greatly augmented the numbers as to lead to much inconvenience and confusion, and induced the committee to raise the age of entrance to 15, and require members to continue their contributions during the adjournment which takes place in the summer months. The numbers for a time considerably declined, but the change soon began to prove beneficial. The number of members since last September had kept gradually increasing, and now amounted to 133 males and 18 females – total, 151. The institution was now open three nights a week, Monday, Wednesday, and Friday, on the two former of which classes met for reading, writing, arithmetic, and grammar. On the Saturday afternoon and on the Friday evening the Institute was open for the perusal of newspapers and periodicals, &c, and all those advantages were to be obtained for the payment of 1s entrance fee, and 1d weekly subscription. Fourteen lectures had been delivered during the year. The

Ladies' Temperance Society passing Fountain Street.

attendance at the classes had been regular, and the voluntary teachers punctual and assiduous in the attendance. During the year there had been 1694 changes of books in the library, besides the periodicals. The library now consisted of 346 volumes. The treasurer's account was satisfactory; £50 7s 3d having been received and £42 1s 5½d expended, leaving a balance in hand of £8 5s 9½d.

After the reading of the report, the meeting was addressed by the Rev. J.H. Ryland, of Bradford; the Rev. J.A. Savage, of Wilsden; the Rev. J. Walters and the Rev. J. Gregory, of Thornton; Mr. J. Leach, vice-president of the Institution; Mr. Cockcroft, of Cullingworth; Mr. J. Crabtree, and Mr. Wood. The various speeches contained much interesting and valuable matter, to which, did our space allow, we would willingly advert, and we trust that the result of the annual *soirée* will be to give a lasting impetus to the good work now going on in the village of Thornton.

Bradford Observer, 25 March 1852

THORNTON. SUDDEN DEATH. On Sunday last an awful instance of the uncertainty of human life occurred in this village. The wife of Thomas Robinson, mason, Thornton, on her return from the Wesleyan chapel in the afternoon, had not proceeded far towards home, before she was seized with a sick fit and almost instantly expired. Mr. Corrie, surgeon, was almost immediately on the spot, but on his arrival the vital spark had fled. The deceased was only about 22 years of age, and though she had not been in a very good state of health for a few weeks, she had not felt anything unusual.

Bradford Observer, 1 April 1852

THORNTON. SERIOUS ACCIDENT. On Friday last, Nathan Hainsworth, of Thornton, delver, met with a serious accident while working in the Delfah [*sic*] Guide Moor, in the township of Allerton. He was carrying a heavy flag, and fell with it on his back. He was very much bruised, and hurt in several places. He was immediately conveyed to the Bradford Infirmary, and on Saturday, owing to one of his knees being so much crushed, amputation of one leg was obliged to be resorted to. He is now gradually recovering.

Bradford Observer, 15 April 1852

THORNTON: WESLEYAN REFORMERS. The Wesleyan Reformers in this village have hitherto occupied, for their Sunday and other meetings, the Lodge-room belonging to the Freemasons; but on account of that place being much too small for them, they have taken the large and commodious room recently built in Commercial Street, and on Sunday last it was opened by two sermons being preached by Mr. Smithson, of York, an expelled local preacher, after which collections were made for incidental expenses, amounting to £7 16s 0½d.

Bradford Observer, 15 July 1852

ROBBERY AT LEVENTHORP BAR, THORNTON. One night last week, about half past ten o'clock, two men, both of them strangers, went into the bar house at the above place, and asked for a bottle of ginger beer, and on the wife going into another place for one, one of the ruffians instantly knocked the bar-keeper, Thomas Pickles, down, demanding his money and ill-using him, and at the same moment the other villain followed the wife and ill-used her, and threatened to shoot her if she made any noise. She told them they had paid the beer-money the day before, but the candle being put out and all in darkness, they ransacked the cupboard and got £3 10s, with which they at once decamped, leaving a larger sum in another pot in the same cupboard. Owing to the noise, and the neighbours being all up, and hearing some thing not right, they began to run to the place, but the ruffians ran off, and though pursued for a considerable distance, could not be taken, nor is any trace of them known.

Bradford Observer, 22 July 1852

THORNTON. FATAL ACCIDENT. Last Saturday afternoon, a melancholy occurrence happened in this village. Mr. Charles Frederick Bailey, druggist, a young man about 22 years of age, went out with a friend at the above time to enjoy an hour's shooting. He was in a field near Alderscholes, at which place there is a coal pit, and in the field where he was shooting there is a vent-pit, but of the existence of which he had not the least idea. It is entirely unfenced off, and the top of the pit is covered over with brush, grass, &c. Unfortunately, Mr. Bailey's eye being intently fixed on a small bird at which he had shot, he walked into the pit, and fell to the depth of 40 yards. Immediate efforts were made to get him out, and every assistance was rendered that it was possible to use, but it is almost unnecessary to add that he was so much injured that when got out life was quite extinct. Both Mr. Corrie and Mr. Hills, surgeons, attended, but there was not the least chance of restoring life, and the body was conveyed to Mr. Jarratt's, the Bull's head, to await the coroner's inquest, which was held on Monday evening, before G. Dyson, Esq., when the following verdict was returned – 'Injuries received from accidentally falling down an old coal shaft.' The jury requested the coroner to write to the overseers of the shaft, Messrs. Bairstow and Wilson, Ovenden, calling their attention to the dreadful accident that had happened, and trusting they would take immediate measures to fence it off, so as to prevent any such lamentable occurrence in future.

Bradford Observer, 19 August 1852

THORNTON – TREAT TO WORKPEOPLE. On Saturday afternoon, another of those small social festive gatherings which ought to bind the interests and kindly feelings of master and servant in closer bands, took place at Thornton. Messrs. Craven and Harrop, merchants and manufacturers, treated all their workpeople employed in the manufacturing department, amounting to upwards of 700, to tea; but 'the cup that cheers and not enebriates [*sic*' was accompanied with ample supplies of roast beef, ham, and other old English fare, and after full justice had been done to the edible department, the joyous company retired outside to enjoy sport and dance, not as in days of yore, on the 'village green,' but the field adjoining the factory. A band of music added to the other enjoyments; order prevailed throughout the proceedings, and after enjoying themselves for a considerable time, the numerous company separated highly delighted with the festivities of the day. About a fortnight ago since the employers [*sic*] in Messrs. Craven and Harrop's warehouse at Bradford had a similar treat, when they partook of tea, &c., in the Athenaeum, Thornton, and then enjoyed cricket, &c., out of doors.

Leeds Mercury, 16 October 1852
AUCTION SALES.
THORNTON. Valuable Farm, Free Inn, Cottages, and Building Land, and Beds of Coal,

By Mr. Davis, at the Black Horse Inn, Thornton, on *Tuesday, the Twenty-sixth October*, 1852, at six o'clock in the evening, subject to such conditions of sale as shall then and there be produced, and in the following or other such lots as may be agreed upon at the time of sale:

Lot 1. ALL that valuable FREEHOLD FARM, situate at Back Denholme, in the township of Thornton, now in the occupation of Mr. Jonas Driver, and comprising a farm-house, barn, and outbuildings, and about 8a 3r 1p of excellent LAND, divided into convenient inclosures, altogether forming an eligible property for occupation or investment.

Lot 2. All that ONE-SIXTH PART or SHARE of and in the valuable BEDS and SEAMS of COAL under Lot 1, and also under certain lands near thereto, now or late in the occupation of Mr. William Driver, comprising in the whole an area of 15 acres, or thereabouts.

Lot 3. All those FOUR COTTAGES or Dwelling-Houses, at New Halifax, in the township of Thornton, in the respective occupations of Joseph Southwaite, John Robinson, Charles Binns, and Matthew Robertshaw.

Lot 4. All those FOUR COTTAGES or Dwelling-Houses, at New Halifax aforesaid, in the respective occupations of John Driver, John Barker, Richard Wood, and Thomas Drake.

Lot 5. All that valuable Piece of BUILDING LAND, situate at New Halifax aforesaid, adjoining Lot 4, and containing 600 square yards.

Lot 6. All that capital and well-accustomed FREE INN, situate at Thornton aforesaid, and known as the Black Horse, containing travellers' room, bar, kitchen, tap room, capacious club room, suitable bed rooms, and convenient and co-extensive cellarage; with good yards, garden, lime yard, piggery, commodious stabling, brewhouse, coach-house, and other requisite accommodations. On this lot are two Dwelling-houses, fitted as shops, and facing the road leading from Kipping-lane to Thornton Heights. There are also Eight Cottages on the premises, which are well tenanted.

This lot offers unusual advantages to a purchaser, the house being free, and doing a lucrative business. Immediate possession may be had, and the vacant ground gives the opportunity of extending the buildings and accommodation of the inn as occasion may require.

Further particulars may be had of Mr. SAMUEL WASHINGTON, Land Agent, Lightcliffe, near Halifax; and at the offices of Messrs. WAVELL, PHILBRICK and FOSTER, Solicitors, George-street, Halifax.

Bradford Observer, 21 October 1852

THORNTON: CHILD BURNT TO DEATH. On Monday last an inquest was held at the Black Horse Inn, before G. Dyson, Esq., coroner, on view of the body of Hannah, daughter of Squire Jowett, a delver. The deceased was about four years old, and a fortnight since last Saturday afternoon she went up stairs into the chamber where there was a fire, to play with some others of the family, when her clothes accidentally caught fire, and she was so burnt that after much suffering she died on Saturday. This is the second accidental death by burning during the last week in the village.

Bradford Observer, 28 October 1852

HILL TOP & SCHOOL GREEN, IN THORNTON, IN THE PARISH OF BRADFORD, TO BE SOLD BY AUCTION, by Mr. DAVIS, at the house of Mr. Jonas Driver, the Black Horse Inn, at Thornton, in the parish of Bradford, on *Tuesday, the 2nd day of November*, 1852, at Six o'clock in the Evening (unless previous notice of Countermand be given), in lots, or as may be then agreed upon, and subject to conditions to be then and there produced.

LOT 1. ALL those Seven Freehold COTTAGES or DWELLING-HOUSES, situate at Hill Top, in the township of Thornton aforesaid, with the Outbuildings, Garden, and conveniences belonging thereto, now in the several occupations of Abraham Clough, Thomas Asquith, and others.

LOT 2. All that Freehold Messuage or DWELLING-HOUSE, situate at School Green, in the township of Thornton aforesaid, and now used as a

Beerhouse, with the Stable, Shed, and other outbuildings belonging thereto; and also the vacant piece of GROUND adjoining or contiguous to the same, now in the occupation of Elias Rawlinson.

LOT 3. All those Four Freehold COTTAGES or DWELLING-HOUSES, also situate at School Green aforesaid, and adjoining or near to the said Messuage, with the outbuildings, gardens, and conveniences belonging to the same, now in the several occupations of Jonas Robinson and others.

The respective Tenants will show the premises, and further particulars may be obtained on application to Mr. WM. THOMAS, Bookseller, Thornton, near Bradford; or to Messrs. HITCHIN & GLEADHALL, Halifax, Oct. 21st, 1852, Solicitors, Halifax.

Bradford Observer, 6 January 1853

THORNTON. WESLEYAN REFORMERS TEA PARTY. On New Year's Day upwards of 400 Wesleyan Reformers of Thornton took tea at their usual place of meeting, the Athenaeum. Mr. James Crabtree occupied the chair at the public meeting in the evening, which was addressed by the local preacher and other friends of Wesleyan Reform. From the report it appeared that the cause at Thornton is in a very flourishing and progressive state.

Bradford Observer, 10 March 1853

THORNTON – A SERIOUS ACCIDENT. Last Saturday evening a serious accident happened on the road leading from Thornton to Bradford, at a place called the Tunnel, opposite Leventhorpe Mill. A cab was returning from Thornton and the night being very misty and dark the cabman got a light at Leventhorpe Bar, but unfortunately it went out just before reaching the dangerous spot where the cab and horse and its driver, as well as a person who was sitting with him on the box, were at once precipitated into the field below the road, a depth of six or eight yards. The horse in the fall became disentangled from the vehicle, which was smashed to pieces, and the driver and the person with him were very seriously injured in several places. The driver was much hurt about the head and his companion had his arm broken in more than one place, but providentially their lives were spared, and it is hoped that the fence at that very dangerous part of a public road will be forthwith put into such a state as to prevent a similar accident in future.

Leeds Mercury, 7 May 1853

THORNTON. MECHANICS' INSTITUTE. Last Saturday afternoon, in the Kipping schoolroom, the members of the above institution had a social tea party, on the occasion of presenting a splendid time-piece to the librarian, Mr. Thomas Barker, for the assiduity, care, and punctuality with which he had zealously discharged the duties of that office for several years. Joseph Craven, Esq., of West House, the president of the institution, in suitable and complimentary terms, presented the testimonial; after which Mr. Barker, in a feeling and grateful manner, acknowledged the favour so generously awarded him, and the meeting was subsequently addressed by several members of the institution, who supported the president's commendatory remarks. After this the social festive pleasures of the evening were continued for a considerable time.

Leeds Mercury, 16 July 1853

KIPPING SUNDAY SCHOOLS. On Sunday last, two sermons were preached on behalf of the above schools, in Kipping Chapel, by the Rev. E. Mellor, M.A., of Halifax. Six additional rooms have recently been built, five of which are occupied by select classes. To meet the heavy expenses of the year, collections were made after the sermons, which amounted to £109 2s 2d.

Bradford Observer, 30 December 1853

Died yesterday week aged 38, Mr. Amos Bower, Alderscholes, Thornton. It is rather singular that he was born, married, and buried on a Christmas-day.

Hamlet of Upper Hoyle Ing.

Chapter Nine
1854

Spiritualism debunked by preacher – Drinkers fight with three-legged table – Purse thrown into field to avoid robbery – Lower Mill for sale

Bradford Observer, 26 January 1854
NOTICE IS HEREBY GIVEN that the partnership lately subsisting between us, THOMAS HARTLEY and JONATHAN ROBINSON, both of Denholme Clough, in the township of Thornton, in the parish of Bradford, in the county of York, stuff manufacturers, carrying on business at Denholme Clough aforesaid, under the firm of Hartley and Robinson, was on the tenth day of May last dissolved by mutual consent. Dated the sixteenth day of January, one thousand eight hundred and fifty-four.
THOMAS HARTLEY JONATHAN ROBINSON
Witness to the signing hereof by the said Thomas Hartley
WILLIAM GEORGE, Solicitor, Bradford.
Witness to the signing hereof by the said Jonathan Robinson
JONATHAN SMITH.
NOTICE IS HEREBY GIVEN that the partnership lately subsisting between us, THOMAS HARTLEY and JOSHUA HARTLEY, both of Denholme Clough, in the township of Thornton, in the parish of Bradford, in the county of York, stuff manufacturers, carrying on business at Denholme Clough aforesaid, under the firm of Thomas and

Joshua Hartley, was on the eighth day of October last dissolved by mutual consent. Dated the sixteenth day of January one thousand eight hundred and fifty-four.

THOMAS HARTLEY JOSHUA HARTLEY

Witness WILLIAM GEORGE, Solicitor, Bradford.

Bradford Observer, 2 February 1854

HIGHWAY ROBBERY. At the Borough Court, on Friday, two persons, named Cornelius Crabtree and Squire Tordoff, were charged with committing a robbery in Thornton Road, on the evening of Thursday week; having robbed Isaac Smithies of a florin, a shilling, and some copper, and Thomas Robinson of 2*s* 7½*d*. The prosecutors were drinking together at several public houses and beer shops in the town on Thursday, and at a rather late hour they left a beer house in Southgate to go home to Thornton. They had been drinking at the last house in company with the prisoners and several of their companions; Smithies, who had long known Crabtree, treating the prisoners and their friends with several quarts of ale. It was at the reputed entreaties of Robinson, that the prosecutors at length quitted the company, as he had not liked their company. They were followed by the prisoners and their companions, who were evidently wishful that they should still continue together, at some other public house. The prosecutors, however, contrived to evade their company. They got away from them, and some time after, they were overtaken in Thornton Road, beyond Messrs. Fairbank's Colliery, by the prisoners and two other persons, knocked down, violently used, and robbed of the money mentioned. The prosecutors afterwards returned to Bradford and gave information of the robbery. The prisoners were committed for trial at the sessions.

Bradford Observer, 9 February 1854

THORNTON MECHANICS' INSTITUTE. The committee of the above institution having made arrangements for the delivery of a course of eight lectures in the Athenaeum, the first of the series was given on Tuesday evening by the Rev. D. Fraser, classical tutor at Airedale College, on 'Burns and his poetry.' It is almost needless to add that in the hands of a lecturer so gifted, the subject was rendered a very interesting one, though it was capable of being rendered much more attractive to a mixed audience by the introduction in various parts of more of Burns's poetry. Mr. Kay occupied the chair. The audience was a numerous and intelligent one; the lecturer had the thanks of the meeting warmly given to him, to which he suitably responded, and the company separated highly gratified.

Bradford Observer, 16 February 1854

THORNTON. Our correspondent sends us the particulars of a social meeting, held on Saturday last, which we have pleasure in publishing, though in somewhat abridged form. The meeting was composed of the young men of a Bible class, conducted by Mr. A. Wood, who invited their teacher to take tea with them, and then presented him with a beautiful and valuable writing desk, suitably inscribed, as a mark of their esteem and gratitude. Mr. Wood has conducted this class for some time; he has been unremitting in his labours, and has been cheered by much success. We may remark, by the way, that well-directed effort in this field of industry always secures an adequate response. Many young men in Thornton are deeply indebted to Mr. Wood for his exertions on their behalf. The meeting referred to was held in Kipping School-room, Mr. Banister Hill presided. Mr. John Speight, on behalf of his class-mates, presented the testimonial to the teacher expressing their grateful sense of obligation to him, in appropriate and affectionate terms. Mr. Wood replied, accepting with much pleasure this token of good-will, urging upon his young friends the importance of those subjects which had for the most part formed the staple of his instructions. Mr. C. Barraclough, Mr. G. Crowther, and others, subsequently spoke, and the evening closed over one of the pleasantest and most suggestive meetings yet held in the same room.

Bradford Observer, 23 February 1854

THORNTON MECHANICS' INSTITUTE. On Thursday evening the Rev. W. Scott, president of Airedale College, delivered a lecture in the Athenaeum, 'on spectres, apparitions, and table moving.' Joseph Craven, Esq., West House, occupied the chair. The lecturer ably showed the absurdity of a belief in such superstitions and folly; and the audience, which was a numerous one, seemed to coincide with the views stated. On the whole the lecture was well received, and at the close a vote of thanks was cordially given to the lecturer.

Bradford Observer, 23 February 1854

Last evening, Mr. T.J. Pearsall, lecturer and agent to the Yorkshire Union of Mechanics' Institutes, delivered the first of his lectures in the Athenaeum, 'on Nineveh and Ancient Art,' with illustrations. The Rev. W. Woodward, B.A., incumbent of Thornton, occupied the chair, and his choice remarks passed a high eulogism on the lecturer for the great ability he had displayed in the lecture.

Bradford Observer, 9 March 1854

HOME MISSIONARY SOCIETY. On Tuesday last the district meeting in connection with the above society was held at Thornton.

Bradford Observer, 9 March 1854

THORNTON MECHANICS' INSTITUTE. The fifth of the series of lectures arranged to be given in the Athenaeum in connection with the above institution was delivered by Mr. A. Wood, schoolmaster, the subject being 'on the progress of civilisation in England.' The Rev. J. Gregory presided, and the lecturer displayed ability of no common order. The lecture was equally as instructive as interesting, and gave much satisfaction to the audience. A vote of thanks was warmly accorded to the lecturer for the very able manner in which he had discharged the duty he had undertaken.

Bradford Observer, 9 March 1854

On Tuesday evening Mr. W.A. Pallister, of Bradford, delivered a lecture in the Kipping Old School, on 'Friendly Societies: their excellence and defects.' After dwelling largely on the insecurity and generally insolvent state - according to his views - of the present friendly societies, the lecturer eulogised the 'People's Assurance Society,' and stated that his object was to form a branch at Thornton in connection with it. A branch was accordingly opened, and Mr. Joseph Greenwood appointed agent. Mr. Wood, schoolmaster, occupied the chair, but the meeting was only thinly attended.

Bradford Observer, 16 March 1854

THORNTON MECHANICS' INSTITUTE. Last Wednesday evening the Rev. Henry Woodward, B.A., Incumbent of Thornton, delivered a very instructive, interesting, and able lecture, in the Athenaeum, on the 'Crusades.' Mr. Hills, surgeon, was called on to preside but business calling him away, the Rev. J. Gregory supplied his place. A vote of thanks was passed to the rev. gentleman for his very valuable lecture, which afforded great satisfaction to the audience.

Bradford Observer, 23 March 1854

THORNTON MECHANICS' INSTITUTE. On Wednesday in last week, Mr. Brady, surgeon, of Bradford, delivered a lecture 'on God's Providence, as revealed in the Architecture and Phenomena of the Earth.' The object of the lecturer was to prove that the earth exhibits evidence of intelligent design – firstly, in the position in which it had been placed with reference to the sun; secondly, in the architecture of its surface; and thirdly, in the phenomena which take place upon its surface. The lecturer commenced his discourse by explaining the laws of motion and the principle of gravitation; illustrated their bearing on the relative distances of the sun, moon, and earth; and proved, from the beneficent results arising out of their present relationship, as affecting animal or vegetable kingdoms, they could not have sprung from the blind operation of material laws, but that these laws must have been mere instruments in the hands of an intelligent voluntary agent. The next topic discussed was that of the cause of the succession of the seasons. This was illustrated by a simple apparatus, and shown to depend on two causes – 1st, the inclination of the earth's axis to the plain [*sic*] of the elliptic; and 2ndly, to the circumstance that the axis always remains parallel to itself. The mode in which the earth is ventilated and watered, or the origins of wind and rain, was next illustrated, and the necessity shown for their perpetual circulation. The elevation of the loftier mountains in the more central regions of the earth were next alluded to, and was shown to be the means adopted by the Creator for tempering the atmosphere in territories which from their great heat would be otherwise uninhabitable. This part of the lecture involved the laws of refraction and reflection of light, which was illustrated by diagrams. The nature and causes of tides formed the next topic for consideration; their laws were plainly and succinctly described, and shown to depend on the relative distances of the sun, moon, and earth. The lecture was tolerably well attended, and the audience evinced a good deal of interest in the various topics discussed. The Rev. J. Gregory occupied the chair, and at the close, on the motion of Francis Craven, Esq., a vote of thanks to Mr. Brady was proposed and warmly responded to by the audience.

Bradford Observer, 27 April 1854

Died Friday last in his 91st year, Mr. Abraham Brooksbank, yeoman, Thornton. The deceased was born, lived all his long life, and at last died, in the same house.

Bradford Observer, 11 May 1854

THORNTON MECHANICS' INSTITUTE. On Tuesday, the above institution held its fifth annual meeting in the Athenaeum. Robt. Milligan, Esq., of Harden, occupied the chair, and his opening address graphically set forth the objects, advantages, and pleasures of institutions formed for the improvement of the mind, and favourably contrasted the working men of this country with those of any other in such matters; after which he called upon Mr. Wm. Kay, the secretary, to read the report, which was again the year of a very satisfactory and encouraging nature, and showed that the institution was gradually progressing in usefulness. Classes had been formed for reading, writing, arithmetic, grammar, geography, and composition, and were well attended. A sewing class had also been formed for the females during the year, and had proved very successful. Twelve valuable lectures had been given by gentlemen during the year on various interesting and instructive subjects. A penny savings bank has also been established during the year which had proved very successful in the objects its promoters had in view. The library continued to diffuse a taste for reading, and the number of exchanges of books this year is 2828. Many of the most popular periodicals and newspapers were also taken in and well read. 32 new works had been added to the library during the year, and, after all expenses had been paid, a small balance was left in the Treasurer's hands. The meeting was most effectively addressed by the Rev. J. Gregory, the Rev. D. Fraser, John Rawson, Esq., E. Kenion, Esq., and Mr. Wood, of Thornton, schoolmaster. Miss Whittam sang several popular airs, and gave great pleasure and satisfaction. Some noble and elevating sentiments were enunciated by the various speakers during the evening, and all passed off with considerable éclat; but there was certainly one thing to be regretted and that was, that there was not a larger audience to enjoy such an intellectual treat.

Bradford Observer, 18 May 1854

ASSAULTING A WIFE. At the Borough Court, on Tuesday, Isaac Dobson, of Thornton, was fined 20*s* and expenses 17*s* for an assault upon his wife Sarah, a resident in Clayton Street, Thornton Road. Mr. Lees appeared for the defendant.

For eight years the defendant and his wife had been living apart from each other, the husband allowing the wife a weekly stipend of 3s 6d for her maintenance. At one o'clock on the morning of Sunday inst., the defendant with others went to his wife's residence, with the intent (it was alleged on his part) to test certain rumours that were afloat about her character; with the intent (said she) of causing her loss and annoyance. However, whatever his intentions were, whilst there he committed an assault upon her, and for this the magistrates inflicted the penalty above stated.

Bradford Observer, 18 May 1854

At the West Riding magistrates' court on Thursday, John Kaye, of Thornton, was charged with a desperate assault upon Wm. Robinson, of the same place. On the 8th instant, the two parties, with others who appeared as witnesses, were seated in a beer house kept by one David Holmes. A trifling dispute arose, in the course of which the defendant seized a three-legged table, and with a threat against the life of the complainant, brought it down upon his (complainant's) head. Kaye put in a denial to this statement, and sought to prove that he was a very ill-used individual. The magistrates, however, decided the case against him, fining him 5s, and expenses £1 14s 6d. He was also ordered to find two sureties for £5 each, and himself to be bound over in £10 to keep the peace for the space of six months.

Bradford Observer, 1 June 1854

PRESENTATION AT THORNTON. The Rev. Thomas Jackson, curate of Thornton, has been appointed to the curacy of Langton, Staffordshire. As he must very soon leave Thornton, those who have known and valued him there, as a faithful, earnest pastor and preacher, have taken an opportunity to present him with a beautiful Timepiece, as a mark of their affectionate esteem. The occasion of the presentation (Saturday week) was made the occasion of passing some pleasant time in his company. His congregation and other friends held a tea meeting in the National Schoolroom, after which, with a suitable address, Isaac Wood, Esq., the churchwarden, presented the memorial to the rev. gentleman. Mr. Jackson replied in affectionate terms at that time, and afterwards (on Tuesday last) when he returned the compliment, and invited 150 of the Sunday school teachers and scholars to feast with him, he again took another opportunity to address them. The rev. gentleman preaches his farewell sermon on Sunday.

Bradford Observer, 15 June 1854

CRICKET. On the 10th inst., a match of cricket was played between eleven of Messrs. Craven & Harrop's employees and eleven of Messrs. Schwann, Kell & Co.'s, when the latter were victorious in one innings, and seven wickets down. Score as follows:

Messrs. Craven & Harrop's Eleven –
F. Gobert 13, 6; J. Welldon 19, 10; Craven not out, 8, 4;

Adkin 0, 18; Spence 2, 10; T. Bell 23, 8; R. Bell 0, 0;
Powell 1, 0; Lee 0, 17; Clapham 0, 3; Wilson 0, and not out;
byes and wides 8. Totals, 159.
Messrs. Schwann, Kell & Co.'s Eleven –
C. Blakey 7, 0; T. Lynes 15, 0; A. B. Kemp not out, 4, 0;
A. Robertshaw 3, 0; J. Atkinson 4, 2; J. Shaw 8, 0;
J. Whitely 8, 7; J. Child 21, and not out 15;
J. Robinson 0, and not out 2; T.H. Moore 0; Z. Constantine 4, 0;
byes and wides, 16. Totals 160.

Bradford Observer, 6 July 1854

TO STONE-MERCHANTS, DELVERS AND BUILDERS, To be let by ticket, at the Boar's Head Inn, in Bradford, in the county of York, on Thursday, the 6th of July, 1854, at six o'clock in the evening (subject to conditions to be then produced), ALL the BED or BEDS of STONE, lying within and under a portion of three several closes of land called the Ing, the Wards End Field, and the Brow, containing 8,500 square yards, being part of the two farms called the Hob End and Spring Holes, situate at Thornton Height, near Bradford, in the occupation of Mr. Samuel Wright and Mr. David Robinson. The above Stone is of very superior quality and a great thickness, free from water, and may be got by open quarry. It is now open to inspection, and a portion of it is in the course of being delved. For further information, apply to Mr. WILLIAM ATKINSON, Clayton, (the owner); or to Mr. HIGHAM, Solicitor, Brighouse, with whom a plan of the estate is lodged. Brighouse, June 14th, 1854.

Bradford Observer, 6 July 1854

ACCIDENT AT THORNTON. On Tuesday, Mr. Simeon Myers, delver, of Thornton, met with a serious accident in one of the stone quarries there. A large stone fell upon him, broke his leg, and otherwise injured and bruised him; but he was immediately taken to the Bradford Infirmary, and is now in a fair way of recovery.

Bradford Observer, 6 July 1854

THORNTON WESLEYAN REFORMERS' SUNDAY SCHOOL ANNIVERSARY. On Sunday last – after two sermons by Mr. B. Porrit, of Heckmondwike; that in the afternoon in the Athenaeum, and that in the evening in the Kipping Chapel – upwards of £20 was collected towards the support of the school.

Bradford Observer, 3 August 1854

THORNTON MAN FOUND DEAD. On Tuesday morning, Oliver Wright, the engine-tenter at the colliery belonging to Messrs. Townend & Wood, was found dead in the boiler house. About half-past five o'clock his son went to fire for him as he was in the habit of doing every morning, and was horror-struck on thus finding his father laid dead. The works were standing, and he is supposed to have gone in during the night, and when asleep, fallen against a step edge, as his face was covered with blood, and his forehead much cut. The deceased was about 63 years of age, and much respected. An inquest will be held at the Black Horse Inn, on Friday next, before G. Dyson, Esq., coroner, but it is not likely that any additional light can be thrown on the unfortunate occurrence.

Bradford Observer, 24 August 1854

THORNTON. ATTEMPT AT HIGHWAY ROBBERY. Last Saturday evening, as Mrs. Wood, of the Victoria Inn, near Keelham Bar, Thornton, was returning from Bradford, she was attacked by a villain whom she did not know, who at once threw her down and attempted to rob her, but her presence of mind was more than a match for his strength. On her leaving Thornton to go home, it was about ten o'clock, and as the night was a very dark one for this season of the year, she thought – as the road was lonely and she might be attacked – she would keep her purse, which contained about £16 17s, in her hand, and in case of need she could throw it into the field. When she had got within half a mile of the house she was attacked, and in the midst of the struggle she threw her purse into a cornfield, where it was found as soon as daylight appeared all safe and right. Had it not been for this fortunate precaution no doubt the villain would have accomplished his purpose, and it is to be regretted that the darkness of the night rendered him unknown.

Bradford Observer, 31 August 1854

THORNTON ROAD BAR. The bar on the Thornton Road is a most formidable barrier to all equestrian locomotion in that direction. If we remember right the toll on a cab is 8*d* or 9*d*. All bars are a nuisance to those who travel, but this bar is emphatically a *great* nuisance; the other bars in the borough are doomed, some are already extinct, and others will be in the course of a few months; but this bar has no seeds of mortality about it: what is certain death to everything else, debt, is the palulum of life to a toll-bar; the Thornton road is in debt, it gets deeper and deeper in debt every year, and therefore its toll-bars are immortal. If the bar were in Wales 'Rebecca' had long since demolished it, but in this well-behaved county it is safe from violence of that kind. It is, however, going to be attacked. The incipient village of Girlington lies just within its reach, and the inhabitants perceiving how detrimental to their interests the toll-bar must prove, are going to see what can be done to remove it. They have convened a public meeting, which is to be held at the Girlington Hotel on Monday to consider what steps it may be advisable to take.

Bradford Observer, 12 October 1854

SUDDEN DEATH. Another awful instance of the uncertainty of life occurred last Sunday at Thornton. About five o'clock in the afternoon of that day, a young man of the name of Isaac Dobson, a weaver, went with two companions to take a walk up the Thornton New Road, in the course of which they all three set off running. But in a very few moments the young man above mentioned fell down and, without being able to speak a word, immediately expired. An inquest was held over him on Tuesday, before Mr. Ingram, deputy coroner, at the New Inn, and the verdict returned was 'Died suddenly from natural causes.'

Leeds Mercury, 14 October 1854

Thornton Lower Mill. – Valuable Worsted Machinery, comprising 300 Pairs of Combs, Drawing and Roving Frames, extra Gill Boxes, Spinning Frames, Power Looms, Heald and Genappe Yarn Machinery, Steam Piping, Cross Shafting, Drums, Guide and other Pulleys, a large Quantity of Gas Piping and Burners, Gallipoli and Sperm Oils, 17 Packs of Soap, Mechanics' and Smiths' Tools, wrought cast Iron and Wood Cisterns, Waggons, Carts, and Farming Implements, neat Phaeton and Whitechapel, &c, &c.

Mr. CARR has been honoured with instructions from Mr. Simeon Townend to offer for unreserved Sale by Auction,

THE whole of the very valuable WORSTED MACHINERY, on the premises at Thornton Lower Mill, near Bradford, on *Tuesday 24th, Wednesday 25th, Friday 27th, and Saturday 28th October*, 1854.

The SCOURING and STEAMING MACHINERY comprise – washing rings, 3 pairs washing rollers, bowls, piping, and taps, steam soap cisterns, steam chests with patent valves and taps, 2 steam closets, 2 boiling cisterns, with creel pegs and crane, 2 steam pans, 30 in. diameter, with pipes and valves, scouring troughs, &c.

300 Pairs of WOOL COMBS, 3, 4, 5, and 6 pitch, with pads.

The PREPARING MACHINERY

is by the first makers, most of it nearly new, consisting of double-headed gill boxes, double-headed sliver gill boxes, Smith's extra superior gill boxes, with tooth and pinion rollers, 10 double-headed drawing boxes, 7 six-spindle roving frames, 11 eight-spindle roving frames, 4 spindle finishers, 6 spindle finishers, dandy rover, double sliver, cans, belting, slubbing, roving, and finishing bobbins.

40 SPINNING FRAMES,

many of them nearly new, varying from 96 to 144 spindles.

HEALD and GENAPPE MACHINERY,
including twisting frames, winding engines, doubling frames, singe plates, steaming chests and apparatus for every process, in drying, – forming together the most complete, efficient, and beautiful establishment for any person wishing to cultivate that trade; pulleys, universal guides, &c.

38 pairs of LOOMS,
15 4-4 looms, 4 5-4 do., 19 8-4 do., by Hodgson and Haley, and Ray and Habershaw; change wheels, wheel racks, spare flyers, spindles, guides, spool bobbins, spare rollers.

4-fold DOUBLING FRAME,
with 12 spindles, indicator, and bobbins to fit; German clock.

Two FOLDING MACHINES,
For 24 spindles, horizontal traverse and patent indicator, double reels, grossing presses, lockers.

290 Yards 2, 3, and 4 in. STEAM PIPING,
cross shafting, most of which is bright; drums, pulleys, and hangers; gas meter; 576 yards gas piping, pendants, and burners, &c.

MECHANICS' and SMITHS' TOOLS,
circular saw and frame, grindstone and frame, vices, benches, stocks, taps, and dies, shears for cutting iron, files, screws, nails, double-geared lathe, 9 inch centre, with tools, cones, and gauntree, universal chuck, anvils, blows, single-geared lathe, cones, tools, and iron-faced gauntree, self-acting double-geared slide lathe, 8½ inch centre, with cones, chucks, rests, tools and iron gauntrees, self-acting fluting engine, tools and index complete, upright drill and tools, rack drill, two emery glazers, screw jack, a complete set of gas pincers and tools, swage blocks, swages, and tools of all kinds, bar, rod, and sheet iron, masons' sieves.

200 GALLONS GALLIPOLI OIL and SPERM OIL,
oil cistern, oil cans, pumps, measures, and savers, 17 packs of soap, a quantity of grease, 12 gross new pickers, 28 reams of grossing paper, 30 lbs. of string, new brushes, skep lurry, on four wheels, wool trucks, loading rack, large and small beams and scales, weighing machines, weights, measuring machines.

COUNTING HOUSE FURNITURE,
double desk and two buffets, mahogany desk, 15 feet long, with 13 drawers and buffet; iron safe, bins, shelves, partitions, two cranes,

School Green Hotel.

wagons, carts, manure barrels, wheelbarrows, trucks, gearing and
farming implements, ladders, yard lamps, a neat phaeton and
whitechapel, two sets of gig harness, &c., &c.
Mr. Carr has pleasure in inviting manufacturers to view this superior
machinery which has been selected with great care and judgement, a
considerable part of which is of the newest construction, in excellent
condition, and worthy the attention of the public.
The sale will commence each day at ten o'clock a.m.
Catalogues may be had on the premises, and at Mr. Carr's Offices,
Queensgate, Bradford, and Harrison-road, Halifax.

Chapter Ten
1855-1856

Sheep stealer arrested in Ireland – £50 a year for Thornton policeman – Vandals destroy plants in Kipping garden – Thornton toll bars to let

Bradford Observer, 18 January 1855

The Rev. H.H. Heap, of Hatfield Hall, Durham, and curate of Horton, has been appointed to the incumbency of Thornton in this parish. Patron the Vicar of Bradford.

Bradford Observer, 22 February 1855

TO SCHOOLMASTERS - WANTED, a MASTER, for the Grammar School at Thornton, near Bradford, in the county of York. The annual income is about £60, for which he will be required to teach the English and Latin languages. Other branches of education are paid for on a scale to be fixed by the Trustees. Application, with testimonials 'as to character and abilities' to be sent, post-paid, to Mr. WM. COWGILL, Land Agent, Darley Street, Bradford, on or before Saturday the 3rd day of March next. The Trustees will meet at the offices of the said WILLIAM COWGILL on *Thursday March Eighth* at eleven o'clock in the forenoon, for the purpose of making the appointment. Bradford, February 9th, 1855.

Bradford Observer, 29 March 1855

THORNTON. On Monday evening the premises of Mr. Jabez Pickles, of Thornton, wool dealer, were broken into, and wool, &c., to the amount of upwards of £20, stolen therefrom.

Bradford Observer, 17 May 1855

DRUNKENNESS AND ROBBERY. At the West Riding Court on Monday, three persons named Matthew Warburton, Emanuel Wilkinson, and Sutcliffe Tyas, were charged with having on the morning of Monday week stolen a quantity of tobacco, and some £3 17s 6d in money, the property of Joshua Northrop, of Fall Bottom, Thornton. The complainant was recently a beershop keeper, and at half-past ten o'clock on Sunday evening week, the defendants went to his house and demanded some ale. They were rather obstreperous, and to induce them to be quiet he offered to give them some ale. On his presenting them with a pitcher of beer, however, they gave him a trifle for it. The party continued at the house till six o'clock on Monday morning, drinking warm ale. At nine o'clock, Northrop discovered that the money which he had previously had in his house was missing. One pound of the sum was in sixpences, and suspicion fell upon the prisoners in consequence of their being afterwards found eating and drinking for many hours at the Black Horse Inn, Thornton, there paying the shot (some 16s or 17s) in sixpences. The complainant stated that after he had locked up the house at six o'clock on Monday morning, he observed Warburton holding up the window while Wilkinson either entered or returned from the house through the window. Northrop admitted that he had himself been very drunk every day from Monday to Friday, and that it was in consequence of the constable of Thornton coming to him when he was sober that he had taken any steps against the prisoners in reference to the robbers. The magistrates determined to deal summarily with the case against Wilkinson and Warburton, being of opinion that no jury would convict in the case, and they therefore dismissed Tyas, and called on the other prisoners to account for their presence in the dwelling at the time they were seen at the window by Northrop. Tyas was called by Mr. Lees on their behalf, but he failed to give any satisfactory account of their movements. The two defendants were each committed for three months each to the House of Correction as rogues and vagabonds.

Leeds Mercury, 18 October 1855

FATAL ACCIDENT. A person, named Atkinson, met with his death from an accident, on Sunday last. Deceased went upon the scaffold of a building in course of erection, at the Old Corn Mill, Thornton, when he fell down, and was so injured that he only survived for about three hours.

Leeds Mercury, 18 December 1855

THE THORNTON SHEEP STEALING CASE. We stated the precise facts of this case a short time since, and they are now borne out, notwithstanding a fallacious attempt by Charnock, one of the constables, to disprove them. Yesterday morning, Jonn. Sutcliffe, woolcomber, of Thornton, was placed at the bar of the West Riding Magistrates' Court before J. Pollard, W. Horsfall, and A. Harris, Esqrs., charged with the robbery. On the 29th November, Mr. William Holdsworth, jun., butcher, of Thornton, purchased eight sheep, four of which he killed, and placed the remainder in a field in the vicinity. On the morning of the following day, he discovered that one of them had been slaughtered and stolen, the skin and offal being left in the field. Information was given to the parochial constables of the circumstances, and John Barker, one of the officers, subsequently discovered portions of the carcase in Sutcliffe's house; while he packed up the meat, he sent Charnock, another constable, with two other men, to apprehend Sutcliffe at a neighbouring beer-house, but their prisoner was, by some unaccountable means, allowed to escape. The Superintendent-constable sought to bring Charnock before the Bench for a wilful neglect of duty, but the Magistrates considered it best to allow the matter to rest until more positive proof could be adduced. In the meantime, Sutcliffe enlisted in the 41st Regiment of Foot, and was sent as part of a detachment to Ireland, where he was followed by Constable Barker, who succeeded in apprehending him, having got his warrant endorsed by the Magistrates at Dublin, near Templemore, in the county of Tipperary. Sutcliffe then said to Barker that he should not have thought of decamping, had not Charnock given him a suggestive push when they got to the door of the beer-house. The prisoner admitted the offence before the magistrates, stating that he had been driven to commit this felony by a want of sufficient food. He was committed for trial at the next York Assizes.

Leeds Mercury, 12 January 1856

ROBBERY ON THE NEW RAILWAY. Thos. Spurr, a middle-aged man, was placed in the dock of the West Riding Magistrates' Court, Bradford, on Thursday, charged with stealing two wheelbarrows. The barrows were the property of Messrs. Smith and Knight, contractors, and were missed by Thomas Wilson, a sub-contractor from the line of the Bradford, Wakefield, and Leeds Railway, now in course of construction, so long ago as the 23rd November. They were found last week at Thornton, by Constable Barker; the brands were partially cut out, and they had been disposed of by the prisoner. The case was summarily dealt with, and Spurr sentenced to three months imprisonment, with hard labour, in Wakefield House of Correction.

Leeds Mercury, 12 January 1856

TRESPASS AT THORNTON. Mr. John Pollard, of Thornton, was summoned before J. Pollard, Esq., A. Harris, Esq., and Capt. Pollard, at the West Riding Magistrates' Court, Bradford, on Thursday last, charged with wilfully damaging the property of his neighbour, Mr. Craven. Mr. Terry appeared for the complainant, and produced a sketch of the land and the township map. It appeared that there formerly existed a fence upon the boundary of Mr. Craven's land, but it had to be taken down in consequence of the land being quarried. Four years ago, a wall was erected on the site of the fence, and this Mr. Pollard pulled down alleging he had right of road. Mr. Driver, the former owner of the land, negatived this assumption;

he disposed of the land to Mr. James Bray, who sold it to the present parties no right of road existing. The damage was laid at 6s. The defendant, who did not appear, was ordered to pay the amount claimed, with the legal expenses.

Bradford Observer, 17 January 1856

TO LET, a FARM, known by the name of the 'Little Hill Farm,' Black Carr, near Thornton, containing about 17 acres of good, sound grazing Land, with a comfortable House, Barn and other outbuildings. For particulars, apply to Mr. J. HIRD, Old Brewery, Bradford.

Bradford Observer, 21 February 1856

ST JAMES'S EPISCOPAL CHAPEL, KENNINGTON. The congregation of this chapel have presented their minister, the Rev. Henry Woodward, late of Thornton, with a purse of sixty sovereigns at the conclusion of the first year of his ministry, as an earnest of their personal regard, and admiration of his zeal and talent. This indeed is a visible and substantial way of evincing applause and appreciation which it were well to emulate, and is really and in truth a golden testimonial.

Bradford Observer, 21 February 1856

THORNTON. APPOINTMENT OF PAID CONSTABLES. On Friday last, a vestry meeting was held at Thornton church, for the purpose of nominating constables for the township for the ensuing year, when it was agreed to have a paid constable for Thornton, and another for Denholme - the former at a salary of £50, and the latter £25, per year - and all fees receivable by them to be returned to the township. Mr. John Barker was chosen for Thornton, and Mr. Eli Foster for Denholme.

Leeds Mercury, 1 March 1856

Free-stone Quarries – Thornton near Bradford. To be SOLD by TICKET, on Monday, Tenth March, 1856, at four o'clock in the afternoon, at the house of Mr. Isaac Wood, Victoria Inn, Thornton. ALL those valuable BEDS of STONE, at Bell Dean and Back Height Quarries, on leases for seven years. For plans and further particulars apply to Mr. Ezra Woodhead, High Ash, Idle, Leeds.

Bradford Observer, 20 March 1856

THORNTON. ELECTION OF OVERSEERS, &c. On Friday last, at a vestry meeting held pursuant to public notice, Mr. Simeon Townend and Mr. Joshua Craven were re-elected overseers of the poor for the ensuing year, and at the same time a Board of Surveyors for the Highways, consisting of nine persons, was elected for the same period.

Bradford Observer, 27 March 1856

THORNTON. WANTON MISCHIEF. Late on Saturday night last or early on Sunday morning, some evil-disposed person or persons destroyed the young trees, shrubs, and plants in the garden and field adjoining the house of and belonging to Mr. Simeon Townend, of Upper Kipping, Thornton. Ten pounds reward is offered for the apprehension and conviction of the offender, but so far nothing has transpired to lead to detection.

Bradford Observer, 27 March 1856

THORNTON. WESLEYAN BAZAAR. A bazaar of useful and ornamental articles has been held in the schoolroom adjoining the Wesleyan Chapel, Thornton, for the benefit of that place of worship. It opened on Good Friday, and was continued on the Saturday, Monday, and Tuesday following. It has been very numerously attended, especially on Good Friday, and the amount realized by sales and admission will no doubt surpass the expectations of its friends and promoters.

Bradford Observer, 27 March 1856

VALUABLE PROPERTY AT BRADFORD AND THORNTON. TO BE SOLD BY AUCTION, by Mr. CARR, on *Thursday the 27th day of March*, 1856, at the Talbot Inn, Bradford, at six o'clock in the evening. ALL that valuable FREEHOLD PROPERTY, situated at Bradford, in the county of York. All those SEVEN DWELLING HOUSES or Cottages, situated in King Charles Street, Otley Road, adjoining each other, in the occupation of Mr. Benj. Whiteley and others. Also all those EIGHT DWELLING HOUSES or Cottages, in Paper Hall Court, running parallel with King Charles Street, in the occupation of Moses Drake and others. Also all those SEVEN DWELLINGS, situated in Paper Hall Court, in the occupation of Reuben Hinchliffe and others. These Dwelling Houses are lately built, are in good repair, near to the centre of the town, and are well supplied with water.

IN THORNTON

All those Two Closes of Land, situated at Thornton, near Bradford, known by the names of Starlight Field, or Height Field, and Upper Field, containing by admeasurement 9,000 superficial square yards, or thereabouts.

These two closes contain a very valuable bed of stone, easy of access; also two good beds of coal, known as the Halifax Hard and Soft Bed Coal, and are approached by three roads, and close to the town of Thornton. Mr. GEORGE HARKER, 55 Joseph Street, Leeds Road, will give any information respecting the property at Bradford; and Mr. JONATHAN JOWETT, of Spring Gardens, Thornton, will show the Land, &c., at Thornton.

For further particulars, apply to Mr. CARR, Auctioneer, Queensgate, Bradford; or to Mr. WARWICK, Solicitor, Knaresborough.

Bradford Observer, 27 March 1856

THORNTON. DENHOLME GATE INN. On Monday, a new Lodge of Oddfellows, belonging to the Independent Order, M.U., was opened at the above splendid inn, by the lodge now established at Peah [*sic*] Pits, near Illingworth, in the Halifax district. There was a very numerous procession of the members of the order from all the surrounding lodges, and after the routine of duties attending the opening had been gone through, the evening was spent in the happy and convivial manner customary on such festive occasions.

Leeds Mercury, 19 April 1856

THE STABBING CASE AT THORNTON. Edward Clough, the young man remanded from Monday under the details fully described in Tuesday's Mercury, was again brought up at the West Riding Magistrates' Court, Bradford, on Thursday (before J. Pollard, W. Walker, J. Hollings, and W. Horsfall, Esqrs.), charged with stabbing William Shaw. Mr. Mossman, the clerk, read over the disposition of the injured man, taken before Mr. Horsfall, who stated the facts very reluctantly. Several young men had met at the house of a Mrs. Beck, in Thornton, of a very doubtful description, and commenced dancing and larking, on which five women, who had been sitting in the house went out. Shaw and another then pulled Clough out of a chair, and dragged him to the door; a quarrel ensued between them, and Clough and Shaw fought and wrestled; during the contest Clough got Shaw's head down between his knees, and while holding him in this position, inflicted three stabs in his chest with a knife. Mr. Hill, surgeon, found him at one o'clock in the morning, suffering from these wounds, and with four inches of the left lung protruding through one of them. Shaw still lies in an exceedingly dangerous state, and it is doubtful whether he will recover, although it was reported that he had improved on Thursday. Shaw's father saw the wounds inflicted on his son, and was therefore produced as a witness against his assailant; but the constables had been compelled to almost drag him out of the coal pit in which he was mining, and when in court scarcely anything could be got out of him. It was at last elicited that he had married the accused's sister, and since the unfortunate occurrence his relatives had told him a solicitor was employed for Clough, and if he (Shaw) attended the Court, whether he spoke the truth or not, they would have him transported. The Magistrates were, therefore, unable to go fully into the case. Clough was further remanded, and the old man Shaw was directed to be taken care of by Mr. Ingham, the superintendent constable, in order that he might not be influenced by his relatives. The Magistrates subsequently set Clough and the witness at liberty, finding it impossible to proceed with the case as it at present stands.

Bradford Observer, 17 July 1856

KIPPING SUNDAY SCHOOL ANNIVERSARY. On Sunday last, after two sermons by the Rev. Joseph Fox, of Manchester, the sum of £23 10s was collected in aid of the funds of the institution.

Bradford Observer, 17 July 1856

THORNTON. SUDDEN DEATH. About a fortnight since, a young man about 22 years of age, a weaver, of the name of Eli Ackroyd, of Thornton, who had for some time been suffering under consumption, being in a very weak state, was advised to try a change of air, and for that purpose went to Cleethorpes. On Thursday last he was returning home, but he had only reached Hull, at which place, as soon as he had left the steamer, he dropped down dead in the street, and almost immediately expired, owing to the rupture of a blood vessel. On receiving the distressing intelligence his poor mother, who is a widow, went to Hull with the intention of bringing his remains home for interment, but finding they were not fit to be removed, he has been interred at the cemetery there.

Bradford Observer, 25 September 1856

THORNTON. SERIOUS ACCIDENT. On Sunday last, a young man, named John Bentham, a weaver, of Thornton, went in company with a relative to see some friends at Moor End, a place near Mixenden. Having spent the day there, and returning home in the evening, which was very dark, he missed his way and fell into a quarry by the roadside, near Mixenden, and in his fall happening to come in contact with a plank, which somewhat arrested his fall, it is probable that to this circumstance he owes the preservation of his life. He laid in the quarry until near twelve o'clock when his groans were heard by some persons passing by, who got a light and had him removed, and on Monday morning he was taken to the Halifax Infirmary, where he now lies, having broken his thigh and arms, and is otherwise much injured. It is to be regretted that he belongs to no benefit society, and has a wife and six small children.

Bradford Observer, 9 October 1856

CLAYTON. FATAL ACCIDENT. On Monday evening, as Mr. John Jarrett, of the New Inn, Thornton, and Mr. John Booth, of Allerton Green, were returning from Wibsey fair in a gig, on leaving Clayton they took up a person of the name of Thos. Saunderson, farm servant to Mr. Samuel Wood, of Thornton, and unfortunately, they had no sooner done so than the driver lost his hold of the reins, and the horse set off at full speed. Saunderson jumped out of the gig, and fell on his head. Mr. Booth was thrown out, but suffered no injury, and Mr. Jarrett kept his seat, and after some time recovered the reins, when the horse became tractable at once, and he returned in search of his companions. This was about six o'clock in the evening. Saunderson was immediately removed to the Bull Inn, Clayton, and medical assistance immediately procured, but his injuries were of so serious a nature that he never afterwards spoke, but lingered until five o'clock the next morning, when he expired. The deceased was a very steady man, and had been about seven years with Mr. Wood, but was a native of Huntingdon. An inquest will be held over his body to-day, at the Bull Inn.

Bradford Observer, 16 October 1856

A VIOLENT FELLOW. At the West Riding Court, on Thursday, a young fellow named Richardson Greenwood was charged with committing a series of assaults, and sundry damage to the injury of several persons at the Bull's Head, Thornton. There were several complaints preferred against him, and it appeared that while in liquor on the 4th inst., he had proceeded through the several rooms of the house and assaulted persons indiscriminately. He was fined in several cases. He was first fined £1, and costs of £1 3s 8d, for an assault upon Joseph Pickles Foster; next, he was fined £1, and costs £1 3s 8d, for an assault upon one Thomas Smith; then, for damaging his wearing apparel, the defendant was fined in damages 5s, and costs; fourth, the defendant was fined £1, and £1 3s 8d costs, for an assault upon one John Hodgson; and last he was fined in damages 5s, and costs 6s, for damaging the wearing apparel of Hodgson. Failing to pay, the defendant will have a period of six months to serve in the House of Correction.

Bradford Observer, 16 October 1856

BRADFORD AND THORNTON TURNPIKE ROAD. NOTICE IS HEREBY GIVEN, that an AUCTION will be held at the Offices of Messrs. Hailstone and Payne, No. 35, Manchester Road, in Bradford, on *Thursday, the 16th day of October instant*, at twelve o'clock at noon precisely, for the purpose of LETTING to the best bidder, at that place, on that day, between the hours of twelve o'clock at noon and two o'clock in the afternoon, in the manner directed by two several Acts passed in the 3rd and 4th years of the reign of his late Majesty King George the Fourth, 'for regulating Turnpike Roads,' the TOLLS for One Year, from the 31st day of October instant, of the Turnpike Road leading from Bradford to Sun Side Cottages, in Thornton, both in the West Riding of the County of York, in the following Lots, that is to say – LOT 1. The TOLLS arising at the several Toll Gates, Side Gates, or Chains erected upon the said road at Baldwin's Mill, Brick Lane, and Whetley Lane, and at the Weighing Machine erected upon the said road, which tolls were let for the year ending the 31st October instant, for £600 above the expenses of collecting the same.
LOT 2. The TOLLS arising at the several Toll Gates, Side Gates, and Chains erected upon the said road, at Leaventhorpe Hall, Keelham, and Shay, which last mentioned tolls were let for the year ending the 31st

New Road, Thornton, looking west.

October instant for £255 above the expenses of collecting the same.
Each of the above Lots will be put up at the above mentioned sums
respectively.
Whoever happens to be the best bidder for either of such lots must at
the same time (if required) pay one month in advance of the rent at
which such lot may be let to such bidder, and give security with
sufficient sureties to the satisfaction of the Public Works Loan
Commissioners for payment of the remainder of the money monthly.
Dated the 1st day of October, 1856. By order,
BARNES & BERNARD
2, Great Winchester Street, London, Solicitors to the Commissioners.
Edward Hailstone, Receiver of the Tolls of the said Road.
N.B. Each bidder will be required to deposit the sum of £20 with the
Secretary or Agent of the said Commissioners, which, in the event of his
not answering to his bidding for either lots, will be forfeited.

Bradford Observer, 30 October 1856

THORNTON. FATAL OCCURRENCE. A most melancholy event happened in
the village on Saturday forenoon. A travelling Scotchman, who has for many years
visited the neighbourhood, was at the Black Horse, and having some services
rendered by an old man named James Beetham, who had been a woolcomber and
was upwards of 73 years of age, and with a mistaken view of rewarding him, gave

him three pennyworth of gin; after that another, then a third, and lastly a fourth, all which he drank in rather a short time, and nearly without water. The poor old man lived in a chamber nearby, where he went, and nothing more was heard of him until near three o'clock in the afternoon, when John Knapton, a friend of his, called to see him, and was horrified to see him sitting up in his chair, frothing at the mouth, unable to speak, and life fast ebbing away. Mr. Corrie, surgeon, was immediately sent for, but arrived too late to render him any effectual assistance. He lingered on till four o'clock on Sunday morning, when he expired. The deceased had been a member of the Kipping church for nearly forty years, and had led a consistent life. On Tuesday an inquest was held at the Black Horse Inn, before G. Dyson, Esq., coroner, when the following verdict was returned. 'Apoplexy from excessive drinking.'

Bradford Observer, 30 October 1856

HIGHWAY ROBBERY. On Saturday night, between eleven and twelve o'clock, as John Robinson was returning home from the court of Foresters, held at the New Inn, Thornton, he was attacked near the Methodist Chapel by two men, one of whom seized him by the throat and so strangled him that he could not cry out, while the other put his hand at once into the pocket in which he generally carries the money received as treasurer to the said court, and at once decamped, with its contents, leaving the poor fellow unable to cry out. They robbed him of £8 7s 10d, but missed five sovereigns which he had in another pocket. He has not the least idea who the men were, and he seems to have been rendered at once unconscious.

Bradford Observer, 27 November 1856

FREEHOLD PROPERTY AT THORNTON. TO BE SOLD BY AUCTION, by Mr. GEORGE POOLE, at the house of Mr. Bentham, the Bull's Head Inn, in Thornton, near Bradford, in the county of York, on Monday the 1st day of December 1856, at Six o'clock in the Evening precisely, subject to such conditions as shall be then and there produced. ALL those Five Freehold MESSUAGES or Dwelling-Houses, together with the Appurtenances thereto belonging, situate at Thornton TOWN END, and now or late in the several occupations of John Robinson (late Dr. Fawthrop), Robinson Murgatroyd, Jonathan Knowles, Charles Varley, and Jonas Wilman. One of the houses contains two Rooms and Scullery on the ground floor, also two Bedrooms and Closet, and is fitted up with cupboards and requisite fixtures; was formerly in the occupation of the late Dr. Fawthrop, and is well adapted for a shop. The other cottages are large, and all supplied with requisite fixtures; and, from being near to several large worsted mills, are always likely to be well occupied. The principal part of the purchase money may remain secured thereon if desired by the purchaser. For further particulars, apply to the AUCTIONEER, at his Office, 116, Westgate, Bradford, or to Mr. F. BUTTERFIELD, Solicitor, Albion Court, Bradford.

Bradford Observer, 18 December 1856

CROFT HOUSE, THORNTON near BRADFORD. The Misses LONGFIELD continue to receive under their care a limited number of Young Ladies, to whose training, moral and mental, they entirely devote themselves; ever endeavouring, by constant supervision, to secure the health, comfort, and happiness of those entrusted to their care. References are kindly permitted to the Rev. Jas. Gregory, Kipping Parsonage; Josh. Craven, Esq., West House; and Josh. Craven, Esq., Prospect House, Thornton; also to the Parents of the Pupils. School duties will be resumed (D.V.) on WEDNESDAY, January 20th, 1857.

Leeds Mercury, 20 December 1856

THE DUTIES OF CONSTABLES. During the hearing of an affiliation case (Emma Asquith, of Thornton, against Joseph North, of Shipley), at Bradford Court-house on Thursday, before the West Riding Magistrates, it transpired that Barker, one of the Thornton constables, had made himself very officious on behalf of the defendant. He offered himself as a witness, and swore that he had seen at least half-a-dozen young men in the complainant's company, that they were all strangers to him, that he had never seen the girl in the company of North, and that she bore a very light character. It turned out, on cross-examination, that North had sought out Barker, who had previously served him with the summons, on Saturday, that they had partaken of some gin together, and that subsequently Barker asked a man named John Robinson to attend as a witness for North and corroborate the above statements. Joshua Pollard, Esq., severely reprimanded Barker for his exceedingly indiscreet conduct, informed him that it was no part of his duty to assist in getting up cases either on the one side or the other, and in conclusion exclaimed, thank goodness we are going to have a rural police. An order for maintenance was issued.

Chapter Eleven
1857–1858

Grand opening concert at the Athenaeum – Weekend at Blackpool for millworkers – Cock-fight ends in brawl with police – Thornton's water stolen by Bradford – Serial bigamist at work

Bradford Observer, 19 February 1857

THORNTON. FATAL ACCIDENT. On Thursday morning, as John Hey, a waggoner, in the employ of Messrs. Feather and Speak, spinners of Haworth, was going to Bradford market, when he was going down the hill towards School Green, Thornton, either from his horse taking fright or some other cause he fell and the waggon went over his neck, and caused instantaneous death. An inquest was held on the body on Friday at Mr. Robt. Holmes's before G. Dyson, Esq. Verdict, 'Died from being accidentally run over by his waggon.' The deceased was a very steady man, married, and only 24 years of age.

Bradford Observer, 19 February 1857

THORNTON MECHANICS' INSTITUTE. On Tuesday evening, a Grand Concert was given in the Athenaeum, Thornton, on the occasion of the re-opening of the above Institution on its removal from the Kipping Old School to the large and commodious building in which the concert was given. Miss Whitham was the principal vocalist, and fully sustained her distinguished reputation. Mr. Hartley presided at the piano assisted by the Celebrated Infant Pianist from the Halifax Concerts, and the Holmfield Orchestral Band, consisting of twenty-one performers. The Thornton Glee Singers added much to the pleasure of the evening. The concert was very numerously attended, and the whole passed off with considerable éclat.

Leeds Mercury, 7 March 1857

IRREGULAR BEERHOUSES. The West Riding Magistrates, at Bradford Court-house, on Thursday, fined John Thornton, a beer-house keeper at Eccleshill, 40s, and the costs, for keeping his premises open after legal hours. Julius Dolby, of Eccleshill, for a similar offence, was also fined 40s, and the expenses. Mr. Pollard, the presiding Magistrate, intimated that he had received an anonymous letter, doubtless intended to influence his judgement on this case; it was a most improper proceeding on the writer's part, and he begged that he might have sent to him no more such communications. Samuel Foster, of Thornton, in the cellar of whose beer-house a rural policeman discovered three men and the landlord at half past four o'clock in the morning, was adjudged to pay a penalty of 40s, and costs, or to be imprisoned for two months.

Leeds Mercury, 7 March 1857

REPREHENSIBLE MISCONDUCT OF AN EX-POLICEMAN. On Thursday, at the West Riding Magistrates' Court, Bradford, John Barker, a middle-aged man, appeared at the bar, charged with the following misconduct. The defendant was for many years the Constable of Thornton, near Bradford, and on the establishment of the West Riding Police, was a short time in the force. In August last, a Mr. Gelder was at the Bull's Head Inn, Thornton, and placed a sovereign on the table; Barker, who was inebriated and probably rather frolicsome, took it up and treated the company with grog to the amount of 10s; next morning he appeared to have no knowledge of the transaction, and those who had enjoyed the treat during his obfuscation entered into a subscription to defray the cost, but it did not reach the amount by 3s, which Gelder promised to make up. On Monday last Barker went to the Bull's Head Inn, 'rather fresh;' Gelder happened to be there; a dispute arose respecting the 3s, and Barker first abused Gelder, then Mr. Bentham, the landlord, and next the landlady, in a most shameful manner. He used towards Mrs. Bentham several disgusting epithets. She remonstrated. 'Well, Mr. Barker, you have got a wife of your own; I don't know that her character is any better than mine; I wish you would let me alone.' He continued his abuse, held up his knob-stick at her, pushed her, and threatened that he would have the landlord 'fined for Sunday next, right or wrong.' Mrs. Bentham then sent for the police, after which he desisted. Mr. Pollard: Why did your husband not take him by the neck, and kick him out of the house? Mrs. Bentham: Because we have such a terror of Barker in Thornton, he has taken so much advantage of us. Mr. Pollard: The Magistrates consider the case is clearly proved, and fine the defendant 10s, and the costs, or one month's imprisonment at Wakefield; and I hope it will be the last time we shall see him here.

Bradford Observer, 16 July 1857

THORNTON. FATAL ACCIDENT. On Friday a little boy called Mallison Bateman, son of Jonas Bateman of Thornton, weaver, was accidentally drowned in a well on the opposite side of the road where he lived. The boy was between two and three years old, and had not been many minutes out of the houses before he was found drowned. Medical assistance was immediately procured, but life was extinct.

***Bradford Observer*, 30 July 1857**
VALUABLE FREEHOLD LAND AND BUILDINGS
AT THORNTON, NEAR BRADFORD
TO BE SOLD BY AUCTION, by Mr. G. HARDCASTLE, at the House of
Mr. Samuel Bentham, the Bull's Head Inn, in Thornton, near Bradford,
in the County of York, on Wednesday, the 19th day of August, 1857, at
Seven o'clock in the Evening precisely, subject to such conditions as
shall be produced at the time of sale.
Lot 1. All those Two CLOSES of Land, in Thornton aforesaid, called the
Upper Dole and the Lower Dole, containing together, by
admeasurement, three acres and 32 perches, or thereabouts (be the same
more or less), and now in the occupation of Samuel Bentham.
Lot 2. All that CLOSE of LAND, in Thornton aforesaid, called the Croft,
with the Dwelling-house and other buildings thereon, containing, by
admeasurement (including the sites of the buildings), three roods and
nine perches or thereabouts (be the same more or less), and now in the
occupation of the said Samuel Bentham, or his undertenants.
Lot 3. All that CLOSE of LAND, in Thornton aforesaid, called the
Yocken, containing, by admeasurement, two roods and 31 perches, or
thereabouts (be the same more or less), and now in the occupation of the
said Samuel Bentham.
All the above lots are most eligibly situated in the large and prosperous
manufacturing village of Thornton, which is distant from Bradford four
miles only, and Lot 1 is immediately adjoining to the large worsted mills
and works of Messrs. Joshua Craven and Sons.
Lots 1 and 2 have a considerable frontage to the turnpike road from
Thornton to Bradford, and part of Lot 2 is also fronting to the Main
Street of Thornton. Lots 1 and 3 are supposed to contain valuable beds
of coal and flagstone.
Mr. Samuel Bentham, the tenant, will show the premises, and further
particulars may be had on application to Mr. WILLIAM PICKARD,
Contractor, Laister Dyke, near Bradford; to the AUCTIONEER,
Bradford; to Mr. JOSEPH SMITH, Land Agent and Surveyor,
Kirkgate, Bradford; or to Messrs. WELLS & RIDEHALGH, Solicitors,
Bradford.
July 25th, 1857.

Leeds Mercury, 8 August 1857

Joseph Mann, of the Raggald's Inn beer-house, in Thornton township, was fined £5 by the West Riding Magistrates, at Bradford, on Thursday, or two months' imprisonment, this being the third offence, for having his house open for the sale of beer at half past eight o'clock on Sunday morning.

Bradford Observer, 13 August 1857

THORNTON. TREAT TO WORKPEOPLE. On Saturday Messrs. Craven and Harrop gave a treat to all their workpeople, at both Thornton and Bradford. A special train took them from Bradford to Blackpool on Saturday morning, and they returned in the same way on Tuesday evening.

Bradford Review, 3 January 1858

TWO OF A TRADE. Joseph Palterman was charged by George Haigh, with threatening to do him bodily harm at Thornton. The defendant was required to find sureties that he would keep the peace for six months.

Leeds Mercury, 9 January 1858

A TIPPLING FARMER ROBBED BY WOMEN. Yesterday, at the Borough Court, Bradford, two young women, named Elizabeth Rushworth and Margaret Donnelly, who had been apprehended by Police-constable Woodhead, were charged by Jonathan Leach, farmer, of Thornton Heights, with having robbed him of £6 16s in silver. The prosecutor stated that he left the Woolpacks Inn, Bradford, between eight and nine o'clock on Thursday night, and was then rather 'fresh.' He had £6 16s 5½d in his pockets. He met with the two prisoners in the street; they offered to find him lodgings, and he accompanied them to a house kept by an old woman named Jane Clark, in Longlands-street. He there sat and talked to the women a short time, after which the prisoners forced him out of the house, one attacking him in the face, and the other *prising* him. He never felt a hand in his pocket, and could not say who robbed him, but, immediately after he had been turned out, he discovered that all his money was gone, except 5½d in copper. The prisoners were subsequently taken into custody at the Washington dram-shop, Cropper-street; one of them had 10d in her possession, and the other 1s. The Magistrates decided that the evidence was insufficient, and discharged the women. The same prosecutor, Jonathan Leach, was robbed not long since in Thiefscore-lane, Bradford.

Bradford Review, 6 February 1858

THEFT BY A FISH HAWKER. Edward Shackleton, an itinerant vendor of cockles, and other shell fish, was charged at the West Riding Court on Thursday, with stealing a bag of corn from the barn of a farmer, called Thomas Hardy, at Storrs, in Thornton. The prisoner was seen leaving the barn at a quarter past six o'clock the same morning, with a bag on his back, by Joseph Hardy, a son of the prosecutor, who followed him across the fields, and saw him deposit it in an outhouse adjoining his own residence. Information was given to the police, and the bag being found in the place described, the prisoner was then taken into custody. He was committed for three months with hard labour, and left the court protesting that he was innocent, if he was hung for it, or died before he came out of the goal [*sic*].

Leeds Mercury, 6 February 1858

STEALING OATS. On Thursday, at the West Riding Court, Edward Shackleton, said to be a fish hawker, was charged with having stolen a sack and about three stones of oats, the property of Mr. Abraham Hardy, corn miller, of Thornton. Shortly after six o'clock the same morning, a youth named Joseph Hardy, nephew of the prosecutor, saw the prisoner leaving a barn at Storrs, Thornton, with a sack containing the oats in question on his back. Information was given to County Police Constable Walker (186), who took the prisoner into custody, at his own house, in the same neighbourhood. The sack and oats were found on the prisoner's premises; the sack was positively sworn to as belonging to Mr. Abraham Hardy, and there could be no doubt that the oats were his property, as they were of the same description as some in the barn. Access to the barn had been gained by opening the door lock, and Mr. Thomas Hardy stated that the same thing had been done five times during the last three weeks. It appeared that the prisoner had been three or four times in custody for various offences, and convicted on two occasions. He was committed for three months to hard labour as a rogue and vagabond.

Bradford Observer, 18 March 1858

THORNTON. On Friday last, a public meeting was held, pursuant to notice, for the purpose of choosing a board of surveyors, nominating overseers, &c. Mr. Isaac Wood, Mr. James Booth, Mr. Thomas Geldard, Mr. Thomas Rouse, and Mr. Jabez Pickles were elected as the board for Thornton; and Mr. John Bailey as surveyor for the hamlet of Denholme for the ensuing year. Mr. Jonathan Knowles, brewer; Mr. Henry Foster, manufacturer; Mr. Jonas Hartley, draper; and Mr. John Overend Wood, farmer, were nominated as overseers of the poor for the ensuing year.

Bradford Observer, 25 March 1858

ANOTHER MILL FIRE – THORNTON – On Saturday night, about nine o'clock, the inhabitants of Thornton were thrown into a state of great excitement by a report that Messrs. Craven and Harrop's mill was on fire. In a few minutes hundreds of people were on the spot, and the unmistakable evidence of a fire in one of the top rooms was apparent. Messengers were forthwith despatched to Bradford and Queenshead for the fire engines, and in a very short time two from the former place and one from the latter were on the spot. In the meantime, however, before the keys could arrive, an entrance was forced into the mill. Abundance of water being at hand, and plenty of willing hands to convey it, the fire was extinguished before it had obtained much hold. According to general opinion, the fire was happily discovered soon after it broke out, for, though the flames spread rapidly, and destroyed £300 or £400 of property in a very little while, yet it was confined to a limited portion of the building, and yielded to the active exertions of a few unprofessional firemen. The services of the fire engines were consequently not required. We are sorry to have to add, that there is no doubt the fire originated in the wilful act of an incendiary. A cotton warp which had been saturated in oil had been placed across three jacquard looms, and then ignited, and the footprints of the incendiary were observed and traced some distance at a place where he had found a secret entrance to the premises. Every effort has been used to discover the guilty party, but hitherto without success. The West of England Insurance Office have offered a reward of £100. Large numbers of people visited the locality on Sunday, to see what could be seen, but we should think their curiosity was hardly repaid. The external indications of the disaster are very slight, and on Tuesday the extensive works resumed their usual operations as though nothing of the kind related had happened: a happy circumstance for the workpeople and all concerned, as much suffering has thereby been providentially averted.

Bradford Review, 27 March 1858

FIRE AT THORNTON, NEAR BRADFORD. On Saturday night, about eight o'clock, a fire was discovered to have broken out in one of the rooms in the factory of Messrs. Craven and Harrop, manufacturers, of Thornton and Bradford. Messengers were despatched for the engine from Bradford, and that of Messrs. Foster, Black Dyke Mills, Queenshead, and about ten o'clock the corporation brigade and engine, under Mr. Olivant, jun. and that from Queenshead, were at the premises, but the fire had been extinguished. Shortly after its discovery, a number of the men connected with the premises, and others, conveyed a large quantity of water in buckets to the looms, etc., on fire, in the very centre of the large room, and by pouring it copiously from the room above, succeeded in extinguishing the flames. Three of the looms were damaged, but not wholly destroyed, the water causing more damage than the opposing element. The injuries, estimated at nearly £300, will be fully covered by insurance.

Bradford Review, 3 April 1858

A DISORDERLY BEER HOUSE. David Holroyd, of Thornton, was charged at the West Riding Court on Thursday by Sergeant Brear, with having drunk and disorderly company in his house, and being himself the most drunken in the lot, on Sunday evening last. As he had been convicted of allowing gambling in his house on the 26th of February last, he was fined £10 and costs, with the alternative of three months imprisonment.

Bradford Review, 3 April 1858

CAUTION TO GAMBLERS. Sunday gambling has for some time past been a great nuisance in the fields and lanes of Thornton, to the annoyance of the orderly people. Five young men, James Butterfield, Robert Horner, Thomas Shaw, William Duckett, and another, who had been seen by Sergeant Brear to play at pitch and toss in Bell Dean, on Sunday last, were fined 2s 6d each, with 10s costs, by the magistrates at the West Riding Court on Thursday last.

Bradford Review, 3 April 1858

WILFUL DAMAGE. Samuel Bairstow, of Leventhorpe, was charged at the West Riding Court on Thursday, with firing a quick thorn hedge in a field occupied by Wm. Rhodes, and the damage was laid at 25s. Mr. Peel in defence admitted that his client had fired the brushwood and dried grass, but stated that he had only done so to clear all off preparatory to the making of a better. It appeared, too, that the summons had originated in the ill-feeling entertained against him by S. Cordingley, Mr. Powell's game-keeper. He was ordered to pay 10s damages, with 10s costs.

Leeds Mercury, 3 April 1858

A BEER-HOUSE KEEPER HEAVILY FINED. At the West Riding Court, Bradford, on Thursday, David Oldfield, beerseller, of Thornton, was charged by Serjeant Briar, of the West Riding constabulary, with having been drunk in his (defendant's) house on Sunday evening, and with having allowed company to assemble therein contrary to law. The charge was proved, as well as a previous conviction in reference to card playing in the defendant's house; and the court fined him £10 and costs, – the term of imprisonment in default of paying the fine to be three months.

Bradford Observer, 8 April 1858

A beerhouse keeper named David Oldfield, residing at Thornton, was on Thursday last fined £10 and costs for being drunk in his own house on the previous Sunday evening; a previous conviction for allowing card playing in his house having also been proved.

Bradford Review, 17 April 1858

ASSAULTING THE POLICE. At the West Riding Court, Bradford, on Tuesday before Robert Milligan and W. Horsfall, Esqs., Ingham Mitchell, a labourer, was charged with assaulting police-constable Richard Naddy, of the West Riding constabulary on the 29th ult., at Thornton. On the day in question about 300 men, of whom the prisoner was one, were assembled at a cock-fight, in a field, at Foreside, Thornton, and the complainant and two other officers went to stop the illegal and barbarous sport, and to disperse the crowd. The three constables were assailed with stones, and the complainant was hit on the head and sides, and injured on the ribs. The prisoner was identified as one of the assailants. It appeared that he was fined £2 and expenses [*sic*] about twelve months ago for assaulting the constables, and he was now convicted in the penalty of £10 and expenses [*sic*]; or in default of payment to be committed for two months to the Wakefield House of Correction.

Leeds Mercury, 17 April 1858

VIOLENT ASSAULT. On Thursday, John Rowlinson, a young man employed at Leventhorpe Mill, in the township of Thornton, was charged at the West Riding Court, Bradford, with violently striking and kicking John Ingham, a fellow workman. The offence was committed on Wednesday. The complainant's eyes and face exhibited marks of the severity of the blows he had received. The court inflicted a fine upon the defendant of £2 and expenses.

Bradford Observer, 22 April 1858

Extracted from the report of an enquiry held at the House of Commons concerning the desire of businessmen from surrounding townships for an extension of limits to the area then served by Bradford Waterworks Company.

Joseph Craven, examined by Mr. Johnston: Was partner in the firm of Joshua Craven and Sons, of Thornton. The population was about 8000. The rateable value of the property was £8500. His firm was rated at £400 or £500. Thornton was four miles from Bradford. At present the water supply was very bad. The feeling in favour of the scheme was general. The water was to be distributed upon the same terms as in Bradford. At present the inhabitants were supplied by wells, which were often at a distance. In the summer water had to be fetched a mile and a half. They had to pump their water 50 yards at great expense. This measure would be a great boon to the town.

Cross-examined by Mr. Venables: They had no constituted authority or means of laying down pipes. Bradford would have to lay them down. It would be in their way, they had to make the line of piping. There was, however, an arrangement for paying a certain percentage on the cost of the pipes which would be spread over the village. The area of Thornton was a very large one, but the persons who would probably be supplied would be in a small area; perhaps 6000 would take the water; they had been robbed of water by Bradford.

Bradford Observer, 22 April 1858

From a lecture given by Rev. J. Fawcett of Low Moor to the Bradford Mechanics' Institute on Tuesday 13th April entitled 'Former Inhabitants of Bradford and Neighbourhood.'

LISTERS.

Amongst those who are worthy of note in connection with our old town and neighbourhood, we must by no means overlook the family of the Listers, who took so prominent a part in the religious movement of the 17th century. We need go no further back than Mr. Joseph Lister, who is mentioned by Oliver Heywood, one of the Nonconforming ministers under the Act of Uniformity of 1662. It appears that he was living at Allerton, in this parish, on the 26th of May, 1682, and on the 4th of June, 1686, when he was visited there by Mr. Heywood. He had two sons; the eldest, David, who was intended by his father for the Nonconforming ministry, was first at school with one David Noble, of Morley, author of a treatise on the Book of Daniel, and who died at Natland,* near Kendal in November 1677; the younger, Accepted, who was born at Allerton, and baptised in March, 1671, and educated under Matthew Smith, at Mixenden, in the parish of Halifax. He was ordained by Mr. Frankland, Mr. Heywood, and Mr. Thorp (all ministers who had been ejected in 1662), on the 6th of June, 1694, at the meeting house in Horton. This Accepted Lister first settled as a minister at Kipping, but removed to Bingley in 1695, from whence he went to Thornton, and finally appears to have returned to Kipping. Oliver Heywood has the following entries relating to him:- '18 March, 1694-5. Called on Mr. Accepted Lister: did a weighty business with him about Bingley.' '11 Dec, 1701: Set myself to write a letter to Mr. Lister, in answer to his concerning that great dispute of his removing from Bingley.' According to the testimony of his friend and neighbour, Mr. Thomas Dickinson, who succeeded Mr. Heywood in his congregation at Northowram, in the Chapelry of Coley, Accepted Lister was 'an excellent preacher; a little helpless body, but a great and sound soul.' John Draton (see Panegyrick on Eminent Persons, in the Life and Errors of John Draton, Nichols's edition, London, 8vo., 1818, p. 421) says, 'Mr. Accepted Lister, of Thornton, in Bradford Dale, is a little man, but one that has a great soul, rich in grace and gifts, of a strong memory, good elocution, *accepted* with God and all good men, and one that serves God faithfully in the Gospel of his Son; naturally careful for the good of souls, and longing after them in the bowels of the Lord Jesus.' On the 11th of April, 1705, Accepted Lister married Mary Whitehead. His widow afterwards (July 21, 1713) married Robert Richmond, minister at Cleckheaton, and on the 18th September, 1728, she married a *third* husband, John Willis, of Wakefield. This same Accepted was buried in the burial ground of Thornton Chapel, the place of which is marked by a stone bearing the following inscription:- 'Here lyeth the body of Mr. Accepted Lister, minister of the Gospel, who exchanged this frail life for a better, February the 25th, 1708, anno ætatis 38, after he had by his abundant labours verified his own motto, '*impendam et expendam.*'

About this time there was a physician living at Thornton, a member of the Kipping congregation, of the name of Dr. Hall, at whose earnest entreaty it was mainly that Accepted Lister bowed to the call of the congregation assembling there to become their minister. This person was also buried at Thornton Chapel, in a grave at the head of the one which contained the remains of Accepted Lister.

It is deserving of notice that Mary, only daughter and heiress of this John Hall, was married to John Firth, of Halifax, whose son Joshua died 17th July, 1709, aged 95. There is a monument to his memory in Thornton chapel, and his granddaughter the Rev. J.C. Franks, A.M., formerly vicar of Huddersfield [*sic* – words including 'married' were presumably omitted by the typesetters] and who still retains property at Kipping.

The Joseph Lister whose autobiography has been so frequently published, with his father John Lister, seem to have been inhabitants of Horton, and by a paper of accounts to have been entrusted with the collection of monies and goods which were furnished by the town of Bradford for the support of the Parliamentarian cause, when the place was besieged and taken by the Earl of Newcastle and his army upon the 2nd and 3rd of July, 1643. By this paper we are enabled to fix a date to that event which has been hitherto in controversy. The amount raised was £288 4s 6d.

It may here be mentioned that the chapel at Kipping was endowed with land and houses with about £30 per annum, and stood, according to tradition, on the site of a barn, at the Western extremity of the village of Thornton. The house which adjoins the barn is yet called 'Kippin.' The word 'Kippin,' says Mr. James, in his 'History of Bradford,' is a corruption of 'Cockham,**' mentioned in Barnard's Survey as being a hamlet to Thornton. This chapel was deserted about 1770, and the present one, bearing that name, was built in the village.

(Mr. Fawcett does not seem to be aware that the chapel built in 1770 has been deserted in its turn, and that within the last few years a much larger and handsomer structure has been raised for the use of the congregation worshipping at Kipping.)

It was David Lister, not David Noble, who died when a pupil at Mr Frankland's academy at Natland near Kendal in 1677.

** *'Cockham' was almost certainly not Kipping but 'Cockan', a lost settlement which was on Clayton Edge.*

Bradford Observer, 22 April 1858

THORNTON, OVENDEN, and OXENHOPE. On Friday, the 7th day of May, 1858, at Six o'clock in the afternoon, with be offered for SALE BY PUBLIC AUCTION, at the Old Cock Hotel, in Halifax, by Mr. JOHN CARR, subject to conditions to be then and there produced. SEVERAL desirable FREEHOLD PROPERTIES, situated in Thornton and Oxenhope, in the parish of Bradford, and in Ovenden, in the parish of Halifax, together with the RIGHTS, EASEMENTS and PRIVILEGES thereto respectively belonging, parcel of the estates of the late Thomas Holmes, Esquire, deceased.

In the Township of Thornton

LOT 1. The MESSUAGE, FARMHOUSE, and TENEMENT, with the Barns, Mistals, Outbuildings, and Appurtenances, situated at Foreside, in Thornton, now occupied in two separate farmsteads by Mr. Joseph Fielding and Mrs. Betty Hoyle. And the several Closes of LAND adjoining and near thereto, and now occupied therewith, containing in the whole 17 days' work or thereabouts.

LOT 2. The Four several Closes of LAND, situated at Foreside aforesaid, called by the names of the Moor Closes, now in the occupation of the said Joseph Fielding and Betty Hoyle, and containing 18 days' work or thereabouts; and the

Three several Allotments of waste LAND, situated to the south of and near the said last-mentioned closes, and adjoining the manor of Ovenden.

LOT 3. The Allotment of new enclosed LAND, formerly parcel of the commons of the manor of Thornton, and the Close or Parcel of GRASS LAND, called the Garden Bed, formerly parcel of the same commons, situated at Foreside aforesaid, the whole containing 15 acres or thereabouts, and in the occupations of the said Joseph Fielding and Betty Hoyle, and formerly in the possession of the late Mr. William Clark.

LOT 4. The several Allotments of LAND, situated at Blackmoss, formerly parcel of the commons of the said manor, and in the possession of the said William Clark, and adjoining northwards on Denholme Park and Stubden Beck, and containing in the whole 45 days work or thereabouts, and now in the possession of the devisees of the said Thomas Holmes.

In the Township of Ovenden

LOT 5. The Two several Allotments or Parcels of LAND, formerly parcel of the waste lands of the manor of Ovenden, allotted to the late Thomas Holmes, Esquire, under the Inclosure Act, and adjoining the allotment to the late Richard Emmott, Esquire, containing together 19 acres and 29 perches or thereabouts, and now in the occupation of the said devisees.

In the Township of Oxenhope

LOT 6. The Allotment of LAND, part of the Great Moor, late parcel of the commons, within the manor of Oxenhope, numbered 69x on the Commissioners' Plan annexed to their award, and containing 35 acres and 34 perches or thereabouts, and now in the possessions of the said devisees.

Further information may be had on application to DICKENSON EDDLESTON, Esquire, Cross Hills, Halifax, and (together with more detailed printed particulars) at the offices of
Mr. ALEXANDER, Solicitor, Halifax.

Leeds Mercury, 1 May 1858

BIGAMY. On Thursday, at the West Riding Court, Bradford, Prestwood Pogson, a middle-aged man, lately labourer in a stone quarry, at Thornton Heights, was charged with bigamy. Serjeant Brier apprehended the prisoner at Lincoln on Tuesday last. It appeared that in 1838 he married Elizabeth Foster, at Nettleton, Lincolnshire, and that some years ago, after she had borne several children, he deserted her. In 1851, he married Hannah Graham, or Grime, a widow, of Thornton Heights, with whom he lived about five years, and then absconded. It also came out in evidence, that about ten months since he was on the point of

Athenaeum Rooms in Commercial Street.

being married at North Shields to a third woman, his lawful wife being still alive. He was committed for trial at the York Assizes.

Bradford Observer, 8 May 1858

THORNTON. DEATH BY BURNING. On Saturday last, an inquest was held at the Victoria Inn (Mr. J. Woods), on the body of William Rushworth, an old pensioner, eighty years of age, who was found dead in his house, his clothes having caught fire. The deceased lived alone in the house; and as there was no reason to suppose that the fire was other than accidental, the jury returned a verdict accordingly.

Bradford Review, 5 June 1858

On Monday evening Mr. Wickham presented a petition to the House of Commons from Thornton and its vicinity, praying that practitioners of the medico-botanical system of medicine may be placed on an equality with doctors of medicine.

Chapter Twelve
1859

Coalminers split up – Famous ventriloquist performs – Giant mushrooms grown in Thornton – Two-headed duck found in field – Eight-year-old boy's fatal slip on ice

Bradford Observer, 6 January 1859

DENHOLME CLOUGH MILL:- TO BE LET, on lease or otherwise, the mill and premises called DENHOLME CLOUGH MILL, situate in Denholme Gate, near the Halifax and Keighley Turnpike Road, in the township of Thornton, at present in the occupation of Mr. Samuel Balme, worsted spinner. The premises may be entered upon the first day of January next. A Plan showing the mill and premises may be seen, and further information obtained on application at my office, Swain Street. By order. (signed) CHARLES GOTT
Water Works Manager &c. Borough Surveyor and Water Works Manager's Office Swaine Street, Bradford, 7th Dec., 1858.

Bradford Observer, 6 January 1859

DISSOLUTION OF PARTNERSHIP. NOTICE IS HEREBY GIVEN, that the Partnership heretobefore subsisting between us the undersigned JONAS CRAVEN and UNICE BENTHAM, carrying on business at Thornton, in the parish of Bradford, in the county of York, as Coal Miners and Dealers, under the style or firm of 'Craven and Bentham,' has been this day Dissolved by mutual consent. The business will in future be carried on by the said Unice Bentham and her son, Robinson Bentham, on their own account, and they will pay and be entitled to receive all debts and sums of money respectively owing from or due to the said firm.

Dated the Twenty-third day of December, 1858.

JONAS CRAVEN

UNICE X (her mark) BENTHAM

ROBINSON BENTHAM

Witnesses to all the signatures, – WILLIAM GEORGE, Solicitor, Bradford. J. G.T. Gant, Solicitor, Bradford.

Bradford Observer, 13 January 1859

THORNTON. On Wednesday last night, Mr. Duncan Macmillan, the far-famed ventriloquist, gave an exceedingly successful entertainment in the Mechanics' Institute. The classical beauty of the remarks made on the nature of oral language and sound particularly struck every one present, while the sound illustrations in his peculiar art, drew forth bursts of applause and laughter from a large and most respectable audience.

Bradford Observer, 27 January 1859

VALUABLE FREEHOLD ESTATE AT THORNTON, NEAR BRADFORD. Mr. THOMAS is instructed by the Trustees under the assignment of Messrs. J. and H. Horsfall to offer for SALE BY PUBLIC AUCTION at the Talbot Hotel, in Bradford, on *Monday, the 14th day of February, 1859*, at six o'clock for seven precisely, subject to such conditions as shall then be produced, ALL that Freehold MESSUAGE or Dwelling-House, now occupied as a Beershop, and known as the High Field Top Inn, with the Barn, Cottages, and other Outbuildings thereto attached. And also, all those several Fields or Closes of LAND, adjoining thereto, and known by the names of the Sun High Field, the Middle High Field, the North High Field, Flatts Hill, the West Flatts, the Long Flatts Top, the Ing, and the Croft, or by what other names the same are known or distinguished. All which Beerhouse, Farm Cottages, Closes or Parcels of Land, are situate at Alderscholes, in Thornton aforesaid, and are in the occupation of Joseph Ackroyd. The fields are good grass land, and are in a high state of cultivation; they are well fenced, and a water course runs through the estate. The estate is situated within half-a-mile of the thriving village of Thornton. The Tenant will show the premises, and further particulars may be obtained of the AUCTIONEER; 12 St. James's Street, Halifax; or of Mr. G ALDERSON SMITH, Solicitor, 17, Park Row, Leeds.

Leeds Mercury, 12 February 1859

THORNTON MECHANICS' INSTITUTE. On Thursday, a lecture on the 'Philosophy of the Breakfast Table' was delivered in the Athenaeum by Mr. Barnett Blake, the agent of the Yorkshire Union of Mechanics' Institute. The lecture was repeatedly applauded throughout its delivery, and at the close a vote of thanks was unanimously awarded.

Bradford Observer, 24 February 1859

THORNTON. ELECTION OF PUBLIC OFFICERS. On Friday last, a public meeting was held in the vestry of Thornton Church, for the purpose of nominating Constables, Overseers of the Poor, Surveyors of the Highway, &c. Mr. Isaac Wood was in the chair. Mr. Jonathan Knowles, jun., and Mr. John Overend Wood were chosen overseers of the poor; Mr. John Bailey surveyor of the highways for the hamlet of Denholme, and a board, consisting of seven, for Thornton. After nominating a sufficient number for constables, and transacting other routine business, the question of the New Burial Ground in connection with Thornton Church was taken into consideration. But, instead of having to devise the best means of raising the money for the payment of the new ground (one acre), and other necessary expenses connected therewith, the meeting was agreeably surprised by Mr. Wood, the chairman, stating that some gentlemen, whose names he was not at liberty to mention, had voluntarily offered to find the requisite amount for both purchasing and enclosing the ground when wanted. After a vote of thanks to the Chairman, the meeting separated, highly pleased with the unexpected information.

Bradford Observer, 7 April 1859

ON SALE, a BAY MARE, 15½ Hands high, 5 years old, accustomed to work in a cart, and run in harness. Warranted sound and free from vice. Apply to S. TOWNEND and Co., Thornton.

Leeds Mercury, 2 July 1859

BREACHES OF THE FACTORY ACT. On Thursday, at the West Riding Court, Bradford, before Timothy Horsfall, Esq., and Captain Pollard, magistrates, Mr. Rickards, sub-inspector of factories, charged Mr. Joseph Craven, manufacturer, of Thornton, with a breach of the Factory Act, in not having kept a school certificate-book, showing the way in which the children under thirteen years of age employed in his factory had attended school day by day. Mr. Rickards said that on visiting the defendant's factory, on the 15th June, finding that at least two children were there employed, he inquired for the school-certificate book, in order to satisfy himself that that important part of the Factory Act had been carried into operation. He was met by the manager with the information that they had no school-certificate book, and the only book in which they registered school attendances of any kind was a book in which they were compelled to keep a

Market Street, looking east.

register of the children. In reply to a question from Mr. Terry, who appeared for the defendant, Mr. Rickards said the book which was kept gave no information in reference to schooling to satisfy the purposes of the act. The defendant was convicted upon each of two informations in the lowest mitigated penalty of 20s, and the expenses. Mr. Francis Craven, manufacturer, of Thornton, was next charged by Mr. Rickards with having made a false entry in his register-book of young persons. The defendant had registered a boy named Eli Jowett as first employed by him on the 4th of April, whereas, on visiting the mill, Mr. Rickards ascertained that the boy had been at work at least a month before that date, and that he was not thirteen years of age until the 3rd of April. Consequently, during that month he was in the eyes of the law a child, and it was Mr. Craven's duty to have had a register-book for him and to have him attending school. Mr. Terry, on the part of the defendant, said it appeared that the overlooker had been guilty of some neglect in this case, but it had been without the knowledge of Mr. Craven, who endeavoured as far as he could to comply with the requirements of the Act of Parliament. The defendant was convicted in the lowest mitigated penalty of £5 and expenses.

Bradford Observer, 25 August 1859

THORNTON FLORAL AND HORTICULTURAL SOCIETY. On Monday evening the above society held its annual meeting at the Black Horse Inn. About 30 sat down for an excellent supper, after which S. Taylor, Esq., surgeon, was called to the chair. The Secretary read a report of the year's transactions, from which it appeared that the society was in a very flourishing state, and had been the means of doing much good in the neighbourhood. The room was tastefully decorated with flowers; and on the table, in front of the chairman, stood a splendid testimonial, which should have been presented to Henry Harrop, Esq., the president of the society, as a token of the esteem in which that gentleman is held; but owing to the state of his health he could not be present to receive it, and Mr. Taylor, Mr. Corrie,

Mr. Clark, and Mr. W. Thomas were chosen as a deputation to present it to him. The testimonial is a beautiful glass flower stand, with wax flowers in the inside, and a suitable inscription on the stand at the bottom.

Bradford Observer, 1 September 1859

EXTRAORDINARY MUSHROOMS. At a house called Heaslecrook, in the township of Thornton, several large mushrooms have grown this year betwixt the flags and the outer wall, in the inside of the house. One has been got there 8 inches in diameter. A friend from Wilsden was at the house last week, and there were two large mushrooms growing, which he measured to 4 inches in diameter.

Bradford Observer, 24 November 1859

Died Thursday last, aged 80, Mr. John Craven, Thornton. The deceased was one of the old handloom manufacturers, and almost the last remaining in this neighbourhood.

Bradford Observer, 22 December 1859

THORNTON. Mr. John Sutcliffe, of School Green, Thornton, has in his possession a remarkable instance of one of Nature's freaks, in a bird; the species to which it belongs being called the grassdrake. The bird was taken last mowing season, in a field belonging to Mr. Joshua Craven, of Thornton. It has two heads, two necks, two beaks, and four eyes.

Bradford Observer, 29 December 1859

THORNTON. KIPPING SUNDAY SCHOOL. On Monday, the Kipping Sunday School had their annual tea party and meeting. In the forenoon, the scholars met for the recital of pieces, chapters, &c., and were regaled with spice cake and tea. In the afternoon, the teachers and friends of the institution took tea in large numbers, and at the conclusion of that interesting part of the proceedings, the company adjourned into the new school room, which was very tastefully decorated with evergreens, oranges, mottoes, &c. The Rev. J. Gregory occupied the chair, by whom, and Messrs. Henry Priestley, Nathan Drake, Abraham Nichol, Briggs Priestley, J. Foster, &c., &c., suitable and effective addresses were delivered. The company was very numerous, and the proceedings passed off with universal satisfaction and pleasure.

Bradford Observer, 29 December 1859

THORNTON. FATAL ACCIDENT. A fatal accident happened to a little boy, about eight years old, on Wednesday, the 21st instant. He slipped on the ice, and, falling on his elbow and the back of his head, the shock produced concussion of the brain, of which he died on the following Friday. The deceased's name was Thomas Rushton, son of Timothy Rushton, but he was not a native of Thornton.

Chapter Thirteen
1860-1864

*Celery thieves caught – Thornton Toll Bar company wound up – Black
Dyke Mills Band plays in village – Hen lays giant egg – Four hundred
attend temperance meeting*

Bradford Observer, 12 January 1860

THORNTON REGISTRATION DISTRICT. The number of deaths (96) for the
last quarter of the year 1859 was again considerably above an average, and was
again owing principally to the prevalence of scarletina, from which cause there
have been 24 deaths, from bronchitis 5, from hooping cough 4, from diarrhœa 5,
phthisis 2, convulsions 15, paralysis 4, natural decay 5, and from other diseases
25. Of these 50 were certified, 10 uncertified, and 36 without legally qualified
medical attendant. Forty-six died under 5 years of age, twenty-one between 5 and 20,
twelve between 20 and 50, ten between 50 and 70, and seven upwards of 71.

Bradford Observer, 12 January 1860

A FREEHOLD FARM AT SCHOOL GREEN, NEAR BRADFORD, TO BE
SOLD BY AUCTION, by Messrs. HARDWICK & BEST, at the Sun Inn, in
Bradford, on *Monday the 16th day of January*, 1860, at 6 o'clock in the evening,
subject to conditions as will then be produced.

A FREEHOLD FARM, situated at School Green, in Thornton, in the parish
of Bradford, now in the occupation of Simeon Spenceley, or his
undertenants, consisting of a Farm-house, with farm buildings, two
cottages, and nine closes of land, known as the Lower Hoyle Ing, and
containing the quantities following, viz.:

The Homestead, including the sites of the farm-house and farm buildings *(acres, roots and perches)*   0 0 37½

The Calf Croft	0 0 22
Garden	0 0 12
The Top Field	1 2 17½
The Front Field	1 1 9½
The Ing	4 0 19½
The Donk Field	1 0 2½
The Lower Spout Field	1 3 30
The Upper Spout Field	1 2 9½
The Near Brooksbank Ing	1 3 8½
The Far Brooksbank Ing	1 1 33½
Cottages &c	0 0 7

The land is bounded on the north side by the stream called Pitty Beck, and contains several springs of water. It is also supposed to contain an excellent bed of coal; and being near the Bradford and Thornton Turnpike Road, within a distance of three miles from Bradford, it affords a rare opportunity for a safe and profitable investment. Further information may be obtained of Messrs. B. BERRY and Sons, Machine Makers, Hall Lane, Bowling, or JAMES WOOD, Solicitor, Hall Ings, Bradford.

Bradford Observer, 8 March 1860

FACTORY INFORMATIONS. At the West Riding Court, on Thursday, Messrs. Francis Craven & Co., worsted spinners and manufacturers, Dole Mill, Thornton, were charged with a breach of the Factory Act, in running the machinery of their works a short time beyond the hour prescribed. On the 30th ult., some slight accident occurred by which the machinery was stopped for about twenty minutes, and in the evening the mill ran about a quarter of an hour beyond the usual time. Mr. Rickards, the sub-inspector of factories, stated that it was only in the case of mills running by water power that any lost time could be recovered. Mr. Terry thought that lost time might also be recovered in the case of mills worked by steam power. Mr. Rickards said that that was the case some years ago, but not now. Mr. Terry, admitting the liability of his clients, observed that, in justice to them, it ought to be stated that, on the day in question, the works were, in their unavoidable absence, left to the control of a gentleman who had not had much experience. He thought, in the first instance, that the time might be made up, but, afterwards having a doubt, he stopped the works at the end of ten minutes. Under the circumstances, he (Mr. Terry) thought Mr. Richards [*sic*] should withdraw the information on the payment of the costs. The lowest penalty of £1 and costs were imposed.

Bradford Observer, 22 March 1860

THORNTON. FATAL ACCIDENT. On Saturday evening a woolcomber named Isaac Farnell, aged 45 years, very unexpectedly met with an untimely end. He had formerly lived in Ovenden but had for some time resided in Thornton, where he and his numerous family had been in the employment of Messrs. Walton & Holroyd. Being accustomed to go on the Saturday to Halifax, he had continued the habit since his removal to Thornton and went every other Saturday to buy his groceries etc. On his return home last Saturday evening in the company of Samuel Bentham, the Thornton carrier, when coming down the Thornton new road, his foot slipped off the causeway, and having his hands in his pockets, he fell down heavily and received such serious injuries in the abdomen that, though medical assistance was called in soon after his arrival at home, he died from the effects of the fall the following day, leaving a widow and ten children to lament their irreparable loss.

Bradford Observer, 5 April 1860

THORNTON. APPOINTMENT OF OVERSEERS AND SURVEYORS. A public meeting was held in the vestry of Thornton church, at which Mr. Jonathan Knowles, junr., and Mr. John Overend Wood were re-elected for the ensuing year; and Messrs. Michael Pearson, Henry Charnock, Phinehas Pearson, William Broadhead, John Hill, James Craven, and John Jarrett, were appointed the board of surveyors for the ensuing year.

GUARDIANS. Mr. Isaac Wood and Mr. Joseph Briggs have been nominated guardians for Thornton. There is no opposition.

SURVEYOR FOR DENHOLME. Mr. John Bailey has been re-elected surveyor of the hamlet of Denholme for the ensuing year.

Mr. John Barraclough and Mr. Joseph Brooksbank have been appointed assessors of the assessed taxes for Thornton.

THORNTON REGISTRATION DISTRICT. The number of deaths (94) for the quarter ending March 31st is yet above the average of corresponding quarters; but scarletina, which has been a principal cause of the excess for several preceding quarters has now passed away, and the severity and frequent changes of the weather have been fatal to the very old and young; but there is not now any epidemic disease in the district. Of the above number of deaths, 16 have been from bronchitis and pneumonia. 10 from scarletina, 11 from phthisis, 17 from teething and convulsions, 6 from dropsy, 6 from enteritis, 10 from natural decay, and 18 from various other causes.

Bradford Observer, 12 April 1860

NOTICE IS HEREBY GIVEN, that the Partnership lately subsisting between us, the undersigned, FRANCIS CRAVEN and BRIGGS PRIESTLEY, carrying on business as worsted manufacturers, at Thornton, near Bradford, in the county of York, under the firm of 'Francis Craven & Co.,' having expired, the same is DISSOLVED by mutual consent. All Debts due to or from the said late firm will be received and paid by the said Francis Craven, who will carry on the business in future on his sole account.

Dated this 31st day of March, 1860.

FRANCIS CRAVEN.

BRIGGS PRIESTLEY.

Bradford Observer, 7 February 1861

THE STOLEN CELERY. In the West Riding Court, on Thursday, three men, named Wm. Clough, George Feather, and Abraham Drake, were charged by John Pearson, of Grandage Gate, with having stolen six sticks of celery from his garden. The evidence against Feather and Clough was doubtful, and they were consequently discharged. Drake was ordered to pay 9d, the value of the celery, together with a fine of £5 and costs, with the alternative of two months imprisonment.

Bradford Observer, 29 August 1861

BRADFORD AND THORNTON TURNPIKE ROAD. To Mr. EDWARD HAILSTONE, Clerk to the Trustees for carrying into execution an Act of Parliament passed in the sixth year of the reign of His Majesty George the Fourth, for making and maintaining a Turnpike Road, from Bradford to Sunside Cottages, in Thornton, in the West Riding of the county of York. We, the undersigned, being two of such trustees, do hereby authorise and require you to call a Meeting of the Trustees of the said Road, to be held at the Sun Inn, Bradford, in the county of York, on Thursday, the 19th day of September next, at 12 o'clock at noon, for the purpose of investigating the affairs and position of the Trust, arranging for the removal of the several Bars and Chains and Weighing Machines upon the said Road, and the sale of the sites and materials of the said Bar Houses, Bars, Chains and Weighing Machines, and for taking such steps for winding up the affairs of the Trust as shall then and there be determined. Dated this 20th day of August, 1861. JOHN FOSTER WM. ROUSE. In pursuance of the above requisition, I do hereby appoint a SPECIAL MEETING of the Trustees of the said Turnpike Road, to be held at the time and place and for the purposes above mentioned. EDWARD HAILSTONE. Clerk to the said Trustees. Bradford, August 21st, 1861.

Kipping Sunday School procession along Market Street.

Bradford Observer, 3 October 1861

AN ALLEGED HIGHWAY ROBBERY AT THORNTON. At the West Riding Court, yesterday, a stout man, named John Smith, shoemaker at Thornton, was charged with having robbed Joseph Crabtree, of this town, on the highway neat Thornton of 4*s* 5*d* on Monday evening last, near eleven o'clock. Crabtree stated that he had been in the beerhouse of Nancy Shackleton, of the same place, from between five and six o'clock until about eleven, during which time he drank seven glasses of ale and was not quite sober, but far from drunk. When he went in he had 5*s* in his pocket, and only spent 7*d*, so that when he left to return to Bradford he had the 4*s* 5*d* in his pocket. When he had gone about 400 yards, he saw a man in drab clothes crouching across the road before him, and cried out 'Holloa, there.' Prisoner then sprung up, and with a severe blow, knocked him down and struck a tooth from his head, and when he was down kicked a deep wound with the toe of his boot in his temple, which was patched up. Prisoner then put his hand into his right-hand pocket and took out his cash. Mrs. Shackleton proved that Crabtree had been in her house as stated, but the evidence of James Ackroyd, watchman to Messrs. Joshua Craven & Son, who saw Crabtree pass, and afterwards heard something like a cry, deposed also that he saw Smith at a short distance behind him, when Crabtree set off running, and this threw something of a doubt upon Crabtree's statement of the prisoner having been crouching on the road so far behind him. Crabtree also said that the prisoner has been drinking in the same room with him in Mrs. Shackleton's the same night, but this the prisoner denied, and said that he had been at Scholes Green, and only left there at half-past ten o'clock. Mr. Terry appeared for the prisoner and cross-examined the witnesses, but though the evidence for the prosecution was nothing shaken and all the witnesses swore to the drab colour of the prisoner's clothes, and though he was an old offender, the bench (W. Peel, Esq.) felt a slight doubt about the matter, and, giving the benefit of doubt, discharged him.

Leeds Mercury, 9 November 1861

ALTERATION OF TURNPIKE TOLLS. The tolls on the Bradford and Thornton Turnpike road have just been abolished, and yesterday there was a grand procession from the New Inn, Thornton, to Denholme Gate, to celebrate the event. The festivity was concluded with an excellent dinner.

Leeds Mercury, 9 November 1861

THORNTON. An additional burial ground in connection with the Church of England, at Thornton, was consecrated yesterday, by the Bishop of Ripon.

Bradford Observer, 2 January 1862

THORNTON. A BLIND SLEEPWALKER. Early on Tuesday morning William Pearson – better known as 'Blind Billy' – a dealer in tea, quite blind, living at School House Green near Thornton, rose from his bed in a dream, threw up the sash of his window on the first floor and jumped out calling 'Murder.' A near relative came to his assistance and found that he was considerably injured having knocked off the cap of his knee. He is, we learn, doing well, though his injuries might have been much more severe.

Bradford Review, 1 March 1862

CONCERT. The Black Dyke mills band gave a concert on Saturday last in the Athenæum, Thornton. The room was crowded. Besides several pieces being played by the band, songs were sung by Mr. Riley, late of Ripon Cathedral, Miss Warburton, Mr. Turner, &c. Mr. J. Bairstow presided at the piano-forte; all the performers acquitted themselves with credit.

Bradford Review, 7 June 1862

ENORMOUS EGG. Last week, a hen of the chittiprat breed laid an egg which measured 6½ inches in circumference, and weighed 3½ ounces. The hen is the property of Mr. Joseph Redman, of Denholme.

Bradford Review, 28 June 1862

TEMPERANCE MEETING. On Thursday evening a temperance meeting was held in the open air, opposite the Kipping school. Mr. H. Haley, of Great Horton, took the chair. The proceedings consisted of addresses, recitations, &c, by Messrs. S. Geldard, of Thornton, G.D. Allot and W. Craven, of Great Horton. Mr. S. Geldard spoke on the safety of abstinence; Mr. Craven recited 'Oh Sally, or Boniface's Lament,' 'The Smoker's Lament.' Mr. Allott recited 'Barnsley as it is, or the Devil's Picture Gallery;' he also gave an address on 'Drunkenness, its Cause and Cure.' The meeting was a good one and very orderly, about 400 people being present; towards the close a few questions were asked by a gentleman of the name of Harrison, as to the action of alcohol on the human system in disease. The meeting broke up after having lasted two hours.

Bradford Observer, 28 August 1862

THORNTON. KIPPING CHAPEL. On Saturday a tea party, in connection with the Bicentenary movement, took place in the old school of Kipping Chapel, after which it was announced that the effort to clear off the chapel debt (upwards of £500) had been successful, and that a surplus of about £20 now remained in hand. After this very welcome intelligence the company adjourned into the new school-room, and the Rev. Jas. Gregory gave a very appropriate and interesting lecture on the subject which had occasioned their meeting together.

Leeds Mercury, 25 October 1862

THORNTON, NEAR BRADFORD. On Wednesday evening a public meeting was held in the Kipping School-room, to take into consideration the propriety of rendering assistance to alleviate the distress in the cotton manufacturing districts. The Rev. J. Gregory occupied the chair, and stated not only the nature and extent of the distress, and the objections made by some parties that it was not yet time to render assistance, but he showed that those objections were utterly groundless and untrue. Resolutions were unanimously passed to divide the village into convenient districts; that the collection be made weekly from house to house; that F. Craven, Esq., be the treasurer; and Mr. Kay the secretary. The Chairman read a note from Joseph Craven, Esq., of Ashfield, who was unable to attend, owing to a prior engagement, offering a very handsome sum as the subscription of Messrs. Joshua Craven and Son. The meeting was afterwards addressed by Mr. G. Townend, Mr. Corrie, Mr. Kay, Mr. Northrop, Mr. Nichol, Mr. J. Toothill, Mr. W. Thomas, and others, including several Lancashire operatives who have met with employment in the village, and a deep expression of sympathy for our suffering neighbours pervaded the proceedings. After a vote of thanks to the Chairman, the meeting was adjourned to the next Saturday evening, to appoint collectors to the respective districts.

Bradford Observer, 5 February 1863

TO LET, the following FARMS, situate in the township of Thornton, in the parish of Bradford:- 'Storr's Farm,' containing 50a 0r 7p, now or late in the occupation of Messrs. Hardy. 'Spring Hall Farm,' containing 11a 2r 27p, now or late in the occupation of Joseph Ackroyd. 'Highfield Farm' at Alderscholes, containing 12a 3r 35p, now or late in the occupation of Joseph Ackroyd. Possession of the Lands may be had at once, and of the Buildings at May Day. Personal application to be made at the offices of GEORGE BELK SMITH, Estate Agent, Bradford.

Bradford Observer, 12 March 1863

THORNTON. Mr. Jonas Craven treated upwards of 160 widows to a good tea in the Kipping Old Schoolroom, and presented each of them with a shilling besides. Simeon Townend & Co. treated all their workpeople to a substantial dinner at the Wellington Inn; and afterwards a splendid timepiece, which had been purchased by the workpeople as a token of the estimation in which he is held by them, was presented to Mr. Walter Townend on his leaving Thornton to commence business in a neighbouring locality. After appropriate addresses and reciprocal congratulations between the employer and employed, the festivities terminated. In the village, the mills and many private houses were decorated with flags &c, and the Dole Mill was very prettily illuminated by F. Craven & Co. There was a splendid star in the Athenaeum, in Commercial Street.

Bradford Observer, 30 April 1863

THORNTON. An inquest was held at the New Inn, Thornton, on Monday, before G. Dyson, Esq., coroner, on view of the body of Mary, wife of Mr. Jonas Driver, who formerly kept the above inn. The deceased, who was in her 58th year, had been in a desponding state of mind for several weeks, and though every attention had been paid to her, she took the opportunity on Thursday last, on pretence of fetching some coals out of the cellar, to put an end to her existence by hanging herself. Life was not extinct when she was found, but though medical assistance was immediately procured, she died the following day. In accordance with the above facts, the jury returned a verdict of 'Temporary Insanity.'

Bradford Observer, 7 May 1863

BURGLARY. On Thursday night or early on Monday morning the house of a person called Hodgson, situate near the parsonage, Schoolgreen, Thornton, was broken into, and a desk containing about 30s in silver was stolen therefrom, and the desk left in an adjoining field. A dress was found in the desk which had not been stolen from the house, and it is probable that the thieves had been disturbed. On the same morning an attempt was made to break into the Rev. Mr. Heap's, the parsonage house, near the same place, but it was unsuccessful. A square of glass had been cut out of the front window with a view to unloose the screw, but fortunately a bar went across in the inside which prevented any further ingress. Nothing has yet been heard to lead to the detection of the burglars.

Bradford Observer, 16 July 1863

Valuable Freehold Estate in Thornton. TO BE SOLD BY AUCTION, by Mr. BENJAMIN THORNTON, at the Black Horse Inn, in Thornton, in the parish of Bradford, in the county of York, on *Wednesday the 28th day of July,* 1863, at Seven o'clock in the Evening precisely, subject to such conditions as will be then and there provided, unless previously disposed of by private contract, of which due notice will be given.

All that capital FARM, situate at Thornton, in the parish of Bradford aforesaid, commonly called 'Black Carr,' with the good farmhouse, four cottages, barn, mistal, stables, outbuildings, conveniences, and appurtenances thereto belonging, and the nine several closes of land adjoining or near thereto called or commonly known by the several names of the Bush Ing, the Low Mall Field, the Mall Field, the Wilcock Field, the North Wilcock Field, the Ing, the Laith Field, the Dial Field, and the Back Field, containing together by admeasurement, including the site of the buildings, 32 days' work or thereabouts, as the same are now in the occupation of Thomas Walker or his undertenants.

The property is known to contain very valuable beds of coal and stone, and is situate in a ring fence, immediately adjoining the Queenshead and Denholme Gate Turnpike Road. The buildings are in good repair, and the premises well supplied with excellent water.

The tenant will show the estate, and further particulars may be had on application to Mr. Wm. MANKS, of Brighouse, the Owner, or at the offices of Messrs. ADAM and EMMET

Solicitors, Halifax. Halifax, 9th July, 1863.

Bradford Observer, 16 July 1863

Thornton near Bradford. Freehold Farm, Buildings, and Land, TO BE SOLD by Auction, by Mr. B. THORNTON, at the Black Horse Inn, Thornton, on *Wednesday the 28th July*, 1863, at Seven o'clock in the Evening, precisely, ALL that Valuable Freehold FARM, with the Dwelling-house, Stable, and other outbuildings, situate at Alder Scholes, and in the occupation of Mr. Joseph Illingworth or his undertenants. The land contains an area of 13a 3r 17p, or thereabouts, lies within a ring fence, is intersected by a stream of good water, and from its contiguity to the densely populated village of Thornton forms an excellent site for a mill or manufacturing premises. A plan of the estate may be seen at the offices of Messrs. E. WOODHEAD and SON, Land Surveyors, 37, Market Street, Bradford, and further information may be obtained from the AUCTIONEERS, at Huddersfield, or from Messrs. LAYCOCK and DYSON, Solicitors, Huddersfield.

Bradford Observer, 13 August 1863

THORNTON FLOWER SHOW. On Monday and Tuesday, the Thornton Floral and Horticultural Society held their eleventh annual exhibition of flowers, plants, fruits, and vegetables, and it is very pleasing to be able to say that this is decidedly the best exhibition there has been since the commencement of the society, and it cannot but be the means of very much improving the taste and increasing the pleasures and enjoyments of those who live in the neighbourhood. The society is open to Thornton, Allerton, Clayton, Wilsden, and Denholme. This year the show of plants and flowers was so large that the room was rather crowded, but the exhibition has been very well attended, and given general satisfaction. Without being invidious, it may be stated that the cottagers stand very well this year in most of the specimens shown, and deserve considerable praise.

Leeds Mercury, 20 August 1863

WANTED, by the Committee of the Kipping Independent Day School, Thornton, near Bradford, a SCHOOLMASTER to take the entire Management of the School. Apply by letter, to Mr. D. Craven, Secretary.

Bradford Observer, 8 October 1863

On Saturday, Messrs. Jonathan Northrop & Co., shawl manufacturers, of Springfield Place, Thornton, treated their workpeople to a tea in their large warehouse. One hundred and ten sat down, and the subsequent part of the evening was very agreeably spent.

Bradford Observer, 28 July 1864

ALLEGED ASSAULT UPON A SCHOOLMASTER AT THORNTON. At the Borough Court, on Thursday (before George Anderton, Esq., Captain Pollard, Esq., H.W. Wickham, Esq., and Wm. Peel, Esq.) Mr. Joseph Craven, of the firm of Messrs. Joshua Craven and Son, manufacturers and spinners, of Thornton, was charged with having, on Wednesday the 6th instant, committed an assault upon Thomas Jones, schoolmaster at Kipping School. Mr. Terry was for the complainant; Mr. C. Lees for defendant.

Mr. Terry said that the complainant was schoolmaster at the school of Kipping Chapel, Thornton, and had been there for some time. The gentlemen connected with that school were satisfied with him. He did not know whether the defendant had anything to do with the school or not, but a number of half-timers, who were employed at his establishment, went to the school, and there had been some misunderstanding arisen about the terms to be paid to the schoolmaster. On Wednesday, the 6th inst., the complainant having made out his bill for the half-timers at the school during the five weeks previously at the rate of 3*d* a head, took it to the counting-house of Messrs. J. Craven and Son. He delivered the bill to Mr. Thomas Laycock, the cashier, who on looking at the bill, observed that the complainant was charging 3*d* a head, and said it would not be paid. He put the account down and went away in what the complainant thought a contemptuous manner. He (complainant) then requested Mr. J. Gregory, one of the bookkeepers, to inform Mr. Laycock, on his return, that if the account was not paid, he would turn off all the half-timers on Monday morning. He then left the counting-house. He had not gone far before he was overtaken by a messenger and requested to return, being told Mr. Joseph Craven wanted to see him.

When he got into the counting-house, Mr. Joseph Craven was there, and had the account in his hand. He said, 'Well, Mr. Jones, this is your account.' The complainant said, 'It is, Mr. Craven.' Mr. Craven said, 'The charge is 3*d* per head.' The complainant replied in the affirmative. Mr. Craven said something about a resolution which had been passed by the School Committee, and the complainant replied that the charge made was in accordance with a subsequent agreement, and immediately looked to see whether he had not the agreement in his pocket-book, and found that he had left it behind. This appeared to so excite Mr. Craven that he called out something which complainant did not hear, in a contemptuous manner, and at the same moment came towards him and struck him a violent blow, which produced a mark for several days. He then seized Jones, as his father interposed and sought to get him away, and the complainant got hold of him to prevent himself from falling. Jones fell to the floor, however, and while down, the defendant struck him several times in the face, causing his nose to bleed profusely. He had hold of his throat with one hand and struck him with the other. The complainant never struck a blow, and he was unable from a defective limb to lift his arm to either his neck or face. Mr. Jones was called and swore to these being the facts.

The defence was that Mr. Jones went to the counting-house of Messrs. Craven and presented his bill to Mr. Laycock. Observing that he was charging three-pence per head Mr. Laycock called his attention to the fact. The complainant replied. 'Yes; the Committee have rescinded the former resolution (by which 2*d* was charged); and you have got a copy of the last resolution.' Mr. Laycock replied, 'No, we have not.' The complainant replied, 'Mr. Joseph has got it;' and Mr. Laycock said, 'No, I don't think he has; he would have told me if he had.' 'Well,' the complainant replied, 'if it is not paid I shall do something I do not like.' 'What is that?' inquired Mr. Laycock. The complainant replied, 'I shall send the hands away at once.' He [Mr. Laycock] thought it was time that Mr. Craven knew something about the matter, which was new to him, and he immediately went to see Mr. Joseph Craven, who returned with him to the counting-house. As the complainant had gone, he was brought back, and interrogated by Mr. Joseph Craven as to the alleged resolution rescinding the former one. The complainant returned evasive answers, and appeared to seek for a document he could not find. The defendant charged him with equivocating, and the complainant grew angry and replied in an offensive manner. The defendant then went towards him, put his hand upon complainant's shoulder, said he would not be insulted in his own counting-house, and told him to go away. At this moment, the complainant seized the defendant by the throat and, closing, they fell to the floor in a scuffle, and were separated in a moment by Mr. Laycock and Mr. Joshua Craven, and as they were raising up the defendant he struck the complainant on the nose. This was the history of the affair, as given by Mr. Laycock and Mr. Joshua Craven. The magistrates dismissed the case.

Bradford Observer, 28 July 1864

THORNTON. Thornton has been badly off for water during the present drought. Some of the wells are dried up; Sidon, Back Field, and Main Street wells do not yield a drop; and Benting, though still running, is so muddy that the water cannot be used. The beck is the merest runlet of water, and even that during only a part of its course; when it reaches the allotments it entirely disappears, leaving the lower part of the channel with scarcely a standing pool. As a result in part, perhaps, of this dearth of the vital fluid, disease has been somewhat prevalent in the village in the form of scarletina among children and of typhus and small pox among adults. Recently there were three funerals in one day, an event almost without precedent in the history of the little township. In this extremity, it is due to Francis Craven, Esq., Dole Mill, to acknowledge his considerate munificence in giving the public a gratuitous supply of water from his own mill-tap between the hours of six and eight each evening. Of this timely boon the people have eagerly and largely availed themselves, hundreds thronging to the tap during the interval specified; and as a consequence the evil effects of the drought have been greatly mitigated.

Leeds Mercury, 5 October 1864

EXTENSIVE FIRE AT THORNTON. Yesterday, Thornton, near Bradford, was the scene of a disastrous fire, a large warehouse being burnt down to the ground in a few hours, and several thousand pounds worth of property destroyed. The warehouse in which the fire occurred adjoined to Dole Mill, being the property of Messrs. Francis Craven and Co., manufacturers, and occupied partly by that firm, and partly by Mr. Josh. Craven, manufacturer. It was four storeys and an attic in height, and of considerable length. The fire broke out about half past eleven o'clock. It is stated that a little girl had been instructed to light a gas stove in the attic, and that she struck a Lucifer match for that purpose, whereupon an explosion took place in consequence of the gas having been turned on some time before. The result was that the room immediately took fire, and the flames rapidly spread to the floor below. The workpeople in the building were placed in circumstances of great danger, and in the excitement of the moment many of them – men, women, and children – effected their escape by means of the crane rope. The hands in the adjoining mill and many of the inhabitants of the village exhibited great promptitude in their efforts to remove such portions of the contents of the warehouse as could be got at, and the greater part of Mr. Joseph Craven's stock, consisting of pieces, shawls, weft, and warp, was thus rescued. The fire apparatus of Messrs. Joshua Craven and Sons, Prospect Mill, was also manned, and brought to bear upon the flames. In the meantime messengers were despatched to Queensbury and Bradford, and within less than an hour from the fire breaking out, the Bradford Corporation, Leeds and Yorkshire, and Black Dyke Mills fire brigades were upon the spot, and at work. An ample supply of water was derived from the mains of the Bradford Corporation Waterworks and from the reservoirs attached to the neighbouring mills. It was, however, soon evident that it would be useless to attempt to save the warehouse, and the efforts of the brigades were then directed to prevent the fire spreading to Dole Mill, which was only separated from the warehouse by a narrow passage, spanned by two wooden

United Sunday Schools parade along Market Street.

gangways. In this they were successful, their endeavours being assisted to some extent by a brisk wind which blew the flames in an opposite direction from the mill. The heat from the burning building was intense, and persons in the highway at fifty yards distance could hardly endure it. Two cottages standing by the road side, occupied by John Smith and Daniel Robinson, were for a time in great danger, and the inmates deemed it prudent to begin removing their household goods. In about three hours nothing but the bare walls of the warehouse remained standing. The principal damage will be sustained by Messrs. Francis Craven and Co., in whose portion of the warehouse the fire originated, and who had a large amount of fancy goods and other valuable property stored therein. The damage to the united stock of both firms is stated at about £5,000, of which Mr. Joseph Craven estimates his portion at £1,000. The building is said to have been worth about £2,000. The whole lot is covered by ample insurances in the Royal Scottish Union, Westminster, and West of England offices.

Chapter Fourteen
1865

Knor and Spel match results in £50 win for Rotherham man —
Policeman leaves for Barnsley with silver watch — Man dislocates neck
chasing rabbit — Cholera epidemic in Thornton — Three nudes and three
prostitutes in fight at pub

Bradford Review, 21 January 1865

District News. THORNTON. SAGAR'S CHARITY. On Tuesday, at
the Victoria Inn, the annual proceeds of this ancient charity were
'doled out,' and distributed by Mr. Isaac Wood, the surviving
trustee, to such persons as are legally entitled to receive the
same, namely poor persons who are not in the receipt of
parochial relief. Many of the recipients expressed gratitude for
the aid thus administered to them during the winter months.

Bradford Review, 21 January 1865

District News. SUNDAY SCHOOL TEA PARTY. On Saturday, the teachers and
friends belonging to the Sunday School at Yews Green, Thornton, in number 120,
took tea together in the school-room. Afterwards a public meeting was held, over
which Mr. Joseph Toothill presided, and addresses were delivered by Messrs.
Jonathan Northrop, Joseph Andrews, J. Sugden, John Wilkinson, and Thos. Brigg,
all of Thornton; and also by Messrs. Edmund Hirst and J. Andrew, of Clayton. On
Monday night the scholars were regaled with currant buns and hot coffee. After
the treat, recitations and music followed. In this school, which is in a thinly
populated part of the township, there are 75 scholars and 25 teachers. A new
school-room is much needed.

Bradford Review, 28 January 1865

District News. TEMPERANCE MEETING. On Monday evening, a temperance meeting was held at the old school-room, in Thornton, over which Mr. Jonathan Northrop presided. The addresses were by Messrs. John Ramsden, and George Jowett. Some beautiful airs were played by the concertina band.

Bradford Review, 28 January 1865

District News. THORNTON. STATE OF TRADE. Numerous and bitter complaints are now made by working people in Thornton, of the want of employment. Some of the mills are running short time, and at others the weavers have a good deal to stand for warps, which is another mode of curtailing the production of goods; and of checking the increase of manufacturers' stocks.

Bradford Review, 4 March 1865

SUICIDE. On Monday last, an inquest was held at the Wellington Inn, Thornton, on the body of Thomas Crossley, a man aged 36 years of age, who resided at Thornton. It appeared that, about half-past 3 o'clock on Saturday afternoon, a youth named Samuel Turner, and two of his companions, found the deceased hanging by his garters in Swaine Wood, Thornton, his knees touching the ground. The lads informed P.C. Peters, who cut the body down. It appeared to have been dead some time. The deceased was last seen by a woman named Ann Sutcliffe, early on the Saturday morning, making in the direction of the place where he was found. A verdict of 'Hanged himself in a state of temporary insanity' was returned.

Bradford Observer, 16 March 1865

EXHIBITION OF DISSOLVING VIEWS. On Thursday evening, Mr. Jones, schoolmaster, gave an exhibition of dissolving views in the Kipping New School-room, Thornton. There was a numerous audience, and all, both old and young, were greatly delighted with what they saw, the views not only being various and numerous, but were exhibited with much tact and ability. The chair was occupied by F. Craven, Esq.

Bradford Observer, 16 March 1865

BAND OF HOPE AND TEMPERANCE SOCIETY. On Monday evening, a meeting of the Thornton Band of Hope and Temperance Society was held in Kipping Old School-room, the chair being occupied by Mr. Jon. Northrop. The room was well filled, and much interest seemed to be felt by the audience. Addresses were delivered by the Chairman, and Mr. Job Holdsworth of Allerton. Numerous excellent performances were given by the Allerton drum and fife band, and the Thornton concertina band.

Bradford Observer, 16 March 1865

EGYPT SCHOOL. On Saturday evening, a public meeting took place in the School at Egypt, Thornton, over which Mr. Jonathan Northrop presided, when addresses were delivered by Mr. J. Ramsden 'on the Bible,' Mr. M. Priestley 'on reading,' and Mr. James Pickles, of Allerton, 'on the advantage of Sunday Schools.' There was a tolerably good audience, and a collection was made in aid of the library fund.

Bradford Observer, 16 March 1865

MECHANICS' INSTITUTE. Yesterday evening, the Rev. J. Gregory delivered his second lecture of a series, on America, in the Kipping New School-room, selecting for his subject, 'American States, their remarkable places and occurrences.'

Bradford Observer, 23 March 1865

ACCIDENTAL DEATH. During the present week quite a gloom has been thrown over the neighbourhood of Hill Top, and indeed throughout the village of Thornton, by the melancholy death of one Henry Ross, a man about 40 years of age. On Friday, while the deceased was at work as a barer at a quarry on Thornton Moor, belonging to Mr. Midgley Priestley, he was caught by a fall of earth and stones, and killed upon the spot. He has left a wife, far advanced in pregnancy, and five small children. The benevolence and kindness of the inhabitants is being exhibited towards the bereaved family to a very large extent. Deceased was a man of good character.

Bradford Observer, 20 April 1865

CRICKET. On Saturday, a friendly game at cricket was played by the Garibaldi United Cricket Club, in Thornton, between the members who are married and those who are single, with the following result, viz:- married, 72; single, 75.

Bradford Observer, 20 April 1865

DANGEROUS ACCIDENT. On Friday, as Mr. Milner, woolstapler, of Westgrove Street, Bradford, was proceeding down Thornton Road at Thornton, in 'a trap,' with four other gentlemen, the horse took fright and darted off at a tremendous speed. The riders were all thrown out, the vehicle being upset, and Mr. Milner was seriously injured; he was taken to Mr. Robertshaw's, and Mr. Corrie, surgeon, was sent for, who dressed the wounds, and the injured man was afterwards taken home in another conveyance.

Bradford Observer, 20 April 1865

ANCIENT ORDER OF FORESTERS. On Monday, the members of lodge 403 of the Ancient Order of Foresters held their annual feast at the Rock and Heifer Inn, Thornton. They number about 100. After the dinner, which was of a very substantial character, a proposition was made that a collection should be made for the benefit of one of their sick members, and the sum of £2 10s was raised. The usual business of the evening was then proceeded with, and a very pleasant time was spent.

Bradford Observer, 27 April 1865

THORNTON 'ROUGHS' AND HOW THE MONEY GOES. On Thursday, in the West Riding Court, Joseph Haggas, who keeps a beerhouse at Hill Top, Thornton, was summoned upon a charge of having permitted gambling in his house. Jonathan Birch, one of the party who were at the defendant's house on the previous Saturday, gave evidence to the effect that card playing was going on nearly the whole of the day, and that stakes were laid to the amounts of 2s 6d, 5s, and even 10s at a time; there was also sparring for money. At length a dispute arose amongst those present, which resulted in a fight between J. Jennings and the defendant. The witness Birch, interfering to prevent the disturbance, was severely assaulted by Henry Haggas and Robert Horner, who kicked him and struck him. Birch was corroborated in his evidence by James Jennings, and another of the party, and by Mary Kendall. In defence, Aminadab Robertshaw and some others were called, who all swore that they were present and saw no gambling. It was evident, however, that these witnesses were not to be relied on, and the defendant was fined £5 and 16s [or 18s?] 6d costs, and Robert Horner and Henry Haggas were each fined 10s and costs for the assault upon Birch. The money was paid.

Bradford Review, 6 May 1865

PRESIDENT LINCOLN. On Sunday morning last a special sermon was preached at Kipping Chapel, Thornton, by the Rev. J. Gregory in reference to the horrible tragedy which has occurred on the other side of the Atlantic. The rev. gentleman took for his text the 2nd verse of the 97th Psalm.

Bradford Observer, 11 May 1865

WANT OF UNITY. It appears that in Thornton there has been no understanding among the shopkeepers as to the hour upon which they shall close their shops; in the window of one shop appears a notice that it is closed at eight o'clock, and in the shop next door there is another intimation that the hour to close is nine o'clock. It would be much better for all parties if they could agree upon one time; early closing is now a popular movement.

Robertshaw's Piano Shop in Market Street.

Bradford Observer, 11 May 1865

Freehold Farm in Thornton. By Messrs. DAVIS & SHOESMITH, at the Denholme Gate Inn, at Thornton, in the parish of Bradford, in the county of York, on *Friday, May 26th* 1865, at Seven o'clock in the Evening, in one lot or more, as may be agreed upon at the time of sale, and subject to conditions to be then and there produced. All that MESSUAGE, Dwelling-house, or Tenement, called 'Foreside Top,' with one Cottage adjoining or near thereto, in Thornton, and all the outhouses, barns, stables, buildings, yards, orchards, gardens, and appurtenances thereto belonging; and also all those nine several closes, inclosures, pieces or parcels of LAND or Ground, to the said messuage or tenement belonging or therewith enjoyed or occupied, containing together by estimation Thirty days' work or thereabouts, more or less, together with the allotment belonging thereto, as the same now are in the tenure or occupation of Mr. Ingham, his assignees, or undertenants. The tenant will show the premises, and any further information and particulars may be had on application to the Auctioneers, or at the Offices of JNO. EDWARDS HILL, Solicitor, Harrison Road, Halifax.

Bradford Observer, 25 May 1865

LOCAL BOARD OF HEALTH. Initiatory proceedings sometime ago were taken in Thornton with a view to the establishment of a Local Board of Health, under the Local Government Act 1858. The sanction of Sir George Grey, the Home Secretary, having been obtained to such proposal, a notice has been issued this week by Mr. Isaac Wood (who has been appointed summoning officer), for the election of this board, which is to consist of twelve members, and such notice states that the nomination papers are to be sent in not later than the 26th instant. A public meeting of the ratepayers has been called, which will be held in the evening of that day, with a view if possible to prevent the expense of a contest.

Bradford Observer, 25 May 1865

SUNDAY SCHOOL SERMONS. On Sunday, the usual annual sermons in aid of the Sunday Schools were preached at no less than three different places of worship in Thornton, namely at St. James' Church, in the morning by the Rev. J. Barber, M.A., incumbent of Bierley, and in the afternoon by the Rev. J. B. Grant, incumbent of Oxenhope, collections £9 19s; at the Well Head School, by Mr. John Hill of Bradford, collection £10 10s 11½d; at the School in Egypt, by the Rev. J.B. Affleck of Yeadon, collection £9 16s 6d. The congregations were good at each place.

Bradford Observer, 1 June 1865

BOARD OF HEALTH. Friday last being the last day for the nomination of persons to fill the office of the members of the newly formed Board of Health at Thornton, a public meeting of the ratepayers was held in the evening of that day in the National School Room, with a view to prevent the expense of a contested election. The chair was occupied by Mr. Isaac Wood, colliery owner, and the meeting was characterised by perfect unanimity, each individual present seeming disposed to carry out the object for which they were met, and it was agreed that the following gentlemen should form the Board, namely:- Mr. Wood, colliery owner; Mr. Joseph Corrie, surgeon; Mr. F. Craven, manufacturer; Mr. Jonas Hartley, gentleman; Mr. Richard Walton, spinner; Mr. Joseph Hardy, corn miller; Mr. Richard Sellers, farmer; Mr. James Lingard, farmer; Mr. Henry Charnock, farmer; Mr. Abraham Craven, farmer and quarry owner; Mr. Michael Pearson, farmer; Mr. Geo. Townend, manufacturer.

Bradford Review, 29 June 1865

THORNTON. SUDDEN DEATH. On Monday, Samuel Moorhouse, a flagfacer, about fifty years of age, died very suddenly. He had been rather unwell, but had walked out on the Sunday.

Bradford Review, 1 July 1865

PRESENTATION. On Saturday last, Mr. Charles Wilkinson, who has been overlooker at Dole Mill, Thornton, for nearly twenty years, on his leaving the situation, was presented by the mill hands with a beautiful electro-plated cruet stand, as a token of the respect in which he is held by them.

Bradford Review, 1 July 1865

PROCESSION OF FORESTERS. On Saturday great stir and commotion was created at Thornton by a magnificent procession, which was made by the Foresters. It appears that the Court Charity Lodge, No. 403, which for twenty years had been held at the Rock and Heifer Inn, Thornton Heights, had decided to move to the Wellington Inn, Thornton. The members of the lodge, about 180 in number, together with the members of other lodges, met at the Rock and Heifer at about five o'clock, most of them being on horseback and wearing the first and second order of regalia; they had also engaged two bands of music, namely, the one belonging to the Bingley Rifle Volunteers, and the Clayton band, both being dressed in uniform. Being marshalled in this style, they presented an imposing appearance. The cavalcade moved in the direction of Thornton village, down the main street, up the new road to the Wellington, where the members of the lodge opened a court and proceeded with the transactions of business.

Leeds Mercury, 4 July 1865

ALLEGED INFRINGEMENT OF THE FACTORY ACT. Yesterday, before the West Riding Magistrates, sitting at Bradford, Mr. C.P. Measor, sub-inspector of factories, appeared in support of informations which charged Messrs. Jonathan Northrop and Co., shawl manufacturers, of Thornton, with employing a number of children without having obtained from a schoolmaster a certificate that such children had attended school, as required by the Factory Act, during the week preceding the date of the informations. Mr. Terry, who appeared for the defendants, took a preliminary objection that their establishment was not a factory within the meaning of the Act. The defendants bought cloth in a dyed and finished state; it was then cut up into lengths, according to the sort of shawl that might be required, and women and young persons were afterwards employed to attach a silk fringe to the shawls. No process of finishing, hooking, lapping, making-up, or packing was carried on on the premises where the children worked. If the Act was enforced in this case, Mr. Terry said it might with equal justice be applied to a tailor or milliner's shop. After hearing Mr. Measor on the other side, the Magistrates decided that Mr. Terry's objection was good, and dismissed the informations. Mr. Meason afterward asked for a case, which two of the magistrates consented to grant, Mr. Terry saying he should be happy to meet Mr. Measor in a superior court upon the point which had been raised.

Bradford Review, 15 July 1865

THORNTON. LODGE FESTIVAL. The members of the 'Highland Laddie' Lodge, No. 244, of the Grand United Order of Oddfellows, held their usual Tea Party and entertainment on Saturday the 5th inst, at the White Horse Inn, on which occasion Widdop's Glee Party were in attendance, from Bingley, and gave at intervals choice selections of favourite music. The proceedings were further enlivened by Messrs. Hardcastle and Fearnside, who contributed greatly to the merriment of the evening, by a continued recital of various instructive and humourous [sic] pieces. Songs were sung by Mr. B. Dobson, and other gentlemen present. The proceedings, which were of a most agreeable character, terminated at twelve o'clock.

Bradford Review, 22 July 1865

THORNTON. KNOR AND SPELL. Last Monday a match at knor and spell for £50 a side took place at a place called Peat Holes, near Thornton, between the well known Coward, of Baildon, and Nelly of Rotherham. The latter came off victor, having in the thirty rises of which the game consisted, obtained a score of 315. Coward, in the same number, got 300.

Bradford Review, 29 July 1865

ROBBERY. On Friday, a robbery took place in the shop kept by one David Brooksbank, Cunning Corner, Thornton. A purse, containing £10, had been placed on the counter, and soon after the money was abstracted and the purse left empty where it had been placed.

Bradford Review, 5 August 1865

LOCAL BOARD. On Friday week a meeting of the Local Board at Thornton was held in the National Schoolroom, the members present being Messrs. F. Craven, chairman, Isaac Wood, Henry Charnock, Michael Pearson, R.J. Walton, A. Craven, J. Lingard, J. Hartley, and Richard Sellers. The minutes of the proceedings of the previous meeting were read and confirmed, after which a number of devices for the seal of the Board were submitted for examination, out of which one was selected, of the following form:- In the centre are representations of a sheep, a mill, and a thorn, the sheep being significant of agriculture, the mill of manufacture, and the thorn having reference to the derivation of the name of the township. Round the border are the words 'Local Board for the district of Thornton.' The Clerk was directed to write to the Borough Surveyor of Bradford, asking him to meet F. Craven, Esq., the chairman, relative to the insufficient supply of water yielded by the Ball Street tap. It was then agreed that the district should be divided, for the purpose of a general inspection of the roads and places where it is alleged nuisances exist.

Bradford Review, 5 August 1865

PRESENTATION. During the present week a silver lever watch and guard, value five guineas, purchased by subscription in Thornton, has been presented to Mr. Peters, who for seven years was sergeant of police and resident in that village, until his promotion to the office of inspector, and his removal to the Barnsley district.

Bradford Review, 2 September 1865

AN ACCIDENT AND TIMELY ASSISTANCE. On Monday, John Pollard, a young man living in Thornton, was running in warm pursuit of a rabbit, at a place called New Halifax, when he fell and his neck was dislocated. He was laid in a helpless position, when it occurred to some of the bystanders as to what had happened to him, and although inexperienced in such matters, the means they adopted set the man all right, with the exception of the shock he received by the fall. The medical man who was subsequently consulted said that the man's life had been saved by his friends.

Bradford Review, 16 September 1865

THORNTON. CHOLERA. English cholera is very prevalent in Thornton, and, in one or two cases in which the results have been fatal, there have been strong symptoms of the same kind of disease which is just now raging in some of the foreign countries.

Bradford Review, 16 September 1865

THORNTON. CRICKET. On Saturday a game of cricket was played on the Manningham ground between the Manningham Second Eleven and the hands at Prospect Mill, Thornton, which was won by the latter, their runs being 77, while their opponents only got 41. Towards this 77, Mr. Josh. Craven, jun., contributed no less than 33.

Bradford Review, 21 October 1865

THORNTON. CATTLE DISEASE. The cattle disease has at length found its way into Thornton. On Saturday, Mr. Phineas Pearson, occupying the 'Intack' Farm, bought a cow at Halifax, and on the following day it was smitten by the disease and died.

Bradford Review, 25 November 1865

THORNTON. PROSPECT MILLS CRICKET CLUB. On Friday evening, at the Wellington Inn, Mrs. Sarah Pearson provided a most excellent and substantial supper for the patrons, friends, and members of the Thornton Prospect Mills Cricket Club; after which a very convivial meeting was held in the Club room. Mr. Thomas Laycock, manager of the firm, very kindly acted as chairman for the evening. The Chairman opened the meeting with a few pertinent remarks; after which Mr. T.H. Wright read the report of the season, showing that the finances were in good condition, having a surplus of above 20s. The club have only played seven matches during the season, four of which they have won, but they hope to make arrangements for more next season. A new cane-handled bat was presented to the highest average scorer who had played in seven matches. The successful competitor was Joseph Robertshaw. A very excellent paper was read by Mr. Augustus Clark, schoolmaster to the firm, on the origin of cricket, and the advantages to be derived from the game, contrasting it very favourably with other outdoor games, and decidedly giving the preference to the good old game of cricket. Songs and recitations were also given by Mr. Mitchell, Mr. Phineas Craven, Mr. T.H. Wright, and several others. At the breaking up of the meeting, three cheers were given in right good style for Mr. and Mrs. Joseph Craven, Ashfield House, and for Joshua Craven, Esq., both senior and junior, and, lastly, for the Chairman.

Barraclough's Hardware shop in Market Street.

Dole Mill after fire.

Bradford Review, 25 November 1865

Preliminary Notice. MR. CHARLES CRAVEN will offer for Sale by Auction, early in December next, several acres of eligible BUILDING LAND, situate to the western side of the town of Thornton, and divided into lots suitable for small capitalists. Plans are being prepared, and may be obtained 14 days prior to the sale on application to the AUCTIONEER, at Shipley; E. WOODHEAD and SON, Surveyors, 37, Market-street, Bradford; or LAYCOCK and DYSON, Solicitors, Huddersfield. 1st November, 1865.

Bradford Observer, 30 November 1865

THORNTON. Another water pipe explosion. On Saturday night there was another explosion of one of the Bradford Corporation water pipes in a field called Kiln Flat in the occupation of Mr. James Booth, and the next morning the breach was repaired without delay. In consequence of these explosions having become of such frequent occurrence the public are beginning to think there must have been some mismanagement by the contractors in laying down the pipes.

Bradford Observer, 30 November 1865

THORNTON. A disorderly beershop. On Thursday last at Bradford before the West Riding magistrates, Thomas Wilson who keeps a beershop at Low Hill, Thornton, was charged with allowing disorderly conduct in his house. P.C. Craven stated that on the 13th instant he, with another officer, visited the house, where they found three men fighting, all of whom were in a state of nudity. One strong powerful man was pummeling the other two in the presence of from thirty to fifty people, including three well-known prostitutes. The defendant, who, it was said, had not been long at the house, was fined 40s and costs.

Bradford Observer, 7 December 1865

THORNTON. BRUTAL ATTACK UPON A SOLDIER. On Thursday, before the West Riding Magistrate, Joseph Fearnside, Riley Jackson, and John Settle, three young men living at Four Lane Ends, Manningham, were brought up on a charge of having assaulted one Samuel Douglas, a soldier belonging to the 55th Regiment of Foot, on furlough with a friend at 'Freaks' in Thornton. The complainant stated that on Sunday he had to go to the post-office at Bradford, and on returning home with two or three friends they called at a beerhouse at Four Lane Ends, kept by Abraham Settle. After leaving, and when about 200 yards from the beerhouse, they were, without any cause, brutally assaulted by a gang of men, 15 or 16 in number. Complainant was overpowered, laid across a wall, and beaten with large stones. He was internally injured, and his clothes were torn, and was liable to a court-martial for damage done to them. He claimed £2 6s damages. He had been informed that the same gang frequently assaulted people who, on Sunday evenings, were going to and fro. They did this for 'amusement.' The Bench made an order for the full amount claimed, and fined the defendants 10s each and costs for the assault, or two months' imprisonment.

Chapter Fifteen
1866

Tea and currant buns at New Road Methodist anniversary – New lamplighter appointed for ten lamps – Farmer fined for taking cow on road to bull – New bus service to Bradford – Dog savages newsagent

Bradford Observer, 4 January 1866

ST JAMES'S CHURCH SCHOOL, THORNTON. About three months ago a Sunday school was commenced in connection with this church; and on Saturday there was a feast for the scholars, when an agreeable entertainment for both mind and body was provided for them; and as this was the first festival held in the National School, a large concourse of people gathered together. On Monday there was a successful tea meeting at the same place, the proceeds being appropriated for the benefit of the church choir. After tea, the Rev. J. Wilson presided, and addresses were delivered by the Rev. Mr. Eyre, of Denholme, Messrs. S. Thewlis, J. Shackleton, and others. The chief feature of the evening was a performance by the choir, assisted by the Clayton choir, of a most excellent selection of sacred and secular music.

Bradford Observer, 4 January 1866

THORNTON. METHODIST FREE CHURCH SUNDAY SCHOOL. On Saturday, all the scholars belonging to the Methodist Free Church, at Thornton, assembled in the school, and were regaled with tea and currant buns; and, on Monday, the teachers and friends, in number about 400, held their annual tea in the school-room. After tea, a public meeting was held. The Rev. D. Maud, of Farsley, who presided, opened the proceedings by making a few brief remarks. The report of the year's operations was then given in the shape of a dialogue, which was recited by two girls and a boy, respectively named Phoebe Howorth,

140

Mary Hannah Barraclough, and Greenwood Southwart. Addresses were delivered by the Rev. T. Biddulph, of Bradford, Messrs. Denis Hird, Wm. Robinson, James Myers, John Southwart, Stephen Geldard, and Michl. Wright. Some other recitations were given, and several pieces of music performed by the choir. Mr. Jeremiah Robertshaw presided at the harmonium. The trays were all furnished gratuitously by the teachers, and the entire proceeds of the tea are to be appropriated to the fund which is being raised for the erection of an organ in the chapel.

Bradford Observer, 11 January 1866

THORNTON. CLUB DINNER. On Monday evening, 74 members of the lodge of Ancient Foresters (Court No. 100), (held at the New Inn, Thornton), with their wives and sweethearts, partook of a good substantial tea, with a variety of etceteras. After which the company enjoyed themselves in various ways. The proceedings terminated with a dance.

Bradford Observer, 11 January 1866

THORNTON near BRADFORD. VALUABLE FREEHOLD
PROPERTY. To be Sold by Auction by Mr. Buckley Sharp at the
Boar's Head Inn in Bradford in the County of York on Thursday the
1st Day of February 1866 at Five o'clock in the Evening (for Six
o'clock precisely) and subject to such conditions as will then be
produced.
The Mansion called West House, situate in Thornton, in the parish of
Bradford aforesaid, lately in the occupation of Mr. Joseph Craven but
now in the occupation of Mr. Rawson, Surgeon, with the stables,
coach house, outbuildings, gardens and grounds thereto belonging;
and also the Dwelling-house called West Cottage situated in
Thornton aforesaid, and now or lately occupied by Mrs. Townend,
with its appurtenances and Two Closes of Land called West Fields
situated in Thornton aforesaid and now or lately in the occupation of
Mr. George Townend.
The Property above mentioned, which is all Freehold, stands in a
pleasant situation adjoining the highway leading from Thornton to
Denholme and contains an area of about 2a 2r 20p. For further
information apply to Messrs. H.W. Blackburn, Accountants, Darley
Street, Bradford; or Wood & Killick, Solicitors, Hall Ings, Bradford.
10th January 1866.

Bradford Observer, 18 January 1866

THORNTON. LOCAL BOARD. On Saturday, an adjourned meeting of the Local Board was held at the board room, the members present being, the chairman, Messrs. Wood, Corrie, Hartley, Lingard, Charnock, Sellers, A. Craven, and Pearson. A highway rate of 1*s* 3*d* in the pound was laid. Tenders for lighting the lamps were given in by the following persons, namely: Craven Robinson, greengrocer, Robert Lingard, labourer, Wm. Whitton, fishmonger, Abel Holdsworth, beer seller, Jonas Marshall, painter, George Wilman, labourer, Joseph Robinson, bellman, Jonas Jennings, labourer, and Jonathan Pickles, labourer. The lowest tender was that of Jonathan Pickles, who received the appointment at 2*s* a week. The number of lamps is only about half-a-score. Messrs. Andrews and Downs, quarry owners, applied to have the permission of the board to raise the road at a place called 'Who could have thought it,' for their own convenience. Their application was granted, with the understanding that they should make a drain to take away the water. The clerk having reported that the bye-laws had received the sanction of the Home Secretary, Sir George Grey, it was ordered that 200 copies of the same should be printed, and 50 additional copies of those relating to slaughterhouses. Cheques were drawn, amounting to £36 7*s* 9*d* in payment of wages, contracts, &c.

Bradford Observer, 18 January 1866

THORNTON. TREAT TO WORKPEOPLE. On Saturday, Messrs. Joshua Craven & Sons, Prospect Mills, gave their workmen their annual Christmas treat in the shape of a good substantial supper, provided by Mrs. Sarah Pearson of the Wellington Inn. After supper, the guests adjourned into the lodge club room, and there spent the evening in a social and friendly way. The toast of the evening, 'Health to the Masters and prosperity to the Firm,' being drunk in a very enthusiastic manner. Songs and recitations followed, by various gentlemen present.

Bradford Observer, 25 January 1866

NOTICE IS HEREBY GIVEN, that on the Second day of April next application will be made to her Majesty's Justices of the Peace, of and for the West Riding of the County of York, assembled at the General Quarter Sessions of the Peace to be held at Pontefract, in and for the said Riding, for an ORDER for turning, diverting, and stopping up a certain highway leading from another highway, from a point near the manufactory and premises there belonging to and occupied by Mr. George Townend, to the Bradford and Thornton Turnpike Road, otherwise the Thornton New Road, respectively lying within the township of Thornton, in the parish of Bradford in the said Riding, which is one hundred and thirty yards in length, and commences at the northern fence wall of a close of land there, called the near Ing, belonging to the Reverend James Clark Franks, Clerk, and now occupied by Jonas Illingworth as his tenant, and which passes through such close of land in a southwardly direction, and ends in the said Bradford and Thornton Turnpike Road, otherwise the Thornton New Road, opposite to the Methodist Free Church, there all in the said township of Thornton; and in place or stead of which said highway, so intended to be turned, diverted, and stopped up as aforesaid, the said James Clark Franks hath, by writing under his hand, proposed and agreed to set out and make a new highway, commencing at the northern fence wall of the said close of land, called the near Ing, on the western side of the firstly above mentioned highway, and passing through such close of land in a southwardly direction up to and ending in the said Bradford and Thornton Turnpike Road, otherwise Thornton New Road, and which said new highway is one hundred and twenty-seven yards in length, all lying within the said township of Thornton, and belonging to the said James Clark Franks, and occupied by the said Jonas Illingworth; a notice is hereby given, that the certificate of two Justices having viewed the said first mentioned or old highway and the line of the proposed new highway, with a plan of the said old highway and of the line of the said proposed new highway, and the proofs thereof will be lodged with the Clerk of the Peace for the said West Riding on or before the first day of March next. Given under my hand this seventeenth day of January, one thousand eighteen hundred and sixty-six.

FRANCIS CRAVEN

The Chairman of the Local Board of Thornton, as Surveyors of the Highways of and within the said Township of Thornton.

Bradford Observer, 25 January 1866

THORNTON. THE ALLEGED FOOTPATH OBSTRUCTION. A short time ago we referred to an alleged obstruction in a footpath at Storr Heights, Thornton, caused by the erection upon it of a machine for lifting stones out of a quarry. The Local Board, it is said, having paid no regard to complaints which were made, on Saturday evening last, some person or persons threw the machine into the quarry, smashing it to pieces.

Bradford Observer, 1 February 1866

To-morrow. Old Mill, Thornton, near Bradford. To Plain and Fancy Manufacturers and others. Sale by Auction of a Manufacturing Plant, under a Deed of Assignment.

J. BUCKLEY SHARP is instructed by the Assignees of Mr. F. Bottomley to Sell by Auction, on *Friday, February 2nd*, 1866, at Half-past Eleven o'clock, a.m., on the premises, Old Mill, Thornton, the whole of the very compact and desirable MANUFACTURING PLANT, consisting of 80 looms (plain and box), with extra gearing and going parts, to adapt them to any requirement of the trade, 30 engines, upwards of 300 sets of healds and slays, together with spare beams, belting, change wheels, shuttles, pickers, weft forks, bobbins and bobbin boards, gas meter and fittings, sundries in office, &c., useful horse, dog cart, by Cheetham, spring wherry, harness, &c.

The Machinery is on view, and Catalogues may be had on application at 29, Well Street, Bradford.

Bradford Observer, 1 February 1866

THORNTON. Presentations. On Saturday the hands employed at Upper Mill, Thornton, about forty in number, held a tea party, at which they presented to Mr. John Robinson, their overlooker, a splendid eight days' timepiece in gilt, under a glass shade, as a testimonial of their respect, he having accepted a situation in Bradford.

Bradford Observer, 8 February 1866

NOTICE IS HEREBY GIVEN, that the Partnership heretofore subsisting between the undersigned MARY HARDY, THOMAS HARDY, and JOSEPH HARDY, carrying on business at Thornton, near Bradford, in the county of York, as Corn Millers and Farmers, is this day Dissolved by mutual consent. All debts due to and owing by the said Firm will be received and paid by the said THOMAS HARDY, who will in future carry on the said business on his own account. As witness our hands, this second day of February, 1866.

MARY HARDY THOMAS HARDY JOSEPH HARDY.

Witness – LATIMER DARLINGTON, clerk to George Mossman, Jun., Solicitor, Bradford.

Bradford Observer, 8 February 1866

THORNTON. LECTURE. On Tuesday and Wednesday evenings, two lectures were delivered in the Kipping School room, Thornton, on 'Geology,' by Mr. W. Richardson, Lecturer to the Society of Arts, London. The Lectures were of an exceedingly interesting character, being illustrated by numerous diagrams, and numerous specimens of sections of the English, Welsh, and Scotch coal fields were exhibited. The Lectures were given under the auspices of the Thornton Mechanics' Institute.

Bradford Observer, 8 February 1866

At the Bradford Court House on Thursday, Benjamin Shepherd, farm bailiff to Mr. John Carter, of Thornton, was fined 20s and costs for driving a cow on the road on the 28th ult. without a licence. When asked about his licence he said that he had not got one, and that he was only taking the cow to the bull.

Bradford Observer, 15 February 1866

THORNTON. A wages case. On Thursday at the West Riding court, Bradford, Mr. R.J. Walton, worsted spinner, was summoned by Elizabeth Ann Kendal, who had worked for him, for the recovery of 3s 1½d wages. Complainant had left in the middle of the week without any notice. This the bench did not justify, but still, as Mr. Walton made no agreement with hands with respect to notice, the bench thought the money should be paid, and Mr. Walton did so without a conviction.

Bradford Observer, 8 March 1866

THE GRUMBLERS. The grumblers in the village of Thornton are at present making bitter complaints against the Board of Health. It is alleged that the carcase of a dead horse has been allowed to remain in a field not far from a footpath for the space of seven weeks, until a great portion of it has been consumed by the dogs, and the stench arising therefrom has been awful. We cannot justify the existence of such a nuisance for such a length of time; but should this charge against the Board be well founded, we would urge as an extenuation of the apparent neglect of the Board the press of business with which they are at present overwhelmed; and we would ask the persons aggrieved to have a little patience until all their machinery has got fairly into operation, and all such matters will no doubt receive proper and timely attention.

Bradford Observer, 12 April 1866

NEW CRICKET CLUB. On Monday evening a meeting of the village cricketers was held in the Kipping School-room, in order to make some new arrangements for the coming season, at which it was agreed that the two clubs hitherto known as 'The Prospect' and 'Dole Mills' clubs should be amalgamated and form one called 'The Thornton United.' They also determined to hold all their meetings in the School-room. A sub-committee was appointed to solicit subscriptions, and to look out for a suitable play-ground.

Bradford Observer, 31 May 1866

THORNTON. Candidates for Local Board. – Isaac Wood, farmer, Upper Headley; Thos. Hardy, corn miller, School Green; E.E. Rawson, surgeon, West House; Jabez Pickles, waste dealer, Hill Top; Joseph Craven, manufacturer, Ashfield; William Briggs, farmer, West Scholes; John Hey, gentleman, Greenclough; Phineas Pearson, farmer, Intake; John Hardy, farmer, Hollings Lake; George Bairstow, joiner, Mountain; Simeon Mann, labourer, Law Hill; Jonathan Bairstow, farmer, Mountain.

Bradford Observer, 21 June 1866

THORNTON. Bradford Livery Stables Company (Limited). This company have begun to run a bus on Saturday afternoons, two or three times, between the New Inn, Bradford, and the New Inn, Thornton, and Saturday last was the first day. The Thornton people are well pleased with the new means of communication.

Bradford Observer, 28 June 1866

A YOUTHFUL DISPUTANT. Thornton has recently been visited by the Mormons, or Latter-day Saints. On Sunday, they held a meeting, and a considerable number were present. An opportunity being given to rebut the arguments advanced, a youth named John Cain, only 17 years of age, a local preacher among the Wesleyans, presented himself, and after carrying on a discussion at some length, succeeded in completely putting his opponents to silence.

Bradford Observer, 19 July 1866

TREAT TO WORKPEOPLE. On Saturday Messrs. D. & J. Craven, shawl manufacturers, Thornton, gave a treat to their hands, about 50 in number. A good substantial meal was provided at the house of one of the partners, at Close Head, after which they indulged in all kinds of out-door recreations and sports.

Bradford Observer, 26 July 1866

THE REGISTRAR OF BIRTHS AND DEATHS. A good deal of excitement prevails at Thornton as to the election of a successor to the late Mr. Edward Kay, registrar of births and deaths. The contest among the candidates who are offering themselves appears to be confined to Mr. Thos. Sunderland, insurance agent, and Mr. Caleb Barraclough, postmaster, both of whom are making great efforts in canvassing the guardians and in seeking the influence of friends.

Bradford Observer, 29 August 1866

THORNTON. Yesterday at West Riding Police Court, Martha, wife of Isaac Holdsworth, claimed sureties of peace from Maria, wife of Robert Robinson. They are neighbours at Well Heads in Thornton and quarrelled on Sunday 19th August, continuing for two days and becoming increasingly virulent. Offensive epithets were exchanged. Complainant protested that she was in bodily fear, defendant having said that she would kill her. Defendant denied she had said that and called on John Shaw and Thomas Birch as witnesses. The faces of both women are familiar to the bench. The defendant's husband was bound over in the sum of £20 for twelve months to ensure his wife keeps the peace.

Bradford Observer, 20 September 1866

On Thursday, before the West Riding magistrates, Daniel Shackleton was charged by William Drake with having assaulted him at Thornton, on the Tuesday night previous. It appears that on the day named the complainant, a young man, by trade a collier, living at Mountain, with another man named John Drake, *alias* Wright, also a collier, had been spending the afternoon at the beershops and public-houses in Thornton. Between eleven and twelve o'clock at night, when he was leaving the Friendly Inn, an attack was made upon them by the defendant and 'Sam o' Pegs,' the latter it appears was not known at the time. Complainant was struck and kicked most brutally, and bruised on the head. Complainant was corroborated by his companion. Mr. J.W. Berry, who appeared for the defendant, called William Smith, a weaver living at Thornton, who said he had been to see his sweetheart, and had not been at a public-house. He saw the parties coming in contact in the street, and heard the complainant cry, 'Come, there is a big chap here (meaning the defendant), we will have a row.' 'Sam o' Pegs' was then seized, and he having called for assistance, 'Jack Harry' went and released him. It was evident, therefore, that the complainant was the aggressor, and the case was dismissed.

Bradford Observer, 4 October 1866

ALLEGED FELONIES. At the West Riding Court, Bradford, on Monday, William Sharp, who has only the appearance of a boy, but who was said to be 21 years of age, was charged with having committed sundry felonies. It was stated by Police-sergeant Craven that several robberies had been committed in the upper part of Thornton, and other places near, and the prisoner was brought up as being a suspected person, and having a house at Thorngate, in which he was living alone. The house had been searched, and various articles had been found which were suspected to be stolen property. A remand was asked for, and the case was adjourned until today.

Bradford Observer, 11 October 1866

A FEROCIOUS DOG. On Monday morning, Mr. Wm. Thomas, news agent, Thornton, went to the Old Mill upon business, when he was seized by a dog, and was severely bit on the hand and wrist, a piece of the flesh being torn off. The lacerated limb was dressed by Mr. Corrie, surgeon, and Mr. Thomas is likely to recover without the loss of any of his fingers.

Bradford Observer, 18 October 1866

AN ACCIDENT. On Tuesday morning, a man named James Dobson, employed as an engine tenter at a coal pit at Keelham, Thornton, belonging to Messrs. I. Wood & Son, by some means got his foot tangled with some portions of the machinery, and it was crushed and mangled most fearfully. He was immediately removed to the infirmary at Bradford.

Bradford Observer, 25 October 1866

TEA PARTY. On Saturday afternoon, the hands in the employ of Mr. R.J. Walton, worsted spinner, Old Mill, Thornton, took tea together at the house of Mrs. Pearson, the Wellington Hotel. After tea a most pleasant evening was spent.

Bradford Observer, 1 November 1866

THORNTON. ANNUAL SOIREE OF THE MECHANICS' INSTITUTE. The annual soiree took place on Saturday, in the Kipping New School-room, Alfred Illingworth, Esq., of Bradford, presiding. After an excellent tea the choir sang a glee, and then Mr. Illingworth delivered an appropriate address, urging the claims of the institute upon the sympathy and support of the public, and expressed his surprise that out of a population of four thousand people the secretary could only report 135 members. The Rev. J.L. Posnett and the Rev. J. Gregory spoke of the advantages the institute was adapted to confer, and urged additional reasons for its patronage and support. The President, Mr. Phineas Craven, then followed with a number of facts and figures, which he defied his hearers to evade or impugn. He acquitted the audience, or at least the greater part of them, of ever being found guilty of taking the slightest interest in the institute, or of manifesting the least concern whether it prospered or not. The village of Thornton contained thirteen public-houses and beershops; and, on a calculation he had made, he considered that three times the amount of the income for one year of the institute was spent in alcoholic drink every week. Mr. Illingworth, who was obliged to vacate the chair before the meeting terminated, in reply to a vote of thanks, deplored that it was in any one's power to produce such startling statistics as Mr. Craven had done; it behoved all, he said, to put their shoulders to the wheel to try to provide a remedy. The musical part of the proceedings was most efficiently sustained by Miss Wheater, Miss Bellwood, Mr. Croxall, Mr. Northrop, Mr. Wilcock, and others. Mr. Moorhouse presided at the pianoforte.

Thornton and beyond, looking north east.

Bradford Observer, 8 November 1866

PRESENTATIONS. For a number of years back Mr. William Clough, overlooker, has held the offices of chapel-keeper, leader, and local preacher in the Wesleyan society at Thornton, and such is the esteem in which he is held, that just now, he being about to leave the neighbourhood, presentations are being heaped upon him. On Saturday evening, at a tea meeting held for the purpose, a valuable skeleton clock, which has been selected from the stock of Mr. Barraclough, silversmith, was presented by the Rev. J.L. Posnett, in the name and on the behalf of the Sunday School teachers; also, several other articles have been given to him by the hands over whom he had control in the mill.

Bradford Observer, 8 November 1866

BOARD OF HEALTH. On Friday evening the usual fortnightly meeting of the Local Board of Health for the district of Thornton was held in the Board-room, Sapgate Lane. Mr. Isaac Wood presided. Several notices having been previously served for the construction of drains in certain parts of the district, it was reported by two of the parties that the neglect to make such drains was solely attributable to their tenants. In the case of the executors of the late Abraham Ackroyd, the Clerk was instructed to take legal proceedings, unless the notice should be complied with at once. Application was made for a supply of water to a slaughterhouse in New Halifax, which was granted. Cheques were drawn for £42 12s. Some discussion took place relative to the erection of a suitable room to answer all the requirements of the Board, but no resolution was arrived at. Further communications were read and agreed upon, relating to water works, the several matters of detail respecting them and for the site now being fully settled.

Chapter Sixteen
1867

New Thornton church to be built next spring – Suicide of young man caught gambling on Sunday – A ludicrous wedding – Man shoots pigeon for damaging crops – Man dies at soothsayer's house

Bradford Observer, 17 January 1867

THORNTON. REBUILDING OF THE CHURCH. We are given to understand that such is the encouragement which has been given to the people at Thornton in their proposal to rebuild the church that the plans have been prepared, and operations will be commenced early in the Spring.

Bradford Observer, 28 March 1867

THORNTON, KIPPING CHAPEL. This place of worship having undergone large alterations, and after having been closed for six months, was re-opened on the 17th of March by three services. The Rev. G.W. Conder, of Manchester, preached morning and evening, and the Rev. J.R. Campbell, D.D., of Bradford, in the afternoon. On Sunday last, the 24th, the Rev. S. Hebditch preached morning and afternoon, and the Rev. D. Thomas, B.A., in the evening, both of Bristol. Yesterday evening, the Rev. Enoch Mellor, M.A., of Liverpool, preached to a large congregation, gathered from all quarters of the district. All these services have been well attended, deep interest in them has been shown, and the collections have been very good. The clearance of a debt, of between £1,100 and £1,200, incurred in alterations, has been effected. The sermons had their prominent excellencies, and each preacher had his distinctive and striking individuality. The service of song, most effectively rendered, added much interest to the public worship.

The cause of Nonconformity at Kipping has the hoar of antiquity upon it, and is bound up with interesting historical memorials. No doubt the Halifax and Bradford churches owe much, if not their origin, to this religious community, and the present occasion furnishes a reason for reviewing the history of the place. The first chapel of which there is any accredited account was built on an estate called Kipping (hence the name of the chapel, which has been removed from its original site) and is now used as a barn. Apart from its associations it is an ugly object to look upon, and in its best days could never have been an inviting place for Sunday services. Could some of the earlier worshippers in the old place rise from the dead and see the present light, chaste and commodious sanctuary, they would stand amazed at the large strides their descendants have made. A chapel on the present site was built nearly a hundred years ago (A.D. 1769), has since had several rebuildings, and many alterations, but not one alteration so perfect as the present one. The origin of this old dwelling-place of Nonconformity is, like the sources of many rivers, not easily determined. Some writers, learned in ecclesiastical matters, refer it to the Long Parliament, in the time of the Commonwealth. There are circumstances favouring this opinion, but it rests on no solid data. Others date its beginning from the Act of Uniformity, 1662. But others say it took its rise from the Five-mile Act, 1665. That it had an earlier date than this is easily proved. It has been favoured by an almost unbroken succession of simple-minded, earnest-hearted, holy ministers of Jesus Christ. There have only been one or two failing links in the chain.

The *Rev. John Ryther* is the first Nonconformist minister of whom we have any authentic account. He had much of the spirit and bearing of the Puritans – a cedar-like man, flourishing even to old age. When the plague and great fire in London happened, he felt a deep sympathy with the sufferers and preached several sermons thereon. High moral courage is always a burning rebuke to daring despotism. His preaching and usefulness rendered him obnoxious to the powers that be, and he was twice committed to York Castle. The bitterness of persecution eventually forced him from a flourishing flock, and he afterwards settled in London, and built a chapel in Broad Street, Wapping.

Some years later, *Mr Accepted Lister* succeeded to the pastorate. He was so lame that he could hardly stand, having broken both of his thighs in his youth, and his lameness was increased by a fall from his horse, which again broke both his thighs. He was eminently distinguished by the depth of his piety, and by varied literary attainments. His father, Joseph Lister, was one of the best specimens of the Puritan character, – a man of sound understanding, of ardent piety, of undeviating integrity, and of inflexible attachment to the cause of Nonconformity. His mother, Sarah Lister, was exemplary for meekness, wisdom, holiness. About the time of his birth, she attained a joyful assurance of her conversion, and, in testimony of which, she called her son Accepted. Joseph Lister possessed considerable property, and gave his son the best education the times could command. Private counsels and benign and hallowing home influences were not lost upon the son.

He became an excellent preacher, and his services were much coveted by neighbouring congregations. He was a remarkably modest man, and though he preached at Kipping, he would not, on account of his physical infirmities, accept the pastoral oversight of the people. For a time he divided his services between Bingley and Kipping, and then confined himself to Bingley, because the house and chapel were under one roof, and his bodily ailments made him a timorous horseman. The people at Kipping so much appreciated his ministry, that they pressed him with earnest importunity to return. They sent (having gained his consent), 30 men and as many horses and carts as brought him and his moveables. After this he lived seven or eight years, and died in 1709. In Thornton Episcopal Church burial ground, there is on his grave stone, this inscription, impendam et espunder. His father, Joseph Lister, wrote his own biography, which has throughout a beautiful simplicity – life-like sketches of the rough times of persecution in which he lived – and it has an interesting account of the Royalists and the Parliamentarians in the siege of Bradford.

Samuel Hulme was the successor of *Mr. Lister*. The inscription to his memory, placed in the chapel, is, '*To the memory of the late Rev. S. Hulme, who was a diligent and successful minister at Kipping forty-six years. He died October 26th, 1756, aged 70, and was interred in Thornton chapel. He had eleven children, viz., seven sons and four daughters who lived to the age of maturity.*' He had two sons who rose to great eminence, both as authors and practitioners in medical science; and the rest of the children received a good education. How this was done, with only £40 a year, is very puzzling according to our present, severest calculations of domestic economy. Judging from such a stand point, we may say, 'The ministry is a good calling, but a bad profession.'

The *Rev. Joseph Cockin* took the pastoral oversight in 1777, and he gave by his powerful ministry a new impulse to religion, not only in Thornton, but throughout this district. Full of vigour and vivacity, he entered upon his labours. His preaching was distinguished for boldness of conception – for freedom of speech, blended with warmth and affection – for apt, homely colloquial illustrations, presented with great animation and zeal – and for warm-hearted, friendly intercourse with the people. These qualities rendered him highly popular and useful, both at home and abroad. He was truly the Whitfield of the West Riding. He continued at Kipping about 15 years, and then removed to Halifax. The people of his first charge have cherished his memory with rare affection. They can speak of him to this day with kindling enthusiasm, although the generation that knew him has, with one or two exceptions, passed away.

Mr. Cockin was succeeded by the *Rev. John Calvert*, a man of a different stamp, but a good man and a useful preacher. During his ministry the chapel was enlarged. He was succeeded by *Mr. Pool*, who held the office of pastor for 16 years with great acceptance; a further enlargement of the chapel took place during his ministry. In 1834, the *Rev. James Gregory*, the present highly-esteemed and excellent minister, accepted the pastorate. He has that he has laboured successfully. We trust that the necessary and effective transformation that has been made will be but the beginning of a new epoch of spiritual prosperity in this ancient and hallowed sanctuary.

Bradford Observer, 11 April 1867

THORNTON. A LAMENTABLE DEATH BY DROWNING. Great commotion prevailed in Thornton on Thursday morning in consequence of a young man, about 18 years of age, named Frederick Murgatroyd, having been found drowned in the mill dam belonging to Messrs. J. Craven & Sons. The particulars of the case are as follows. For some time back numbers of young men have congregated together on a Sunday in a field situate at Storr Height, in the occupation of Mr. Daniel Aykroyd, butcher, for the purpose of gambling. Mr. Aykroyd, being determined to put a stop to such proceedings, went on Sunday morning to the field in question, accompanied by a policeman and another person, and there they found the deceased with a number of other men. They all ran away, but not before their names had been obtained. It appears that deceased had wandered about all day, and at night he must have thrown himself into the dam in question, as his 'billycock' was found on the dam bank early on Monday morning. Deceased was considered a very respectable young man, was well respected by his masters, and the event is deeply regretted by all who knew him. An inquest has been held, at which an open verdict was returned.

Bradford Observer, 16 April 1867

THORNTON. WESLEYAN REFORMERS' NEW CHAPEL. The Wesleyan Reformers, who have hitherto met for public worship in the Athenaeum, having recently decided to build on the ground purchased by them some time ago on the New Road side, the foundation stone for the new chapel was laid by James Drummond, Esq., of Bradford, on Good Friday. The usual formalities on such occasions were gone through; and the Rev. J. Gregory of Thornton; the Rev. J. Hanson of Bradford; the Rev. Mr. Parnaby; Mr. Thomas Myers of Horton, and others, took part in the proceedings. After the tea, there was a public meeting in the Athenaeum, and the evening was spent in a very interesting and profitable manner.

Bradford Observer, 18 April 1867

Death of a patriarch. On Saturday the remains of old John Wilkinson of Intake, Thornton, one of the village patriarchs, were deposited in the graveyard at Thornton Chapel. The deceased, who was ninety years of age, was formerly carrier to the late Mr. David Wright, a noted manufacturer; and in autumn every year for sixty-seven years, he went regularly a-harvesting for a few weeks into the East Riding. Latterly he obtained his livelihood as a dealer in poultry and has until recently attended the Bradford market.

Bradford Observer, 13 June 1867

THORNTON. A LUDICROUS WEDDING. On Tuesday morning, nearly the whole of the population of the village of Thornton turned out to witness a scene, of the origin and consummation of which the following is a brief description:- It appears that in this locality a person known by the cognomen of 'Shocker' has for a number of years been living with a woman in a state of 'tally'-ship. His neighbours not savouring this state of morals, have often remonstrated with him upon his wickedness; and he always urging his poverty as an excuse for his sin, a short time ago they prevailed upon him to enter into an agreement to the effect that, if his friends would provide him with a suit of clothes and pay the expenses of his wedding, he would 'take Mary for better or for worse.' This agreement having been drawn up and ratified in proper legal form, a subscription was entered into with a view to its being carried out. Success appears to have attended every effort, for on the morning in question 'the happy couple' left the village for the parish church at Bradford in the following style: a vehicle had been provided of large dimensions, with four wheels, to which a pair of horses had been attached; the driver being a postillion. In the front of the carriage was exhibited a board, suspended at a considerable height, upon which was inscribed, in large characters, 'Shocker's wedding.' Under the inscription, 'Shocker' and his intended wife were very comfortably seated, the happy bridegroom being adorned with his new subscription suit of clothes, which consisted of a hat with silver girdle, a blue coat, trimmed with yellow aplets and lace, red shrog breeches, with a black stocking on one leg and a white one on the other. The latter part of the carriage was occupied by a number of persons with tin whistles, tin cans, and other instruments of mock music, the sounds of which were mingled with the shouts and laughter of the numerous throng. In this fantastic style the party proceeded to Bradford, and upon the bride and bridegroom presenting themselves at the hymeneal altar at the Parish Church, the officiating clergyman refused to proceed with the ceremony until a change of dress had been procured for the bridegroom. This was speedily procured, and the bridal knot was quickly tied. The party then returned to Thornton, where a surplus of the subscription which had been made was spent in drinking appropriate toasts, such as 'Happiness and long life to "Shocker" and his wife,' 'The single married, and the married happy.' Much merriment prevailed during the evening.

Bradford Observer, 13 June 1867

SUNDAY SCHOOL FESTIVITIES. The usual Whitsuntide festivities were held on Monday and Tuesday, by the teachers and scholars of the various Sunday Schools in Thornton. Those belonging to the Church held a gala in a field at School Green, and those of the New Road Congregational Church walked in procession to Well Heads, where they enjoyed themselves in similar manner in rural sports. The Wesleyans occupied a field at West Scholes belonging to Mrs. Hannah Briggs; and the Kipping School were in another field at the same place. Refreshments were provided in each case on the ground, consisting of tea, coffee, milk, and currant buns; and in the evening they all returned home well tired with their athletic exercises.

Leeds Mercury, 14 June 1867

SHOOTING PIGEONS AT DENHOLME. Yesterday, before the West Riding Court, sitting at Bradford, Robert Horsfall was summoned on the charge of having feloniously fired at and killed a pigeon, the property of Aaron Bailey. Mr. J.G. Hutchinson was for the complainant, and Mr. Ferns, of Leeds, defended. Aaron Bailey, the complainant, keeps a public-house at Emanuel Heights, not far from a farm occupied by the defendant's father, Mr. Timothy Horsfall, who resides at Field Head House, Denholme. It was stated that the complainant was in the habit of having shooting matches at his house, for which purpose he kept a large number of pigeons. The pigeons were turned out early in the morning, and betook themselves to Mr. Horsfall's farm, where it was alleged the birds had committed great damage, more especially in a field of lentils, of which cereal pigeons were said to be very fond. The complainant had been frequently warned that if he did not abate the nuisance the pigeons would be shot, but he disregarded these warnings, and accordingly on the 31st ult., Mr. Robt. Horsfall fired at a flock of pigeons which had gathered in one of his father's fields, and killed one of them. Hence the ground of complaint, and it was also alleged for the complainant that after the pigeon was shot, the defendant was taking the dead bird away with him, but this was denied. Mr. Ferns, while admitting that his client had shot the pigeon, maintained that the bench had no jurisdiction, as defendant was merely protecting his property from injury, and in support of the position he took, quoted a somewhat similar case in which the Court of Queen's Bench reversed a decision of justices, who had convicted a person of shooting pigeons to protect his crops from injury. After the points raised had been discussed, Mr. Timothy Horsfall was called, who stated that he had gone to complainant's house, and on several occasions had told him that if he did not keep his pigeons from the barn they would be shot, as they had for a long time past been an intolerable nuisance. Bailey denied this statement point blank, admitting, however, that he had received notice of one of his sheep straying on to the farm, but Mr. Horsfall maintained that since then he had seen Bailey several times, and cautioned him, which Bailey, however, as persistently denied. The bench, evidently much annoyed at the contradictory statements of the witnesses, dismissed the case.

Bradford Observer, 27 June 1867

'THORNTON ROUGHS.' On Thursday, some of the 'Thornton Roughs' were required to appear before the West Riding magistrates at Bradford, upon charges of assault. Wm. Shaw, who has been several times before the Bench, was fined 30s, including costs, for having assaulted James Haggas. A charge was also preferred against Isaac Jowett and Wm. Clark, of their having assaulted Edward Clough, which was dismissed, although the complainant exhibited marks of ill-usage, his face being covered with plasters.

Bradford Observer, 25 July 1867

ABUSE AND AN ASSAULT. On Thursday, at the West Riding Court, Bradford, William Sunderland was charged by Sagar Wade, a collier, with having assaulted him. Complainant and defendant both live at Thornton, and on Wednesday week the complainant called at the Highfield Inn, a beershop kept by one John Hey, where the defendant was. Soon after he (complainant) had sat down, he was told by another man that if he spoke a word that night he would 'catch it.' 'Happen not,' said the complainant, whereupon the defendant came up to him, 'slapped him in the face,' threw him on the floor, and kicked him; he also jumped upon him with his knees. Mr. Berry, who appeared for the defendant, in cross-examination brought out the facts that the complainant was drunk, and that he had previously on the same night had a row with one 'Sam o' Pegs.' Timothy Butterfield was called as a witness for the defendant, who stated that the complainant was drunk, because he came in scratching his head. Witness also swore that complainant called the defendant a d—d scamp, and a thief, and this was what gave rise to the disturbance. John Hey, the landlord, was also called, who stated that the complainant had had a 'do' at another house that night. This witness concluded his evidence by offering to bet a wager with the bench that his was the most respectable public-house in Thornton. The defendant was fined 2s 6d and costs.

Leeds Mercury, 23 August 1867

SUDDEN DEATH AT WEST SCHOLES, NEAR THORNTON. Mr. Joseph Watson, ironmonger, of Halifax, forty-five years of age, died somewhat suddenly at the house of Henry Metcalfe (better known as 'Harry Mack'), West Scholes, a small place, lying at the bottom of the deep valley between Thornton and Queensbury. Metcalfe is a herbalist, and has the credit amongst the credulous of being able to see further into futurity than most people, and consequently he is visited not only by the ailing in body but also by those are anxious as to their future prospects in life. Although possessed of little book learning, 'Mack' is thought to be profoundly versed in the art and mystery of unravelling the tangled skein which enshrouds humanity, and the desire for a 'peep into the future' is so strong even in the present day, that 'Mack' is said to receive visits from

Gasworks Lane, looking west to Thornton.

persons in all ranks of society, who come long distances to consult this bucolic 'seer,' even as far as the distant hilly region of Settle. What with his herbs and his predictions 'Mack' is reputed by the country people to drive, in more senses than one, a 'strange amount of business.' On Tuesday evening, Mr. Watson called to see 'Mack,' but for what purpose has not transpired, although it is said that he had been engaged in litigation, and had had a great deal of trouble. After Mr. Watson had been in the house a while he was taken ill, and was afterwards seized with a fit, when 'Mack' sent for a medical man, who speedily attended, but, not withstanding everything was done for the unfortunate man, he expired at three o'clock on Wednesday morning.

Leeds Mercury, 1 October 1867

THORNTON MECHANICS' INSTITUTE, NEAR BRADFORD. The thirty-third annual soirée of this society was held on Saturday evening, in the Kipping School-room. The chair was taken by Mr. Arthur Briggs, of Apperley Bridge. The secretary read the report, which showed the success that has attended the efforts of the committee during the past year. They had removed into new premises, consisting of news-room, class-room, and club-room, all of which have been fitted up in a comfortable and substantial manner, and have been well attended. The number of members is 128, showing a large increase; and the number of volumes in the library is 658, which the committee are glad to state is well used. The chairman in his opening remarks drew attention to the syllabus of lectures and entertainments to be given during the coming winter season, and more particularly mentioned that 'On the life of Charlotte Brontë,' by Mrs. Balfour. He was glad to see they had a female class. He also drew attention to the much felt want of better technical education amongst our artisans and working men, and concluded by expressing his opinion that such societies were calculated to do much good; and he hoped that the inhabitants of Thornton would avail themselves of the advantages of their institute, and that it would continue to flourish. The meeting was also addressed by Mr. Byles, the Rev. J. Gregory, and Mr. P. Craven. The speeches were interspersed with singing and music by Miss Wheater, Miss Scholes, and Messrs. Pickles and Northrop. Mr. Moorhouse presided at the pianoforte.

Chapter Seventeen
1868

New reservoir for Thornton – An exhibition of dissolving views – New co-operative butcher forces down meat prices – Man jailed for blacking policeman's eye – Thornton Feast in full swing

Bradford Observer, 9 January 1868

A SOLDIER IN TROUBLE. On Friday, in the Court of the West Riding magistrates, one Greenwood Knapton, a soldier belonging to the 26th Regiment of Foot, and now on furlough in Thornton, was charged by Rowland Varley, a tailor living in that village, with having assaulted him. Mr. Hutchinson appeared for the defence. It appears that on the night of the 21st ult., the complainant, who is a respectable tradesman, had gone to the Black Horse Inn upon business. The defendant was also there, and while sat in the kitchen the defendant began to create a disturbance, and the complainant seeing this suggested his removal, whereupon he was forcibly ejected into the street. The complainant stayed a short time after this, and upon going away he found the defendant at the door outside, who immediately made an attack upon him – striking and kicking him – inflicting serious injuries. The complainant, upon the suggestion of the Bench, agreed to compromise the case with the defendant's friends upon the receipt of 20*s*, and the costs.

Bradford Observer, 9 January 1868

TO CONTRACTORS, WATERWORKS CONTRACT, No. 1. The Thornton Local Board are prepared to receive Tenders for constructing and making watertight a proposed service RESERVOIR, and other Works connected therewith, in their district. Plans and specifications may be seen, and other information obtained, at the office of JAMES LUMLEY, Esq., C.E., 16 Kirkgate, Bradford, from TUESDAY, January 14th, to WEDNESDAY, January 22nd, between the hours of Ten o'clock a. m. and Four p.m. each day. Sealed Tenders, endorsed 'Service Reservoir,' to be sent to me, the undersigned, not later than Four o'clock p.m. on Thursday, January 23rd. No allowance made for Tenders, nor will the Lowest or any be necessarily accepted. WM. COCKREM, Clerk to the Local Board, Thornton, near Bradford, Yorkshire, 1st January, 1868.

Bradford Observer, 16 January 1868

On Friday, in the Court of the West Riding Magistrates, Thomas Wilson, a beerseller at Mountain, Thornton, was summoned upon a charge of having been drunk and riotous, and fined 5s and costs, or fourteen days. At the same time and place Thomas Redman, a barer at Thornton, was charged by Jonas Jowett of the White Horse [sic] beershop, Hill Top, Thornton, with having broken eight squares of glass in his windows on Christmas Day, and for this offence he was fined 10s damages and 8s costs, or fourteen days.

Bradford Observer, 16 January 1868

LOCAL BOARD OF HEALTH. The usual fortnightly meeting of the Local Board for the district of Thornton was held on Friday evening, in the Board-room, in Sapgate Lane, the members present being Messrs. J. Hartley, J. Pickles, J. Lingard, H. Charnock, T. Geldard, J. Corrie, A. Craven, and I. Wood. In the absence of the chairman (Mr. J. Craven) Mr. H. Charnock occupied the chair. After the usual routine business, an application was made for the registry of a slaughterhouse in New Road, belonging to the Co-operative Butchers' Society. The matter was referred to the Sanitary Committee, with a request that they would view the place and report as to its eligibility. Complaint was made of a drain connected with a house belonging to Mr. Priestley Jowett which, it was alleged, was detrimental to health. This case also was transferred to the Sanitary Committee. A conversation took place relative to the desirability of having a new system of drainage for the town, but no resolution was adopted. Cheques were drawn amounting to £41 2s 6d.

Bradford Observer, 16 January 1868

PUBLIC COMPLAINTS. Numerous complaints are made in the village of Thornton as to the limited time that the public water taps are allowed to be open, and also as to the small number of public lamps which are supplied in the streets.

Bradford Observer, 23 January 1868
LEGAL NOTICES

NOTICE IS HEREBY GIVEN that a Separate Building, named THE ATHENÆUM. Situated in Thornton, in the Parish of Bradford, and the County of York, in the district of Bradford, being a building certified according to the law, as a place of religious worship, was on the 15th of January, 1868, duly Registered for SOLEMNIZING MARRIAGES therein, pursuant to the Act of 6th and 7th, William IV, c.85. Witness my hand this 20th of January, 1868. JOHN DARLINGTON, Superintendent Registrar.

Bradford Observer, 23 January 1868
STRANGE TREATMENT OF A BOY. On Monday evening as Frederick, son of Mr. Robinson Ackroyd, a boy only seven years old, was passing down Commercial Street, Thornton, he was met by a tall, rough looking man, whom he did not know, who, after speaking to the boy, threw him in an ashpit at least seven feet deep, and it was with the greatest difficulty that the lad could extricate himself from his perilous position. Nothing has since been heard of the man, and it is a matter of great surprise in the village what could have been his motive in the committal of this strange and unaccountable act.

Bradford Observer, 6 February 1868
THE RECENT STRONG WIND. On Saturday an unusually strong wind blew at Thornton, by which some of the squares in the windows of Kipping Chapel were broken and the ventilators upon the roof damaged; also a beautiful headstone which had been erected in the graveyard, in memory of the late Mr. Thomas Priestley, was blown down and broken to pieces.

Bradford Observer, 6 February 1868
WESLEYAN SCHOOLROOM. On Thursday evening an interesting exhibition of dissolving views was given in the Wesleyan Schoolroom, Thornton, by Mr. Bottomley, photographer, of Bradford, to a crowded audience.

Bradford Observer, 6 February 1868
ENTERTAINMENTS. On Saturday evening an entertainment consisting of addresses, recitations, and music, was given in the Wesleyan Reform Chapel, Mountain, by 'The Egypt Lifeboat Crew.' The leader of the band was Mr. Sutcliffe. Also, a similar entertainment was given the same evening in the schoolroom connected with the Methodist Free Church, Thornton, by 'The Eccleshill Man-of-War Crew,' under the command of Captain Crooker. The programme contained twelve recitations, besides a number of readings and several addresses. The captain and crew appeared in uniform.

Bradford Observer, 13 February 1868

CO-OPERATIVE BUTCHERS' SHOP. The co-operative society which has been established in Thornton for the purpose of carrying in the business of butchering, has this week commenced operations. An agent has been appointed and the shop has been opened.

Bradford Observer, 20 February 1868

A LECTURE. On Tuesday evening the Rev. J.P. Chown, of Bradford, delivered his popular lecture 'the Philosopher's Stone in daily use by all persons' in the Kipping School, at Thornton, to a large audience, under the auspices of the Thornton Mechanics' Institute.

Bradford Observer, 20 February 1868

On Saturday evening, a lecture was delivered at the Athenaeum, under the auspices of the Young Men's Mutual Improvement Society, by Mr. Samuel Hird, one of the members. The subject of the lecture, 'Chemistry,' was aptly illustrated by numerous experiments. The lecturer, who is only a young man and entirely self-taught, exhibited such a knowledge of his subject as much surprised his audience. He is a working man who by his savings has accumulated a considerable number of valuable instruments, by the aid of which he gives his experiments.

Bradford Observer, 5 March 1868

THE BUTCHERS. The establishment of a co-operative butchers' shop at Thornton has resulted in keen competition in that trade, and the price of meat has been considerably reduced. On Saturday beef, best cuts, was selling at 7d per lb, other cuts as low as 4½d, and legs of mutton 5½d per lb. The cattle previous to their being killed are paraded through the streets adorned with blue ribbons.

Bradford Observer, 2 April 1868

CAUTION TO HOUSEKEEPERS. On Saturday, the upper part of the townships of Thornton and Allerton was visited by two men who pretended to be hawking combs, their real object being robbery and plunder. At Spring Holes they entered the house of Mr. James Gaythorpe, during the temporary absence of the family, and took away a watch and guard of the value of £4. At another place, under similar circumstances, they took away 14s 6d out of a drawer in a cottage; and in a house at Upper Green while ransacking the drawers they were pounced on by a neighbour woman, who sent them reeling down the doorstones with more kicks than halfpence. Had information of these depredations been given to the police immediately, there might have been a chance of the felons being apprehended.

Foundation stone at Bell Chapel.

Bradford Observer, 4 June 1868

WHITSUNTIDE HOLIDAYS. In the village of Thornton Whitsuntide holidays are always anticipated with much pleasure and are enjoyed right heartily. On Monday, at about noon, sounds of music were heard at a distance, which came from the band belonging to the Bingley West Riding Volunteers, who were the precursors of a large procession of Ancient Foresters on horseback, dressed in most grotesque forms. They had started that morning from Cullingworth Gate and come by way of Denholme and Well Heads. Most of the horses appeared little accustomed to saddles and bridles, being more like elephants than hacks. After going down the Main Street and up New Road, they halted at the house of Mrs. Jarratt, the New Inn, and after here partaking of lunch they re-formed and proceeded via Wilsden and Harden to the place where they had started, where dinner was provided for the members of the lodge which is held there – lodge 100, 'brotherly love' – held at the New Inn, Thornton, returning to dinner in their own club-room. The number of members in this lodge is stated to be 320. The teachers and scholars belonging to the different Sunday schools on this day celebrated their annual festivities and galas, their proceedings being similar to those of former years, with this exception – the scholars belonging to New Road Congregational Church had this year distributed amongst them an abundant supply of 'spice sticks' which had been manufactured by certain amateur confectioners among the teachers; and the children in the Wesleyan School had given to them a large stock of nuts. These were both in addition to their tea and buns.

Bradford Observer, 4 June 1868

LOCAL BOARD. On Friday evening last, the usual fortnightly meeting of the Local Board for the district of Thornton was held in the board-room in Sapgate Lane, the members present being the Chairman, Messrs. I. Wood, Thomas Geldard, Henry Charnock, James Lingard, Richard James Walton, Jabez Pickles, Abraham Craven, Jonas Hartley, Joseph Corrie, and Thomas Hardy. After the reading of the minutes of the previous meeting, a plan for the erection of out-offices by Mrs. Robinson in Main Street was examined and approved; also plans for the erection of stables at Fawthrop's Hotel beershop were submitted, and it was ordered that the place should be inspected. A long discussion took place relative to the property of parties having crossings in New Road, which is macadamised, and as to whose duty it should be to repair the same, which resulted in a notice of motion to be submitted at the next meeting, viz: 'That all crossings put down for public convenience at the expense of owners of property shall afterwards be kept in repair by the Board.' Cheques were granted for wages, £20 10*s* 2*d*, and in favour of Messrs. Naylor, Bros., for £240, on account of their contract for the new reservoir. This being the last meeting in the official year, the names of retiring members were announced to be Messrs. H. Charnock, R.J. Walton, J. Corrie, and J. Hartley, and as these are the only gentlemen nominated for the ensuing year, the election will fall upon them without a contest. The plan and particulars of the intended sale of building ground were gone over; some alterations were made therein, and the matter was then adjourned for a fortnight.

Bradford Observer, 4 June 1868

ALLEGED ASSAULT UPON A TOWNSHIP OFFICIAL. On Friday, in the Court of the West Riding magistrates, Jonathan Clay, a farmer living in Denholme, was charged by Joseph Robinson, *alias* 'Joe Boggard,' with having assaulted him. Complainant stated that he had lived in Thornton, in which township he sustained the various important offices of bye-law man, pinder, town crier, bill sticker, &c. On Saturday, the 9th inst., having been at Denholme posting bills, he called at the Denholme Gate Hotel, and here he met with the defendant, who began to abuse and insult him for having, in the discharge of his official duties, pushed down a wall which has been put up by him (the defendant). The quarrel was kept up for some time, and at length the complainant, upon going away through a dark room, was followed by the defendant, who, in pushing him about and striking him, had committed serious injury upon him, so that he had been unable to turn himself in his bed since. The complainant here put in a certificate from Mr. Lee, surgeon, which stated the two of his lower ribs had been fractured. David Hainsworth was called by the complainant as a witness, and his evidence being in favour of the defendant, he was denounced as a traitor, and told that he had been bought over by the defendant. For the defence, William Rusbey, the waiter at the inn, and James Smith, a labourer, were called, both of whom swore that the complainant was not followed out by the defendant; all they saw was the defendant striking the table with his 'cudgel;' he never was in the dark room with the complainant. The Bench being of the opinion that it was impossible for the complainant to say who it was that assaulted him if the room was dark, and that he must have made a mistake, dismissed the case.

Bradford Observer, 4 June 1868

NEW ROAD CONGREGATIONAL CHAPEL. The subscriptions for the erection of the New Road Congregational Chapel are being carried on with much energy and success. Mr. Joseph Craven, of London, has recently put down his name for £1000, and has also given a large piece of ground (nearly two acres) as a site for the chapel.

Bradford Observer, 25 June 1868

OPEN-AIR SERVICES. On Sunday two sermons were preached in the open-air at Yews Green, by Mr. W. Bell, of Bradford, in aid of the funds of a Sunday school conducted there. The congregation were large, and the collection amounted to £16 0*s* 10*d*. This is a branch school connected with Kipping Chapel, Thornton. No school-room has yet been erected, the school as well as occasional religious services being held in a cottage.

Bradford Observer, 2 July 1868

NEW ROAD CONGREGATIONAL CHURCH, THORNTON. On SUNDAY NEXT, July 5th, 1868, the Rev. DAVID ARTHUR, of Aberdeen, Will preach in the Morning, and Rev. Wm. M. ARTHUR, M.A., the recently elected pastor of the church, in the Evening. Services to commence at 10.30 a.m. and 6.30 p.m.

Bradford Observer, 2 July 1868

THORNTON. SUDDEN DEATH. Yesterday week, Mr. Medley Leach, of Thornton, was seized with a fit and never spoke afterwards. He lingered until Sunday, and then died. He was in the 77th year of his age.

Bradford Observer, 2 July 1868

THORNTON. Some time ago, before the days of the local boards, Mr. Jonas Craven, of Thornton, was at considerable cost in conveying a stream of water in pipes from a distance to his own house, and now that an unprecedented scarcity of water exists in the village, Mr. Craven throws open his taps at certain hours of the day, and allows the inhabitants generally free access to them. This is a boon which is highly appreciated.

Bradford Observer, 16 July 1868

YORKSHIRE PENNY SAVINGS BANK. On Saturday a demonstration was made in Thornton in connection with the Thornton branch of the Yorkshire Penny Savings Bank. The depositors, 160 in number, met in the National schoolroom about half-past four o'clock, from whence they walked in procession to a field opposite the Friendly Inn, headed by the drum and fife band from Great Horton playing lively airs. Here an hour was spent in amusement and recreation. Afterwards they went to the Athenaeum, where an excellent tea had been provided. In the evening a public meeting was held in the same room, Mr. Parkinson, National schoolmaster, occupying the chair. Mr. F. Craven gave a brief history of the institution, from which it appeared that it was formed in the year 1857, and for several years was carried on in connection with the Mechanics' Institute. A few years ago it was made a branch of the Yorkshire Penny Savings Bank, and since that time its success and beneficial results have increased every year. The institution is now carried on in the National School; its managers being Mr. Thomas Dobson, Mr. John Pollard, and Mr. Sutcliffe. Addresses were delivered by Mr. Alfred Booth, Mr. E. Ackroyd, and also by Mr. Peter Bent and another gentleman, who attended as a deputation from the central branch at Leeds.

Bradford Observer, 16 July 1868

THORNTON. LOCAL BOARD. The usual fortnightly meeting of the Thornton Local Board was held on Friday evening:- present the chairman, Messrs. J. Hartley, T. Hardy, J. Corrie, J. Pickles, R.J. Walton, T. Geldard and T. Wood. After the usual routine business had been transacted application was made for the improvement of the public well at Spring Holes, in consequence of the scarcity of water. After much discussion the matter was referred to the Waterworks Committee to direct such works as they deem fit. A plan for the building of out-offices by Messrs. J. Stephenson & Co., near Sapgate Lane, was approved. A plan for enclosing a piece of ground and building thereon by P. Leach, at Spring Holes, was rejected. A general district rate at 10*d* in the pound was laid, also a highway rate at 1*s* 8*d* in the pound. Complaint was made of the pollution of water by a drain on property belonging to Mr. Thos. Thwaites at Main Street. The Sanitary Committee were instructed to inspect the place. It was ordered that notice be served upon A. Toothill for the removal of a nuisance at The Bricks. Some mortgage deeds were executed by the Board, and cheques were drawn amounting to £254 8*s*.

Bradford Observer, 30 July 1868

THORNTON. KIPPING CHAPEL SUNDAY SCHOOL. The anniversary was held on Sunday. The Rev. Enoch Mellor, M.A., of Halifax, preached two most impressive sermons, morning and evening; and Mr. John Hill, of Bradford, gave an excellent address in the afternoon, to parents, teachers, and scholars. A very large congregation assembled both morning and afternoon, but in the evening the place was packed to the very doors, and not a few were obliged to go away, unable to get even a standing place. The collection amounted to upwards of £146. The people attending the old place of worship are very cordially carrying on their work, with a quiet but strong determination to maintain, and if possible to increase, the efficiency of its agencies.

Bradford Observer, 30 July 1868

THORNTON. ASSAULTING A LANDLORD AND THE POLICE. On Monday, at the West Riding Court, before Messrs. J. Pollard and T. Peel, a man named James Stansfield was brought up on the charge of assaulting Mr. W.W. Harrison, landlord of the Black Bull, Denholme, about twelve o'clock on Saturday night. The prisoner, who was the worse for liquor, was requested by the landlord to leave his house, but he refused and struck the complainant frequently. The complainant's statement was corroborated, and a further charge was then preferred against the prisoner by P.C. Downham. This officer went to the assistance of the complainant, and the prisoner thereupon commenced a violent assault upon him, striking him, kicking him, and giving him a shocking black-eye. There were five previous convictions against the prisoner, and he was now committed for one month to the House of Correction for each assault.

Bradford Observer, 6 August 1868

THORNTON. A CABBY AND HIS FARE. On Monday in the Court of the Borough Magistrates, Mr. Fred Whitley, woolstapler, Green Mount, Thornton, was summoned by John Lee, a cab driver, for 10s, being his fare for taking him from Bradford to Thornton. Complainant stated that on Saturday night, the 25th ult., he was sent for by the defendant to the Pack Horse Inn, Westgate, at about eleven o'clock; after waiting there for some time he drove him to Thornton, having had to wait for him a considerable time at the Girlington Hotel, where he called. When he arrived at Thornton it was 1.5 a.m. The ordinary fare, with the charges for waiting and the after time, would be 9s. The defendant offered 4s and refused to pay any more. The defendant had retained Mr. Terry to defend him, but to no purpose. He was ordered to pay the amount claimed, with 14s costs.

Bradford Observer, 13 August 1868

THORNTON. A STACK FIRED BY A BOY. On Friday night, a hay-stack, the property of Mr. Thos. Silson, a small farmer at Thornton Heights, was discovered to be on fire, and before the flames could be extinguished the stack was entirely consumed. It was afterwards ascertained that a boy named Thos. Dixon, only six years of age, had that afternoon purchased a box of matches at a shop in the neighbourhood, and had set fire to the stack. When the boy's mother was spoken to about it, we are told that she was exceedingly insolent and abusive to the farmer. The value of the stack was £25.

Bradford Observer, 13 August 1868

ANNUAL FEAST. On Tuesday, the village of Thornton was full of excitement and commotion on the occasion of the annual feast. Shows, riding machines, photographic establishments, shooting galleries, nut stalls, bazaars, and all the other etceteras of a village feast were in attendance, and received extensive patronage. The sixteenth annual exhibition of the Thornton Floral and Horticultural Society has been held. The competitors have been numerous, but the show has not been equal to previous years as regards quality, owing to the extreme drought. This was particularly noticeable in gooseberries; notwithstanding there were some good specimens in almost every class. As usual the show was succeeded by a gala.

Thornton Mills and St James's Church.

Bradford Observer, 5 October 1868

A 'STORMY PETREL.' One day last week a man named Knapton, in gathering mushrooms in a field near to Pinch Beck, Thornton, found a stormy petrel. The bird was alive when picked up, and was able to hop about, but it died soon after. It is now in the possession of Mr. Wm. Coldwell of Thornton Hall who, in curing it, found two pellets in the feathers, indicating that it had been shot.

Chapter Eighteen
1869

Man lives with horse in cellar – New street to be named James – Triplets born at Black Carr – People having their bumps felt – Horse cuts its own throat

Bradford Review, 2 January 1869

KIPPING, THORNTON. Christmas-day was one of more than usual interest to the good friends of Kipping. In the morning, the children were regaled with the unwearying fare of buns and tea. In the afternoon, the teachers and friends laid seize [*sic*] to more elaborate provisions, when nearly 500 united in the attack. The meeting and entertainment were (contrary to previous custom) held in the chapel. The success consequent upon the adoption of the plan was so signal as to determine the promoters to hazard the experiment again. The programme consisted of recitations, one of which was graphically rendered by 'young men and maidens,' speeches by the Superintendent, Mr. Jonathan Northrop, Mr. N. Drake, Mr. Joseph Toothill. Mr. James Gregory, jun., Mr. John Wilkinson, Mr. Joseph Andrews, and Mr. Edward Horsfall. 'The centre of the glittering ring' sat the pastor, Rev. J. Gregory, who presided over the meeting. Mr. Joseph Northrop, the secretary, read the report from which it appears that the school numbers 600 scholars.

Bradford Observer, 7 January 1869

THORNTON. THE CHURCH BAZAAR AT THORNTON. By the bazaar which was held last week in the National School, in aid of the fund for rebuilding the church, the sum of £290 has been realised.

Bradford Review, 9 January 1869

CROFT HOUSE SEMINARY, THORNTON, NEAR BRADFORD. The Misses Shaw receive a limited number of resident pupils. Their school duties will be resumed (D.V.) on Tuesday January 19th. An articled pupil required. References kindly permitted to the Revd. F.H. Heap, Incumbent of St. James's; the Revd. James Gregory, Independent Minister; and the Revd. J. Nelson, Wesleyan Minister.

Bradford Observer, 11 January 1869

LOCAL BOARD. On Friday evening the ordinary monthly meeting of the Local Board for the district of Thornton was held in the Board-room, Sapgate Lane, the members present being Mr. Thomas Geldard, Mr. R.J. Walton, Mr. Thos. Hardy, and Mr. Jabez Pickles. In the absence of the chairman, Mr. Walton presided. The usual routine business having been disposed of, a report was given by the Sanitary Committee of their inspection of a cellar adjoining to the new road, in the occupation of one Thomas Greenwood; it was represented as being in a very filthy state, not fit for human habitation, a heap of manure and a horse being kept therein; it was resolved that notice should be given by the clerk to remove the same at once. Complaint was made of a privy adjoining the Woodman Inn, being a nuisance, and the Sanitary Committee were instructed to inspect the same. Certain plans of certain buildings were deposited, which were ordered to lay over until next meeting to allow time for inspection. It was reported that no arrangement had been come to with regard to the projected improvement of the highway at the place called Squirrel, inasmuch as the land is about to be sold. Cheques were drawn amounting to £104 9s 9d. It was agreed that several other matters of business should be allowed to stand over for discussion at a meeting when there should be a fuller attendance.

Bradford Observer, 11 January 1869

THORNTON. AN IMPROVEMENT. The bridge over Pitz [sic] Beck which separates the townships of Allerton and Thornton had long been in a very dilapidated and dangerous state, and it had been made much more so by the recent laying down of the pipes of the Allerton Clayton Gas Company. All danger, however, is now removed, a substantial skew bridge having been constructed. A still further improvement might be effected by the Thornton Local Board by the lowering of the causeway, which is not only narrow, but also runs for some distance upon a considerable elevation from the level of the highway on the Thornton side of the bridge.

Bradford Review, 27 February 1869

CLAYTON, THORNTON AND ALLERTON GAS COMPANY. On Friday week a meeting was held at the Rock Inn, Clayton Heights, to consider the price charged for gas in the district, which is supplied by the Clayton, Thornton and Allerton Gas

Company, and to see if it were possible to agree upon some method of obtaining a reduction. The chair was occupied by Mr. James Leach, of Thornton, who stating [sic] the object of the meeting. The matter was then discussed, some of the speakers stating that they did not consider the gas very good, as well as being high in price. It appeared from the statements which were made that the terms upon which gas is supplied are a payment of 5s per thousand feet, meters being supplied, the use for which 9d per quarter is charged. This charge was compared with that of other companies, and ultimately a resolution was adopted unanimously to the effect that those assembled would pay no more that 4s per thousand for gas and 6d per quarter for the use of the meter.

Bradford Observer, 11 March 1869

LOCAL BOARD. On Friday night the usual fortnightly meeting of the Local Board for the district of Thornton was held in the Board-room in Sapgate Lane, the members present being Mr. Abm. Craven, Mr. R. Sellers, Mr. Tho. Geldard, Mr. R.J. Walton, Mr. J. Lingard, Mr. H. Charnock, Mr. J. Pickles, and Mr. J. Corrie. Mr. Walton was called to the chair and, after the usual routine business had been gone through, a plan which had been deposited by Mr. A. Binns, for the erection of a paraffin warehouse at Mountain, was examined and approved. Plans which had been deposited by the Messrs. Peel Brothers & Co. for the erection of a block of houses upon the Upper Kipping estate were disapproved, the drainage not being shown. A long discussion took place relative to the place which had been prepared for a new street, to be called James Street, to extend from the New Road to the waterworks reservoir which is proposed to be built by Messrs. Peel Brothers & Co. The question to be decided was as to whether or not the sewerage from Hill Top should be taken down the new street. It was ultimately agreed to appoint a deputation from the Board to meet the owners of the property relative thereto. Cheques were drawn amounting to £119 6s 10d. Some discussion took place touching certain chemical works having commenced near to the coal pits in the New Road, and it was agreed that the owners thereof should be required to furnish the Board with plans.

Bradford Review, 27 March 1869

THORNTON. A TRIPLE BIRTH. The other day, Sarah, the wife of Mr. John Ambler, contractor, living at Black Carr, gave birth to three living children – all boys.

Bradford Observer Supplement, 1 April 1869

ALLERTON. CRUELTY TO A HORSE. On Monday, at the Court of the West Riding Magistrates at Bradford, Thomas Robertshaw, living at Thornton, was charged with using cruelty to a horse belonging to Robert Dalby, farmer, of Crossley Hall, Allerton. It appears that on the 20th instant Miss Dalby heard a noise in her brother's stable, and upon giving an intimation to this effect to her brother, he went there and found the defendant, who had hold of the horse's tongue and was beating the animal on the head with a hame. Under the tongue it was found there had been a cut in a longitudinal line, and it was much swollen; and upon the facts of the case coming to the ears of the police, on Tuesday, Inspector Hey, of the West Riding Constabulary Force, along with Mr. Hodgson, Borough Inspector of Cabs, went to the farm, taking with them Mr. Carter, veterinary surgeon, Bradford, and they found the horse's tongue in a bad state. The defendant was fined 40*s* and costs, £3 3*s* 10*d*, with the alternative of two months' imprisonment. The money was paid.

Bradford Review, 24 April 1869

PHRENOLOGY. During the past week a course of lectures has been delivered in the National School, Thornton, by Professor Graham, the author and practical phrenologist, of Birkenhead, on 'Man, or how to improve the social and moral condition of the people.' The lecturer showed that a great amount of the ignorance, crime, and misery might be averted if the science of phrenology was more understood and practically applied. He denounced the use, moderate or otherwise, of intoxicating drinks, snuffing, and tobacco, as detrimental to the physical and intellectual progress of man. A number of person of both sexes, who were nominated from the meeting, were examined publicly at the close of the lectures. The delineations of character were pronounced to be accurate by the parties themselves. The lectures were illustrated by upwards [of] 200 diagrams of noted characters, and were listened to with interest and thoughtful attention. Mr. Graham was heartily thanked for his humourous, instructive, and practical lectures.

Bradford Observer Supplement, 29 April 1869

THORNTON. ACTION TO RECOVER FOR ASSAULT. On Friday, at the Bradford County Court, before Mr. W.T.S. Daniel, judge, John Briggs, farmer, Thornton, sought to recover damages for injuries sustained by him through an assault committed on him by John Firth, brewer, of Thornton. Mr. Terry appeared for the plaintiff, and Mr. Berry defended. From Mr. Terry's statement and the plaintiff's evidence, it appeared that on the 5th day of February, the parties were at the West Schole Gate beerhouse, at Thornton, along with the defendant's father-in-law. Firth and his father-in-law got to high words, and then to fighting, and the defendant assaulted the old man. Plaintiff interfered to prevent mischief, and then the defendant turned on him, challenged him to fight, knocked him down, and beat him on the face and body. His face was black for a fortnight after, and he was unable to attend to his work for that time. He had also suffered from a pain in his side. In cross-examination, the plaintiff admitted that he was 'rather fresh' at the time the affair took place, and that his own cousin pulled him off the defendant; but he denied that he had ever struck him. A witness, named Cushworth, was called for the plaintiff, who stated in cross-examination that Briggs got hold of the defendant and held him against the wall before the defendant touched him at all. The judge observed that the plaintiff appeared to have been the worse for liquor, and that he committed the first assault. Another witness, named Sugden, gave evidence similar to that of Cushworth, and then his Honour remarked that the case amounted to this, – that there had been a fight, and the plaintiff got the worst of it. He therefore gave a verdict for the defendant.

Bradford Review, 10 June 1869

THORNTON LOCAL BOARD. On Friday evening, the annual meeting of the Local Board for the district of Thornton was held in the board-room, Sapgate-lane, the members present being – Mr. Thomas Geldard, Mr. R.J. Walton, Mr. I. Wood, Mr. Henry Charnock, Mr. James Lingard, Mr. Abraham Craven, Mr. Joseph Corrie, Mr. Thomas Hardy, and Mr. Jabez Pickles. The results of the contested election, which has just taken place, was found to be as follows:- Mr. Isaac Wood, Upper Headley, 291; Mr. Joseph Craven, Ashfield, spinner and manufacturer, 239; Mr. Thomas Hardy, School Green, corn miller, 107; Mr. Jabez Pickles, Hill Top, gentleman, 153; Mr. Francis Craven, Kipping House, manufacturer, 119; Mr. Wm. Wood, Headley, farmer, 105; Mr. Edwin E. Rawson, West House, surgeon, 81; Mr. William Bunting, Prospect House, manufacturer, 78; Mr. Jon. Northrop, Ball Street, manufacturer, 64; Mr. George Townend, Woodlands Cottage, manufacturer, 63; Mr. Jos. Sunderland, New Road, tailor, 43; and Mr. John Northrop, Springfield, manufacturer, 35. There being five vacancies, including the one caused by the death of the late Mr. Jonas Hartley, the five first-names, who had the greatest number of votes, were declared duly elected, and they made the usual declaration. It was then moved and seconded, in complimentary terms, that Mr. Joseph Craven, of Ashfield, should be appointed chairman for the year. The resolution was carried unanimously, with much applause. In the absence of the chairman elect, Mr. Walton was called upon to preside. The resolutions of the last ordinary and special meetings were read and confirmed. The several committees for the year were then appointed as follows:- Waterworks Committee; John Craven, J. Wood, T. Geldard, H. Charnock, R.J. Walton, A. Craven, and J. Pickles. Sanitary Committee; J. Corrie, R. Sellers, Francis Craven, J. Pickles, T. Hardy, R.J. Walton, and Thomas Geldard. Building Committee; Francis Craven, T. Geldard, Jabez Pickles, A. Craven and T. Hardy. Lamp Committee; H. Charnock, R.J. Walton, R. Sellers, J. Pickles, T, Hardy, and J. Corrie. Plans for the erection of four cottages by John Broadhead, at Spring Holes, were approved; and cheques drawn amounting to £60 6s. It was ordered that a sewer be constructed from West House to the Pinfold.

Bradford Observer, 18 June 1869

THORNTON. A Disorderly Beerhouse. Yesterday in the court of the West Riding magistrates before Mr. H.W. Ripley, Mr. G. Anderton and Captain Pollard, Jonas Butterfield, who keeps the Union beerhouse in Thornton, was summoned on a charge of harbouring disorderly company. P.S. Duncan, who preferred the charges, stated that he visited the house on Saturday night after eleven o'clock, and found there several females, who had been known in Bradford as disreputable characters. There were also men in company with them. The house, continued the complainant, was one of the very worst class, and many complaints having been made respecting it, he had more than once given a caution to the defendant. The defendant was convicted in the full penalty of £5 and costs, with the alternative of two month's imprisonment.

Bradford Observer, 1 July 1869

DRAWING AND SPINNING MANAGER WANTED, a thoroughly qualified MAN to fill the above position. To a person of character and experience in the preparation and spinning of long wools a liberal salary will be given, and none other need apply. All communications will be treated in entire confidence, and must be made to JOSHUA CRAVEN & SON, Prospect Mill, Thornton.

Bradford Observer, 2 July 1869

UNLICENSED DOGS. Yesterday, in the West Riding Court, Bradford, Jonathan Northrop, of Ball Street, Thornton, was summoned by the excise officers upon a charge of keeping a dog for which he had no licence. The officer, who was called to prove the charge, stated that when he saw Mrs. Northrop at Thornton, she stated that the licence was in the possession of her husband, at his warehouse in Bradford; and when he saw the defendant, he said it was in the care of his wife at Thornton. At length, however, an admission was made that he had not taken a licence out. The defendant was represented in Court by Mr. Terry, whose excuse for his client was excess of business and consequent forgetfulness. Northrop was fined 50s, including costs. Robert Cundall, of Leventhorpe Mill, for a similar offence, was mulcted in the same sum.

Bradford Review, 3 July 1869

THE PASTORATE AT KIPPING. Mr. Frederick Hall, of Airedale College, has accepted the cordial and unanimous invitation of the Church assembling at Kipping, Thornton, near Bradford, to become co-pastor with and successor to the Rev. Jas. Gregory.

Bradford Observer, 6 July 1869

NOTICE.- Mr. Jonathan Northrop, of the firm of J. Northrop & Co., shawl manufacturers, Thornton, wishes to state that he is not the Jonathan Northrop lately fined for keeping a dog without licence, and inserts this notice to prevent further inquiries. *Advt.*

Bradford Observer, 6 August 1869

THORNTON. AN ASSAULT BY A 'KING.' Yesterday, at the Court of the West Riding Magistrates, at Bradford, Wm. Smith, of Thornton, who is styled 'King of Wellheads,' was charged by John Farrar, alias 'Mustard John,' a very old man, with having assaulted him. It appears that on the day named complainant, in passing in his road, met the defendant, who gave him a blow on the head with his fist. The complainant remonstrated with him, telling him that he had often struck him inside his house, but he would not be struck outside, not even by 'a king.' The defendant, who denied the charges, was fined 5*s*, and 10*s* 6*d* costs.

Bradford Weekly Telegraph, 7 August 1869

Local and District News. SCARLETINA is very prevalent and fatal in Thornton at present.

Bradford Review, 14 August 1869

A HORSE CUTTING ITS OWN THROAT. On Sunday a fatal accident happened to a valuable horse belonging to Dr. Lee, of Thornton. It appears that the animal was grazing in a field, at the top of which stands a shed which is covered with thick glass. The roof of the shed is level with the field, and the horse having stepped upon the roof of the shed fell through, and when discovered it was found dead, its windpipe having been cut through by the glass.

Bradford Weekly Telegraph, 28 August 1869

Local and District News. THOS. GODDY, of Thornton, and James Cunliffe, of Bradford, were, at Bradford West Riding Court, on Thursday, fined £1 5*s* and 12*s* 6*d* costs and 1*s* damages each, for having trespassed in a wheat field at Allerton.

Bradford Weekly Telegraph, 4 September 1869

Local and District News. FATAL ACCIDENT IN THE HOLLING COAL PIT. On Monday morning, the 23rd inst. [*sic*], an explosion of gas occurred in the Hollings coal pit at Denholme which resulted in the death of Thomas Tidswell, the deputy underground viewer. Tidswell, it appeared, had gone down the pit at six o'clock for the purpose of making the customary examination before the men were allowed to go down. When he was going along the windgate with a light, a quantity of gas was ignited and he was much scorched. He was able to go home, and was attended by Dr. Rawson of Thornton, and after lingering until Monday last he died. Deceased was fifty-six years of age.

Bradford Weekly Telegraph, 25 September 1869

Local and District News. JONAS HEY, an old man about ninety-two years of age, was found lying dead at the foot of the cellar steps of the house he lived in at Thornton, on Monday.

Bradford Weekly Telegraph, 2 October 1869

Local and District News. A PUBLIC tea and meeting was held in the Wesleyan Chapel, Thornton, in recognition of the Rev. Edward Salt, the new pastor. There was a good audience, and several interesting addresses were delivered. The proceedings are to go to the circuit fund.

Bradford Weekly Telegraph, 2 October 1869

Local and District News. MR. ISAAC WOOD, farmer, Thornton, was on Friday presented with a silver pint jug, subscribed by the smaller ratepayers of the parish as a mark of their appreciation of the manner in which he has for many years discharged various public duties in connection with the parish.

Bradford Observer, 15 October 1869

SHOOTING GAME WITHOUT A CERTIFICATE AT THORNTON. Yesterday, at the Court of the West Riding Magistrates, at Bradford, Ingham Mitchell, a farmer living at Foreside, Thornton, was summoned for shooting game, he having no game certificate. Elizabeth Hall, who was the only witness, stated that she was the wife of John Hall, who is game watcher under Sir Henry Edwards. On Friday, the 8th inst., she saw the defendant in his own field shoot a grouse and kill it. The bird flew about thirty yards, and then it fell dead in the field. Witness never saw the defendant take the bird away. The defendant called Joseph Fielding, a farmer living near to him, who said he heard the report of a gun on the day in question; was sure the gun was not fired by the defendant, he being with him at the time. This being all the evidence, Mr. Ball submitted to the Bench a list of previous convictions, and the defendant was fined £5, with the alternative of two months.

Leeds Mercury, 19 October 1869

SOIRÉE OF THE THORNTON MECHANICS' INSTITUTE. The annual soirée of this Institute was held on Saturday evening in Kipping New School-room. Mr. Councillor A. Holden was in the chair, and he expressed his sympathy with that and kindred institutions generally, and his pleasure in knowing that it was in a flourishing condition. The report showed that last year there were 100 members, 16 subscribers, and 4 life members, total 120; but there were now on the books 117 male members, 33 females, 25 subscribers, and 5 life members, making up a total of 180, and being an increase of 60. The volumes in the library were 810, being an increase of 170 volumes; the issues of the year were 1,608, showing an increase of 378 on the past year. 24 members attended the female class, conducted gratuitously by Miss Pearson, and the average was over 15; but, owing to the schoolmasters in the village being engaged, classes could not be formed for the male members. Although the question of a new building had been laid aside it was hoped, as there was a want of increased accommodation, that the difficulty of obtaining a suitable site would be surmounted. The financial statement showed that there was a balance of £1 7s 6½d due to the treasurer. Addresses were delivered by Mr. A. Illingworth, M.P., Mr. W. Robertshaw (Allerton), Mr. W.P. Byles, and Mr. A. Briggs. A musical party from Bradford, composed of Miss Myers, Mrs. Lincey-Nalton, Mr. Pickles, and Mr. Wood, with Mr. G. Hirst at the piano, performed several selections of music, which were warmly received, and several encored. The usual complimentary votes closed the proceedings.

Bradford Weekly Telegraph, 4 December 1869

Local and District News. A carter named Joseph Broadhead, living at Thornton Heights, was, at the Bradford Borough Court on Friday, fined 5s and costs for having been drunk while in charge of two horses in Bridge Street on Wednesday last.

Bradford Observer, 14 December 1869

At the Bradford Borough Police Court, yesterday, James Robertson, a quarryman, living at Thornton, was sentenced to three calendar months' imprisonment for assaulting a little girl called Mary Ann Clinton.

Bradford Observer, 18 December 1869

ALLEGED FRAUD AT THORNTON. Yesterday, at the Bradford Borough Court, William Kay, of Southfield Square, commission agent, was brought before Alderman Law, having been apprehended by warrant on the charge of having, 'by means of a certain false pretence, obtained from one Thomas Dawson, a certain valuable security of the value of £16, with intent to defraud.' Mr. J.H. Wade, who appeared for the prosecution, applied to have the case remanded, and Mr. Robinson, for the prisoner, concurred in the application. No statement of the charge was made, and no evidence was called; but we understand it is alleged that the prisoner, as the officer of a South Lancashire Building Society, which has a branch in Thornton, obtained possession of a number of depositors' cards, under the pretext that it was necessary to send them to the headquarters of the society, and afterwards received from depositors various sums of money, for which he gave informal receipts on separate slips of paper. These sums he is charged with having appropriated to his own use. On the question of bail Mr. Wade observed that, if granted, it ought to be of a very substantial character, as, according to his instructions, the defalcations complained of would amount to a very large sum – probably a thousand pounds. In answer to Alderman Law, the Chief Constable stated that Kay had been imprisoned for some months in York Castle as a fraudulent bankrupt. Alderman Law said that under the circumstances he felt constrained to fix the bail at a high amount. The prisoner would be released from custody on entering into his own recognisances in the sum of £500, and finding two sureties of £500 each. The case was then remanded until Wednesday next.

Bradford Observer, 20 December 1869

ACCIDENT AT ALLERTON. On Saturday morning, a melancholy accident happened at the worsted mill belonging to Messrs. Holmes, Robertshaw & Co., at Allerton. A young woman named Rose Ann Rennard, living at Churn Milk Row, Thornton, while engaged in attending to a preparing box for woolcombing, got her hand entangled in that part of the machine called the fallers. She uttered a loud scream, and some one who was near, seeing the position the poor girl was in, instantly stopped the machine by throwing off the belt, but the girl was still held fast by the hand, the fallers, which contain a number of teeth or pins, having penetrated to their full length. Fortunately, however, Mr. Holmes, one of the

Grocery shop at the corner of Market Street and Ball Street, 1913.

partners in the firm was in the room at the time, and he, understanding the nature of the machine, proceeded at once to take it to pieces, and thus the girl was released. A cab was then procured by Mr. Holmes, who took her to the Bradford Infirmary, where the numerous wounds made upon her hand and arm by the teeth were properly dressed by the house surgeon, and she was afterwards taken home in a cab. Credit is due to Mr. Holmes for the care and attention which he exhibited towards the poor girl in her misfortune. Had not the machine been stopped when it was the consequences would have been much more serious.

No Rennards were in the 1861 census for Thornton but by 1871 there was a John Reynard (census reference RG 4488 ED 1 Schedule 108), aged forty-seven, woolsorter, born in Rushworth, with his wife Mary Ann, aged forty-six, born in Thornthwaite, and their seven children, of whom the oldest was Rose Ann, aged nineteen and a worsted weaver, who had been born in Bradford. The next five children were born in Ripley, but the four-year-old youngest girl was born in Thornton. This family was at Lowtown, which is on Leaventhorpe Lane between Leventhorpe Hall and the Leventhorpe mills. Was Churn Milk Row therefore part of Lowtown?

Chapter Nineteen
1870-1871

Thornton prospering in textiles and quarries – Craven treats 500 workers – Earl of Ripon to lay church foundation stone – Fourteen year old whipped for purse stealing – A female burglar

Bradford Observer, 24 January 1870

THE PROJECTED NEW CHURCH AT THORNTON. A few weeks ago, we stated that the building committee in connection with the proposed new church at Thornton had selected as the site for the building a piece of ground near to the place called Green Mount, at the entrance to the village. It appears that in order to carry out this decision, it was necessary that a joiner's shop should be pulled down, and the deputation which had been appointed to wait upon the owner thereof, in order to treat for the same, have found it impossible to do so, owing to the sum required for it. The committee have therefore rescinded their former resolution, and have finally determined that the new church shall be erected directly opposite the old one, on the north side of the new road, and Messrs. Healey, architects, have received instructions to prepare plans and specifications, and to advertise for tenders for the works.

Bradford Observer, 24 January 1870

LOCAL BOARD AT THORNTON. On Friday evening, the usual fortnightly meeting of the Local Board for the district of Thornton was held in the Board-room, Sapgate Lane, the members present being Mr. J. Craven (chairman), Mr. R.J.

Walton, Mr. J. Lingard, Mr. Abraham Craven, Mr. Thomas Hardy and Mr. Jabez Pickles. After the usual routine business had been gone through, a notice was directed to be served upon the representatives of the late Jonas Robinson to remove an alleged nuisance caused by depositing ashes and refuse at Backfield. The Clerk was also directed to serve a notice upon Robinson Driver and Sarah Driver for the removal of an alleged nuisance in Canada, caused by an ashpit. A third notice was ordered to be served upon Mr. Benjamin Robinson, requiring him to provide proper drainage to his beerhouse, by the new road. Complaint was made of the injury done to the road at Egypt by the water coming from a drain at the Rock and Heifer Inn. It was also stated that the public were not sufficiently protected from accidents in passing the quarries; and after some conversation in reference thereto, a deputation from the Board was appointed to inspect the place and report to the next meeting. The consideration of the Aire and Calder Conservancy Bill was resumed, and the general opinion of the Board appeared to be that the Government ought to be parties to bring in such a measure, and that the Board should decline to take any action in opposition thereto further than an expression of opinion, believing that the Bill will be withdrawn by the promoters. A cheque was drawn for £54 7s 6d.

Bradford Observer, 22 February 1870

IMPROVEMENTS IN THORNTON. The village of Thornton has for some time back enjoyed much prosperity. The mills and manufacturers have been in full operation, and we are told that hands are now becoming scarce. The quarry owners and the stone merchants, too, are having a good run of business, and as one of the results of this briskness of trade, buildings have been springing up in various parts of the township. But the improvements which have been effected, and the increase of population which has taken place, is most apparent in the village itself. Here numbers of new streets have already been formed, new mill sheds have been erected, the streets are now lighted with gas, and there is a good water supply. A new church is about to be built, advertisements for the tenders of contractors having been issued. The erection of a new Congregational Chapel is already in progress, and the new Mechanics' Institute project is being promoted vigorously and with every prospect of success. The site has been selected, and three architects are competing in the preparations of plans. In addition to these buildings, we are informed that during the ensuing spring the erection of a new weaving shed and at least 150 cottages will be commenced.

Bradford Observer, 7 March 1870

FESTIVITIES AT THORNTON. On Friday, Mr. Joshua Craven, junr, of the firm of Messrs. J. Craven and Sons, manufacturers, attained his majority; that day, being the weekly pay day, each of the employés, from the manager down to the short-timer, 500 in number, on the receipt of his or her wages, was presented with a handsome gratuity, varying in amount according to the position of the recipient, and in the evening they all sat down to a substantial knife and fork tea, which had been provided for them in the New and Old Kipping School-rooms. After tea they adjourned to a spacious room at the works, which had been fitted up for the occasion, and here they enjoyed themselves in various ways for several hours. Dancing was evidently the favourite amusement, the music being rendered by the Thornton Brass Band. At one stage of the proceedings, Mr. Thomas Laycock called for three cheers for the Messrs. J. Craven and Sons, which were heartily given, with one cheer more; and Mr. Joshua Craven, junr., in responding, expressed the pleasure which it afforded him to be with then on that joyous occasion. He hoped that the good feeling and the mutual goodwill, which had so long existed among them would be perpetuated, and it would ever be his aim to do everything he could in promoting the welfare and the happiness of those by whom he was surrounded. Mr. Joshua Craven, senr., said he was proud of his grandson, and it was a gratification to him to see the day that he attained his majority. He hoped that he would be blest with a long and useful life. Mr. Joseph Craven spoke in eulogistic terms of the workpeople. The firm, he said, had during the last thirty years become extensively known, and he attributed this in a great measure to the character of their workpeople. He then proceeded to give those present some wholesome advice as to the future, recommending them all to live holy and useful lives. We may state that on this festive occasion no intoxicating drinks were allowed, pure water, lemonade, and other teetotal beverages being used. Twelve hundred oranges were distributed during the evening.

Bradford Observer, 7 March 1870

NOTICE IS HEREBY GIVEN, that the Partnership subsisting between us the undersigned, WILLIAM SMITH, JOSEPH SOUTHWART, ALFRED SOUTHWART, and JOHN JOWETT, as Stone Merchants, at Thornton, in the parish of Bradford, in the county of York, under the Firm of 'Southwart, Smith & Co.' has been this day Dissolved by mutual consent, so far as regards the said William Smith only; and all Debts owing to or by the said Firm, will be received and paid by the said Joseph Southwart, Alfred Southwart, and John Jowett, who will continue to carry on business as Stone Merchants in co-partnership, at Thornton aforesaid, under the Firm of 'Southwart & Jowett.' The said William Smith will henceforth carry on business on his own account at the Quarry at Egypt, in Thornton aforesaid. Dated this Fifth day of March One thousand eight hundred and seventy. WILLIAM SMITH
JOSEPH SOUTHWART
ALFRED SOUTHWART JOHN JOWETT
Witnesses to all the Signatures:- H.F. Killick, Solicitor, Bradford. J.W. Moore, Solicitor, Bradford.

Bradford Observer, 4 October 1870

ALLEGED THEFT BY A BOY AT DENHOLME. Yesterday, at the West Riding Court, Bradford, a young boy named James Coventry was charged with stealing a purse containing 7s 8d, the property of James Binns, of Denholme. About five weeks ago the boy went to Denholme in a destitute state, after coming from Liverpool. He was charitably taken in, and work was found for him by the prosecutor. On the 2nd inst., however, he ran away, and took with him a purse containing the amount named, belonging to Binns's wife. Information was given to the police, and Sergeant Duncan traced the lad to Halifax. After searching about the various streets, he met with the prisoner in South Parade and took him into custody. The prisoner was remanded till Thursday next.

Bradford Observer, 5 October 1870

We understand that the corner stone of the new church at Thornton is to be laid with Masonic honours, by the Right Hon. Earl de Grey and Ripon, on the 26th inst.

Bradford Observer, 7 October 1870

A BOY STEALING A PURSE AND MONEY AT DENHOLME. Yesterday, at the West Riding Court, a boy, fourteen years of age, named James Coventry, was charged on remand, with having at Denholme stolen a purse containing 7s 8d, the property of James Binns. The particulars of the case appeared in our Tuesday's impression. The lad was now sentenced to be well whipped in the area of the Court House, and afterwards to be handed over to the care of his mother, who was in court.

Bradford Observer, 17 October 1870

ACCIDENT TO A BOY AT THORNTON. On Friday evening an accident happened to a boy named Sebert Tidswell, son of Thomas Tidswell, a collier, at Thornton. The father had been to purchase a quantity of blasting powder, which he required to use at his work the following day. He incautiously placed the package, which contained three ounces, on a table in the house. Almost immediately he went out, leaving the boy alone in the house. Having ascertained what the package contained, he placed it on the hearth, and, applying to it a piece of blazing paper, the powder exploded, and the lad was shockingly burnt in different parts of his body. Dr. Rowson [*sic*], surgeon, was immediately sent for, and applied such remedies as were necessary. The boy is now likely to recover.

Bradford Observer, 24 October 1870

ACCIDENTAL DEATH AT THORNTON. On Friday a fatal accident happened to a child named Ellen Borwick, about two years old, the daughter of John Borwick, a weaver living at Canada in Thornton. It appears that the mother, having lifted a pan of boiling water from the fire, and placed it on a chair, left the house for a minute or two, and during her absence the child got hold of the pan and pulled it off the chair, spilling all the water upon herself. She was shockingly scalded. Mr. Cogan, surgeon, was called in, but his services were of no avail as the child died on Saturday morning.

Bradford Observer, 25 October 1870

THE NEW CHURCH AT THORNTON: MASONIC CEREMONY. On Wednesday the memorial stone of St. James's Church will be laid with Masonic ceremonial. Earl de Grey and Ripon, Grand Master of the Freemasons of England, and Provincial Grand Master of West Yorks., taking the chief part. A Provincial Grand Lodge will be opened in the Kipping school-room, which will be kindly lent by the Congregationalists. It is expected that there will be a numerous attendance, brethren being present from all parts of the province. After the opening of the Grand Lodge, the memorial stone will be laid, its place in the new edifice being just at the opening of the chancel. The vessels for corn, oil, and wine will be brought down from London by the Grand Tyler of the Grand Lodge of England; and he will also have charge of the historical mallet (the property of the Lodge of Antiquity, No. 2), used by King Charles the Second at the laying of the foundation stone of St. Paul's Cathedral, when he presided at that ceremony. It is known as 'Sir Chris. Wren's mallet.' The trowel to be used, which will be presented to Lord de Grey and Ripon, is a very beautiful piece of workmanship, and will be on view all day at the establishment of Manoah Rhodes & Son, Westgate. It is of silver gilt; and the design is an elegant one. Towards the point of the trowel his lordship's arms are engraved, and below the arms the following inscription:- 'This silver gilt trowel to be presented to the Right Honourable the Earl de Grey and Ripon, Viscount Goderich, Baron Grantham, and a baronet, Lord President of Her Majesty's Council, Knight of the most noble Order of the Garter, and Grand Master of the ancient, free and accepted Masons of England, on the occasion of the laying of the memorial stone of the church of St. James, Thornton, near Bradford, October 26th 1870.' After the ceremony the brethren will return to St. George's Hall, Bradford, where there will be a banquet.

Bradford Observer, 20 December 1870

A BAZAAR in aid of the Funds of the New Road Church, will be held in the ATHENAEUM, THORNTON, on MONDAY, December 26th, 1870, and two following days. The Bazaar will be opened each day from Three p.m. to Ten p.m. Admission: On Monday, 1s; Tuesday and Wednesday, from Three to Six o'clock, 6d; after Six o'clock, 3d. Season Tickets for Bazaar, 1s 6d. N.B. Omnibuses will run on the 26th, 27th, and 28th from the New Inn, Bradford, for the Bazaar, leaving at 2.30 and 5.30, returning at 4.0 and 9.30 p.m.

Bradford Observer, 20 January 1871

A FEMALE BURGLAR AT THORNTON. Yesterday, in the West Riding Court, Bradford, before Mr. J. Pollard, Mr. G. Anderton, Mr. H.W. Ripley and Captain Pollard, a woman who gave the name of Eliza Jane Walker was charged under the following circumstances:- Alfred Southwart stated that he was a stone merchant at Thornton. On Tuesday night he went to bed at about eleven o'clock, having previously locked the door and made all safe. At about half-past one he was awoke by the continuous barking of his dog, and upon getting up and going downstairs, he found the prisoner attempting to secrete herself in the kitchen. He then sent for P.C. Duncan, and gave her into custody. It was afterwards ascertained that the prisoner had affected an entrance at the cellar grate. After this evidence, Mr. Ball applied that the prisoner might be remanded, intimating that he might be able to prefer other charges against her. She was therefore remanded until Monday.

Bradford Observer, 30 January 1871

THE SCHOOL BOARD QUESTION AT THORNTON. On Saturday evening a public meeting was held in the Foresters' Hall, Denholme, in the township of Thornton, which was one of a series of meetings now being held with a view to the establishment of a school board for that township. There was a good attendance. The Chair was occupied by the Rev. E. Salt, Wesleyan minister. The Chairman, after having briefly stated the object of the meeting, introduced Mr. Joshua Craven, jun., who spoke at some length and with considerable ability in explanation of the various clauses of the Education Act. He showed the great need that existed in Thornton for additional educational facilities. He also answered a number of objections which were raised against the establishment of a school board. At the close of Mr. Craven's address the meeting was thrown open for discussion. Various questions were put by Messrs. Moor, Pickles, Illingworth, Hy. Foster, and others, both of a general and local bearing, to which replies were given, after which a resolution was submitted by Mr. W. Atkinson to the effect that it would be advisable to establish a school board. The motion was seconded by Mr. Joseph Illingworth. Several amendments were proposed; and at length it was agreed that the meeting should be adjourned to that night fortnight, for the further consideration of the matter.

Bradford Observer, 3 April 1871

THORNTON LOCAL BOARD. On Friday evening last, an ordinary fortnightly meeting of the Local Board of Health for the district of Thornton was held, the members in attendance being Messrs. Henry Charnock, Isaac Wood, James Lingard, Francis Craven, Jabez Pickles, and John Hill. Mr. Craven presided. A plan by Mr. David Pickard for the erection of some outbuildings at Hill Top was approved. Complaint was made that serious damage was being done to the road leading from Queensbury to Denholme Gate by the laying down of water mains belonging to the Bradford Corporation, the road being left in a slovenly state after the work had been executed. The Clerk was instructed to communicate with the contractor, and require him forthwith to reinstate the whole length of the road which had been used. A complaint was also made of the bad state of the road in Mill Lane, caused by the servants of the Bradford Corporation making excavations to repair damage to the water mains. The Clerk was directed to write to the Bradford Corporation calling their attention to the matter. A petition to Parliament in favour of the Bradford and Thornton Railway Bill was signed, and the seal of the Board was affixed thereto. Cheques were drawn amounting in the aggregate to £136 11*s.*

Bradford Observer, 6 April 1871

OPENING SERVICES GOOD FRIDAY, NEW ROAD
CONGREGATIONAL CHURCH, THORNTON. The OPENING
SERVICES of this church will take place as follows:-
On FRIDAY, April 7th, the Rev. E. MELLOR, D.D., Halifax, will preach
in the Morning; and the Rev. A. HANNAY, London, in the Evening.
Services commence at 11.0 a.m. and 6.0 p.m.. On Sunday, April 9th, the
Rev. J.G. Rogers, B.A., London, will preach Morning and Evening. On
Sunday, April 16th, the Rev. Professor SCOTT. LL.B., Manchester, will
preach Morning and Evening. On Sunday, April 23rd, the Rev. R. Tuck,
B.A., Bradford, will preach in the Morning; and the Rev. J.R.
CAMPBELL, D.D., Bradford, in the Evening. Services to commence each
Sunday at 10.30 a.m. and at 6.30 p.m.. Collections in aid of the Building
Fund will be made at the close of each of these Services.

Bradford Observer, 8 April 1871

NEW CONGREGATIONAL CHAPEL AT THORNTON. Yesterday, a beautiful new chapel, which has been erected by the Congregationalists, was opened at Thornton. The position in which it stands is a pleasant and most advantageous one – being on the north side of the new road near to Kipping Lane. Here the ground gradually rises, and the building has been placed at a distance of about fifty to sixty yards from the road. The architectural style of the chapel is the early decorated Gothic. It has three entrances in the front and over the central one are three double-light windows, which are of geometrical tracery of bold design. At the south east angle of the building stands a tower, containing a staircase to the gallery – provision being made for a spire, and a corresponding staircase in the form of a porch or transept. The sides of the chapel are much enlivened by two large three-light windows, with traceried heads, surmounted by gables. There are also three two-light windows, with traceried heads, of elegant design. The Building Committee, it seems, unfortunately have not yet seen their way to the erection of the spire, which would have added much to the beauty of the design; it is intended to be built 115 feet high. The tower, which has only been carried a portion of that height, has been covered in with lead. The length of the building inside, including vestibules, is 90 feet, and the width is 40 feet. The galleries are supported by eight iron columns carried up to the roof, which is formed in the centre by carved ribs, and rises at the crown to the height of 35 feet, leaving a sufficient space above the ceiling for ventilation. The organ chamber is placed on the east side, and forms a small transept. Corresponding with this is a vestry and transept on the west side. The organ chamber and the vestry are divided from the chancel by a finely decorated open screen. At the north or chancel end of the building there is a lofty arch, opening into an apex, which is paved with encaustic tiles. The windows are filled with finely fluted glass, which softens the sun's rays, and in this manner serves the purpose of blinds. The pews are open benches, made of pitch pine and stained. The pulpit, which is erected in the chapel, corresponds with the other fittings, both in the material of which it is made and the design. A powerful organ is placed in the organ chamber. It was bought in Liverpool at a cost of £270. The instrument contains forty stops, with three manuals and pedals, and has until recently been used in the Rev. Stowell Brown's Chapel, Liverpool. Its original cost was £800. The chapel with its galleries affords accommodation for 650. The total cost of the building is £3205, exclusive of the ground, and the completion of the spire is estimated to cost £300. The site upon which the building has been erected was given by Mr. Joseph Craven, of Clapham, who supplemented the gift by a donation of £1000. Other subscriptions were given, amounting in the aggregate to £750; proceeds of a bazaar, £180; leaving a deficiency of £1275. A cheque for £50 has been remitted by Sir Titus Salt, Bart., in aid of the collections at the opening services. The architects are Messrs. Andrews & Pepper, Bradford; and the contractors are Messrs. Drake & Son, stone masons; Mr. J. Shepherd, carpenter and joiner; Mr. C. Nelson, plumber; Mr. B. Dixon, plasterer; Mr. T. Nelson, slater; Mr. H. Briggs, painter; Messrs. Haley, ironfounders, all of Bradford. The heating apparatus has been supplied by Mr. Thos. Milner, Hillside, Bradford. The opening services (as previously stated) were commenced yesterday morning. There was a large and influential congregation, including many of the ministers and other leading gentlemen from the neighbouring towns. The service was commenced by the Rev. W.M. Arthur, the minister of the place, who, after the singing of the hymn, 'Light up this house with glory, Lord,' &c, offered up a prayer and read suitable portions of scripture.

The sermon, which was a most elaborate discourse, was given by the Rev. E. Mellor, D.D., of Halifax. The collection was then made. Another sermon was preached in the evening by the Rev. A. Hannay, of London. The opening services will be continued tomorrow (Sunday).

Bradford Observer, 1 May 1871

On Friday evening, an ordinary meeting of the Thornton Local Board was held, the members present being Mr. John Hill, Mr. Jabez Pickles, Mr. Henry Charnock, and Mr. G.G. Rawson. The chair was occupied by Mr. Charnock. The following plans were submitted, examined, and approved, namely:- a plan for the erection of farm buildings, at Hill Top, by Mr. Robert Appleyard; a plan for the erection of some outbuildings at Pearson Place, adjoining the new road, by Messrs. D. & J. Craven; a plan for the building of a house and grocer's shop, by Mr. Benjamin Wilkinson at Hill Top. It was agreed that orders should be given for 560 tons of limestone, and 200 tons of dross, for the repair of the roads during the ensuing year, and that a number of handbills should be issued by the Clerk inviting tenders for the leading of the same from Bradford. Some alarm having been caused in the district owing to a strange dog, supposed to be mad, having been ranging about the neighbourhood, it was resolved that application should be made to the magistrates to issue a notice requiring all dogs to be confined from the 1st day of May to the 1st day of November next. Cheques were drawn in payment of accounts amounting to £129 2s 4d.

Bradford Observer, 4 May 1871

Freehold Property at Stream Head, near Thornton, in the parish of Bradford, in the county of York. By Mr. ROBERT SUTCLIFFE, at the Pack Horse Inn, Westgate, Bradford, on *Thursday the 18th day of May,* 1871, at Five (for Six) o'clock in the Evening, precisely, subject to such conditions as will be then and there produced, and read.

The following FREEHOLD PROPERTY, in two Lots, namely:-

Lot 1. All that small and compact MILK FARM, situate at Stream Head, near Dean Lane, between Thornton and Wilsden, in the parish of Bradford aforesaid, called Stream Head Farm, comprising a good four-roomed dwelling-house, outbuildings, cottage, and about eleven acres of pasture and meadowland enclosed in a ring fence.

Lot 2. All that small and compact MILK FARM, adjoining Lot 1, called Hessle Crook Farm, comprising a good two-roomed dwelling-house, outbuildings, and about eight acres of pasture and meadow land enclosed in a ring fence.

The property is situated about three quarters of a mile from the villages of Thornton and Wilsden, and about four miles from the town of

Bradford. It can be inspected on application to Mr. Joseph Pollard, the present occupier of both Lots. For further particulars apply to the AUCTIONEER at his Offices in Market Street, Bradford; or at the offices of Messieurs RAWSON, GEORGE & WADE, Solicitors, Kirkgate, Bradford.

Bradford Observer, 9 May 1871

THORNTON SCHOOL BOARD. The attempts which have been made at Thornton to avoid a contest in the election of a School Board have been unsuccessful. Fifteen persons have been nominated, the number required being seven. The poll has been fixed to take place on Friday, the 19th inst. The following are the names of those nominated:- William Atkinson, painter and glazier, Denholme Lane; Henry Charnock Travis, farmer, Thornton; Wm. Clapham, farmer and wheelwright, Denholme Lane; David Craven, shawl manufacturer, Close Head, Thornton; Joshua Craven, the younger, worsted spinner and manufacturer, Ashfield, Thornton; Wm. Margerison, relieving officer, School Green, Thornton; Henry Edward Foster, manufacturer's clerk, New Road, Denholme; Wm. Pickles, waste dealer, Wicken, Thornton; Midgley Priestley, stone merchant, School Ridge, Thornton; Edwin Elsworth Rawson, surgeon, West House, Thornton; Joseph Shackleton, draper, Thornton; John Sutcliffe, manufacturer, Salt Pie, Thornton; Isaac Wood, farmer, Headley, Thornton; and George Townend, manufacturer, Woodlands, Thornton. The excitement on the subject appears to be increasing, and a smart contest is likely to take place,

Bradford Observer, 19 May 1871

KIPPING SUNDAY SCHOOL ANNIVERSARY, THORNTON. On Sunday, May 21st, 1871, SERMONS will be Preached, Morning and Evening, by the Rev. CHARLES VINCE, of Birmingham; an ADDRESS to the Scholars in the Afternoon by Mr. A.S. WARD, of Bradford. Services to commence at 10.30, 2.30 and 6.30.

Bradford Observer, 15 June 1871

Thornton near Bradford, Valuable Freehold Building land, By Mr. JOSHUA ROBERTSHAW, AT THE Bull's Head Inn, in Thornton, in the parish of Bradford, on *Friday the 30th day of June*, 1871, at Six for Seven o'clock in the Evening, precisely, subject to such conditions as shall be then and there produced, and in one Lot, A Valuable PLOT of BUILDING LAND, situate and adjoining the Thornton Reservoir and James Street, on the west side of the village of Thornton, containing 969 square yards or thereabouts. The land is situate on an incline sloping to the south, and commands a picturesque view of the surrounding

Leaventhorpe Inn: landlord and family.

country. For further particulars, apply at the Office of the Thornton Local Board, where a plan may be seen. By Order, WM. COCKREM, Clerk to the said Local Board. Thornton June 12th, 1871.

Bradford Observer, 19 September 1871

NEW ROAD (THORNTON) IMPROVEMENT SOCIETY. The members of a friends of the New Road Congregational Young Men's Mutual Improvement Society, Thornton, met at tea in the Athenaeum on Saturday last. After tea an entertainment was given by the members of the society, the programme consisting of glees, songs, and readings. It was supported by Messrs. J. Moore, P. Leach, W. Harper, F. Horsfall, and others. The chair was occupied by the president, Mr. Nathan Driver, who in his address referred briefly to the progress of the class, and hoped many more would join it. The report showed that at the commencement of the class they had twelve members, seven have been added since, six have left, leaving thirteen still on the books; average attendance, eleven. The entertainment lasted two hours and a half. At the close a vote of thanks was given to the chairman and the performers.

Leeds Mercury, 17 October 1871

THORNTON (BRADFORD) MECHANICS' INSTITUTE. The annual soirée of the members and friends of this institute was held on Saturday evening, in Kipping school room, Thornton, preceded by tea in the new institute. Mr. Councillor Briggs Priestley (Bradford) presided. A report, read by Mr. S. Drake, showed that the numbers had increased by 87, numbering 298, compared with 211 in the previous year. 74 persons attended the classes, 30 males and 44 females. The issues from the library were 2,429 compared with 1,912 in the previous year. The news and club room had been well attended, but the lectures were not so successful in point of numbers in attendance, although they left a profit of 18s 6d. The receipts were £111 10s 1½d, and the expenditure £105 10s ½d, leaving a balance of £6 0s 1d. The efficient aid rendered by the voluntary teachers was acknowledged. The prizes were presented, after an address from the Chairman, and Mr. C. Pollard, late secretary, received a writing desk and a cabinet atlas for his exertions on behalf of the institute. Addresses were delivered by Mr. W. Pickles, Rev. J. Gregory, Mr. S. Smith (Keighley), and by Mr. J. Craven, jun., the latter stating that there was a deficit of £400 or £500, but after what had been done in the past he had no fear of its being cleared off in two years or less. When the incubus was removed, they might proceed to the erection of a commodious lecture hall. The evening's entertainment was enhanced by the performances of a musical party, consisting of Miss Amy Empsall (Mrs. Eckersley), and Mr. Thornton Wood, with Mr. Moorhouse at the pianoforte. The attendance was large, and the customary vote of thanks closed the proceedings.

Chapter Twenty
1872-1876

Insufficient wagons at new railway station — Liberal Club established — Vet dies suddenly — James Street School opens — Billiards and bagatelle for the poor

Bradford Observer, 3 February 1872

BRADFORD AND THORNTON CARRYING COMPANY. A general meeting of the Bradford and Thornton Carrying Company (Limited) was held in the company's office yesterday, Mr. Francis Craven chairman. No financial report was presented, inasmuch as the company has only been a short time in operation; but a favourable account was given of the traffic, which was stated to be gradually increasing. A satisfactory statement was made as to the working of the road steamer. It was stated that the company had been obliged to decline several large orders owing to a want of wagons, and it was resolved to purchase more. The former directors of the company have been re-elected, and an auditor appointed. Mr. John Littlewood, for many years in the employment of the London and North-Western Railway Company, was appointed traffic manager.

Bradford Observer, 18 March 1872

PERFORMANCE OF THE 'MESSIAH' AT THORNTON. On Saturday evening, this grand oratorio was given with great effect in the Methodist Free Church, Thornton. The performance was promoted by the ladies of the congregation, in augmentation of the funds of a bazaar to be held at Easter for clearing the debt of £300 on the place, and we are glad to announce that financially as well as musically it was successful, the chapel being filled. The band and chorus numbered 100 performers, including many members of the Bradford Festival Choral Society, the principals being Misses Baldwin and Broadbent, soprano and contralto, and Messrs. Illingworth and Rawnsley, tenor and bass, with Mr. Robertshaw at the organ, and Mr. Southwart, conductor. Of the instrumentation it is enough to say that it was under the leadership of Mr. Scholey, and was one of the chief features of the performance. The tenor solos were carefully sung by Mr. Illingworth, especially the recit and air, 'Comfort ye' and 'Every valley;' he, however, lacked energy in 'Thou shalt break them.' His voice is of pure quality and well adapted for sacred music. Mr. Rawnsley's efforts seemed to be well appreciated by the audience. His voice is a little rough, but his delivery and enunciation might be copied with advantage by some bassos of greater pretensions. He was especially successful in 'But who may abide,' 'The people that walked,' and 'Why do the nation,' the latter being delivered with great vigour. 'The trumpet shall sound' was spoiled by the trumpet accompaniment. Of the lady principals, Miss Baldwin showed a little unsteadiness in her first aria 'Rejoice greatly,' but improved considerably, and rendered very nicely 'Come unto Him,' 'But thou didst' and 'I know that my Redeemer,' the latter being her best effort. Miss Baldwin exhibits considerable sympathy in her singing, but would be improved by a more distinct enunciation. Miss Broadbent's best airs were 'He shall feed' and 'He was despised,' the accompaniment to the latter being very tasteful. In the choruses, however, lay the great strength of the performance. The trebles were somewhat weak; apart from this, the fine body of tone and admirable precision were all that could be desired. As the various choruses were uniformly good, it is needless to enumerate separately; we must, however, name 'For unto me' and 'Lift up your heads' as especially fine. We believe the whole of the performers gave their services gratuitously, and the ladies' committee must be congratulated on having been able by such kindness to give a performance perhaps never surpassed in Thornton.

Bradford Observer, 21 March 1872

THE BANKRUPTCY ACT 1869. In the County Court of Yorkshire, holden at Bradford of JONATHAN NORTHROP, of Thornton, in the county of York; SAMUEL TETLEY, the younger, of Bradford aforesaid; WILLIAM HARRISON TETLEY, of Bradford, and GEORGE HERRING WARD, of Wakefield, in the said county, Manufacturers, co-partners, carrying on business at Bradford aforesaid and at Mill Holme, near Skipton, in the said county, under the style or firm of 'J. Northrop & Co.', Bankrupts. An Order of Discharge was granted to Jonathan Northrop, of Thornton, in the county of York; Samuel Tetley, the younger, of Bradford aforesaid; William Harrison Tetley, of Bradford, and George Herring Ward, of Wakefield in the said county, and to each and every of them who was adjudicated bankrupt on the 10th day of October 1871.

GEO.ROBINSON, Registrar.

TERRY & ROBINSON. }

JAMES GREEN. } Attorneys for the said Registrar.

Bradford Observer, 26 March 1872

BOARD SCHOOL AT THORNTON. We understand that the two schools recently established by the Thornton School Board have exceeded the expectations of that body in the number of scholars who have voluntarily joined. Although established but three weeks ago, there are 170 scholars on the books in the girls' school, and a somewhat lesser number in the boys', both schools having passed the self-supporting point. The schools are held in the Wesleyan Reform and Kipping schoolrooms, a temporary arrangement during the erection of proper buildings, and are superintended by a committee of non-members appointed by the School Board.

Bradford Observer, 26 March 1872

THORNTON LIBERAL CLUB. The inauguration of this club took place on Saturday evening, and proved a very successful and enjoyable effort. A substantial Yorkshire tea was first served in the Athenaeum, of which over 100 partook, and at the meeting afterwards there was a large attendance. The club is not yet in full operation. Rooms, however, have been taken, which will be comfortably furnished and supplied with newspapers, &c., and reference library. Officers have been appointed – Mr. Francis Craven being president, and Mr. David Craven, secretary. Although the club is but thus in embryo, some fifty persons have already signified their desire to become members, and this number will be much increased. After tea, Mr. Joseph Craven (Ashfield) took the chair and gave an elaborate sketch of the work to be done by a Liberal Club, and expressed the hope and belief that his ideal would be realised in the one they had met to inaugurate. The meeting was also addressed by Mr. Robert Kell, who advised the Liberal party to still hold aloft the flag under which so many conquests had already been obtained – 'Peace, retrenchment, and reform' – by Mr. J. Raffles, of Birmingham, who pointed to his own town as an example of what might be done by organisation; by Mr. Alfred Illingworth, M.P.; Mr. John Hill, of Bradford; Mr. William Pickles, and others. A very earnest and hearty feeling pervaded the entire proceedings. We understand that Mr. Holden's Thornton committee have paid the whole of the expenses incurred in the recent contest.

Leeds Mercury, 9 April 1872

To be SOLD by AUCTION, *At the House of Joseph Greenwood, Innholder in Thornton, near Bradford, on Monday the 22ᵈ of April inst., betwixt the Hours of Two and Four in the Afternoon, subject to such Conditions as shall be there produced,*

The Following Freehold Estates, of Mr. RICHARD STOCKS, a Bankrupt, and late in his own Possession:

Lot I. A FARM, at *Denholme Clough*, in Thornton aforesaid, consisting of a new-erected Messuage, Barn and 9 Acres of Land thereto belonging, together with the Benefit of a Lease of 7 Acres of Land lying near to the said Messuage, during the Remainder of a Term of 21 Years, granted to the said Mr. Stocks by the Trustees of Thornton School, at a small annual Rent.

Lot II. A Close adjoining on the South-side of the Lane leading between the Town of Thornton, and Denholme-Clough, containing 3 Acres.

Lot III. A Farm at Thornton aforesaid, called *Malt Kiln*, consisting of a new-erected Messuage, Cottage, Barn, and 11 Days Work of Land contiguous thereto.

Joseph Rushworth, who lives at Denholme Clough, will shew the Premises there, and Abraham Butterfield, who lives at Malt Kiln, will shew the Premises there. N.B. Lot II will be put up with Lot I, if more agreeable to the Company at the Time of Sale.

Also, To be SOLD by AUCTION.

At the House of Mr. Newsome, in Guiseley, on Friday, the 19th of April inst., between the Hours of Two and Four in the Afternoon, subject to such Conditions as shall be there produced,

Four Closes, situate at Yeadon, near Guiseley, called *Ley Fields*, containing by Estimation 10 Days Work, and late in the Possession of the said Mr. Stocks – Mr. David Long, of Yeadon, will shew these Closes.

For further Particulars enquire of Mr. John Balme, of Horton, near Bradford, or Mr. Wm. Smith, of Bradford, Assignees of the said Bankrupt's Estate and Effects.

Bradford Observer, 18 April 1872

Marriages: CRAVEN-FOSTER. April 17, at St. Paul's Church, Denholme, by the Right Rev. Bishop Bryan D.D., Vicar of Bradford, assisted by the Rev. M.J. Wilkinson, M.A., Vicar of Denholme, Alice, fourth daughter of the late Henry

Foster, Esq., of Denholme, to Joshua, son of Joseph Craven, Esq., of Ashfield, Thornton.

Bradford Observer, 22 April 1872

SUDDEN DEATH AT THORNTON. On Friday last an aged man named Jonas Wilman, of Main Street, Thornton, well known as a cattle doctor, died very suddenly in his own home. Deceased had not been well lately, but followed his occupation. On the day named, however, he kept the house while his family were absent, and was found dead in a chair on the return of one of them, having apparently been dead some time. It is supposed he had broken a blood vessel.

Bradford Observer, 23 April 1872

MARRIAGE CELEBRATION AT THORNTON. On Saturday the workpeople of Messrs. Francis Craven & Co. were treated to a trip to Morecambe, in celebration of the marriage of Mr. Joshua Craven, jun.. The excursionists, to the number of some hundreds, including Mr. Craven's Sunday school class, the committee of the Mechanics' Institute, and other invited friends, were conveyed to Bradford by conveyance, and accompanied by the Thornton brass band, left the station soon after seven o'clock. On arriving at their destination, the numerous company disposed of themselves according to inclination until dinner time, when the adult male employés were entertained at dinner at the Queen Hotel, the females and young people being provided for in other ways. A sumptuous dinner was also served at the North Western Hotel for the heads of the firm and the chief guests, at each of which place the best wishes were expressed for the future happiness of the newly-married pair. The excursionists returned in good time, grateful for the opportunity afforded them of an early visit to the sea. In the afternoon the aged and young persons, and those not desirous of joining the excursionists, were entertained for tea in the Mechanics' Institute.

Bradford Observer, 11 June 1872

On Wednesday last four children of John Hindle, a poor man belonging to Thornton, in the parish of Bradford, attended the Infirmary at Leeds, to which they were recommended by Mr. Barnard. The patients have been dumb (and of course deaf) from infancy, and upon inspection by the faculty, they were deemed incurable.

Leeds Mercury, 9 April 1873

THORNTON (BRADFORD) MECHANICS' INSTITUTE. Efforts are being made to clear off the debt of £400 on the new building erected in 1870. A tea party and meeting was held on Saturday evening with this object. The meeting, which was held in Kipping New School, was presided over by Mr. Joseph Craven.

The attendance was large. Resolutions were agreed to expressive of thankfulness for the commodious premises that had been provided for educational and literary purposes, and urging the claims of the Institute to general support. Addresses were delivered by Mr. W. Pickles, Mr. J. Craven, jun., Mr. D. Sharp, Mr. J. Northrop, and others. The chairman offered to give £1 for every £5 raised towards reducing the debt. A musical party enlivened the proceedings.

Bradford Observer, 12 August 1873

SALE OF PROPERTY AT THORNTON. Last night, Mr. Buckley Sharp offered for sale at the Commercial Inn, Bradford, a quantity of land situated at Thornton, being a portion of the estate of the late Miss Teal, of Shipley. There was a very large attendance. Mr. Sharp in describing the property said that there were good beds of stone underneath the land. The first lot comprised two closes of grass land situated at Bell Dean in Thornton and contained, with parts of Upper and Lower Heights Roads, 13,611 square yards. The first offer was 6*d* per yard, and after some rather sluggish bidding the sale was declared open at 1*s* per yard, and, finally, the lot was knocked down to Mr. W. Moulson at 1*s* 0½*d* per yard. Lot two, a similar piece of grass land, measuring 10,728 yards, was withdrawn at the reserve price. The third lot was a farmhouse, in the occupation of Mr. Thomas Leach, with barns, stable, mistal, and other outbuildings, and two closes of grass land. The total area was 3 acres 2 roods and 7 poles. The first bid was £300, and after a rather sharp competition it was knocked down for £565 to Mr. William Watson, Bradford.

Leeds Mercury, 27 December 1873

THORNTON SCHOOL BOARD – KEELHAM SCHOOL. To BUILDERS – Persons willing to give TENDERS for the various WORKS required in the ERECTION of SCHOOL BUILDINGS, MASTER'S HOUSE, and BOUNDARY WALLING, at Denholme Clough, may see the plans and obtain bills of quantities at our offices, from Wednesday, the 24th inst., to Wednesday the 31st inst., on which latter day sealed tenders, endorsed 'Keelham School,' are to be delivered to us, not later than noon.- By Order. MILNES and FRANCE, Architects. Bradford, Dec. 22nd, 1873.

Leeds Mercury, 19 November 1874

NEW BOARD SCHOOL AT THORNTON (BRADFORD). The School Board of Thornton have engaged in the erection of three schools, one at Thornton for 400 children, another at Denholme for 400, and the third at Denholme Clough for 180. The new school at Thornton was opened on Saturday, and although computed to accommodate 400 scholars, yet at the Government estimate there is room for 557. The school buildings, plain and unpretentious, are built in James-street, Thornton, from the designs of Messrs. Andrews and Pepper, architects,

Bradford, at a total cost, inclusive of land, of £4,177. Warming and ventilation have had due attention, and there are roomy playgrounds, both open and covered, 2,581 yards being devoted to this purpose. A master's house is placed at one corner of the buildings. The school was opened on Saturday afternoon by Mr. Joshua Craven, jun., chairman of the board, and there were also present Mr. W.E. Glyde, chairman of the Bradford School Board, and others. The children who had attended the temporary school were subsequently examined in the new place by Mr. Tapp (master), Mrs. Brown (schoolmistress), and Miss King, who has charge of the infants. Tea was afterwards served in the Methodist Free Church Schoolroom, and a meeting was subsequently held in Kipping New Schoolroom, Mr. J. Craven, jun., presiding. Addresses were delivered by the Chairman, who thought the board was exonerated from the charge of reckless or extravagant expenditure, and they had provided a most efficient teaching staff; and by Mr. Glyde, Mr. W.E. Foster, of Denholme, Mr. W. Pickles, and others.

Bradford Observer, 7 January 1875

NOTICE IS HEREBY GIVEN that the Partnership heretofore subsisting between us, the undersigned David Jennings, Nathan Jennings, and Richardson Jennings, as Stone Merchants, at Thornton in the parish of Bradford, in the county of York, or elsewhere, under the style or firm of 'N. Jennings & Bros.' or under any other style or firm, has been this day Dissolved by mutual consent, and that all debts due or owing to or by the late firm will be received or paid by the said Nathan Jennings. The said David Jennings and Richardson Jennings will henceforth carry on the business of Stone Merchants at Moscow, Thornton aforesaid, in co-partnership, under the style or firm of 'R. & D. Jennings.' The said Nathan Jennings will henceforth carry on the business of a Stone Merchant at Storr Heights, Thornton aforesaid, in his own name and on his own account. Dated the Fifth day of January, 1875. DAVID JENNINGS NATHAN JENNINGS RICHARDSON JENNINGS Witness – J.W. Moore, Solicitor, Bradford.

Leeds Mercury, 22 May 1875

Died:- GREGORY.- May 18th, at his residence, 17, Apsley-crescent, Bradford, aged 71 years, the Rev. James Gregory, late minister of Kipping Chapel, Thornton.

Leeds Mercury, 20 October 1875

Portraits of the late Rev. James Gregory, one of the founders of the Thornton (Bradford) Mechanics' Institution, and of Mr. Joshua Craven, who died at the early age of 25, when president of the institution, have been subscribed for, and placed in the building. The portraits are in oil, enlarged from photographs taken by Mr. Albert Sachs, of Bradford, and have been executed with great care.

Bradford Observer, 14 April 1876

A CHILD SERIOUSLY BURNT AT THORNTON. On Wednesday afternoon, Sarah Harriet Simpson, a girl twelve years of age, living with her father at No. 12, Pinchbeck, Thornton, was sitting asleep in front of the kitchen fire when her clothes became ignited. She rushed screaming into the street, and the flames were extinguished by some of the neighbours. The girl, however, had received severe burns, and had to be removed to the Bradford Infirmary.

Bradford Observer, 1 July 1876

To be Sold by Auction. Thornton.

Valuable Freehold Property in Thornton. By Mr. J. Ackroyd, at the house of Mr. William Bennett, the Black Horse Inn, Thornton, in the parish of Bradford, in the county of York, on Tuesday the 4th day of July, 1876, at Seven o'clock in the Evening precisely, subject to such conditions of sale as shall be then produced. All that Freehold MESSUAGE and Dwelling-house, with the garden, yard, and outbuildings thereto belonging, situate at the junction of Knowles Street, in Thornton aforesaid, with the public highway leading from Thornton to Well Heads; which said premises comprise in the whole (including a moiety co-extensive therewith of Knowles Street aforesaid) an area of 270 square yards or thereabouts (be the same more or less), and are now in the occupation of Mrs. Hannah Foster. The Dwelling-house, which is well and substantially built, contains ample cellaring, sitting room and a good kitchen on the ground floor, and two good bed-rooms over. It is in good repair, supplied with gas, and pleasantly situated within a few minutes' walk of the intended railway station at Thornton. The completion of the line of railway from Bradford to Thornton is sure to enhance the value of the property at the latter place, hence the present affords an opportunity not often occurring of securing a desirable investment there. For further particulars apply to the AUCTIONEER, at his Offices, Haworth; or to J.W. MOORE, Solicitor, Bradford.

June 23rd, 1876.

Bradford Observer, 17 July 1876

THORNTON ENDOWED SCHOOL. TO BE LET, the several works required in the Erection of new SCHOOLS and Master's House at Thornton, near Bradford. Plans and specifications may be seen and Bills of Quantities obtained at our Offices, Tyrell Street, from THURSDAY, 20th inst., to THURSDAY, 27th Inst., on which latter day Tenders are to be delivered to us. The lowest of any Tender will not necessarily be accepted. T.H. HEALEY, F. HEALEY Architects. Bradford 12th July, 1876.

Bradford Observer, 27 July 1876

THE ACCIDENT AT THORNTON. The little boy, Edwin Burkitt, who was run over by a stone waggon at Thornton, on Monday evening last, died at the Bradford Infirmary at half-past seven o'clock yesterday morning. The child had sustained a compound fracture of the right thigh, and his right arm was so dreadfully mangled that it was found necessary to amputate it soon after his admission to the Infirmary.

Bradford Observer, 12 August 1876

THORNTON UNITED CRICKET CLUB. CRICKET MATCH, GALA, and ATHLETIC SPORTS. On Tuesday August 15th 1876. THORNTON UNITED v. NEW WORTLEY, with Mr. H. LOCKWOOD. Wickets pitched at 10.30 a.m.. Several valuable Prizes will be competed for at the Gala. Admission:- Cricket Match and Gala 4d; Gala only 3d. See Bills.

Bradford Observer, 16 August 1876
CRICKET. SATURDAY'S MATCHES

THORNTON v. BOWLING OLD LANE. Played at Thornton, and resulted in a victory for Bowling Old Lane, with six wickets to fall. Score:-

Thornton. Bowling Old Lane.

H. Green c Parkinson b Gascoigne 1 W.C. Dixon b J. Smith 17

G. Smith b Gascoigne 4 W. Parkinson c Robinson

b. J. Smith 0

W. Jennings run out 2 M. Hillas b J. Smith 1

J. Smith b Yewdall 0 J. Long c G. Smith

b. J. Smith 4

F. Robinson run out 3 J.H. Yewdall not out 3

F. Craven c Long b Gascoigne 5 W. Beaumont not out 7

N. Appleyard b Yewdall 4

J. Broadbent c Denison b Yewdall 5 To bat – M. Crowther,

J. Barstow b Gascoigne 2 T. Denison,

T. H. Leach b Gascoigne 1 J. Robinson,

C. Illingworth not out 2 J. Blakey,

J. Gascoigne.

Extras:- 11 Extras:- 9

Total 40 Total for 4 wickets 41

Bradford Observer, 16 August 1876

BRADFORD AND THORNTON RAILWAY. CAUTION. The Police have strict orders to TAKE INTO CUSTODY any persons found Trespassing on these Works, or carrying away any material therefrom. By Order. Messrs. BENTON & WOODIWISS.

Bradford Observer, 17 August 1876

THORNTON FLOWER SHOW. The twenty-fourth exhibition held by the Thornton Floral Society took place on Tuesday last, in a field lent for the occasion by Messrs. Peel Brothers. The show is open to competitors residing within three miles of Thornton, but apparently excited little competition amongst local exhibitors, of plants especially. There was, however, an excellent collection of stove and greenhouse plants contributed by Mr. Joseph Fox, of Lidget Green, to which an extra prize of £4 was awarded. The attendance was upon the whole considered good, seeing that in an adjoining field a cricket match and gala was being held, got up by the Thornton Cricket Club. The present being 'Tide week' at Thornton offers some explanation why two events like those named should be held upon the same day, but in future it might be well to avoid a recurrence of the circumstance. The Thornton brass band was in attendance, and a gala, comprising a race for a silver cup, closed the proceedings. The following is a list of the principal prize-takers in the various departments:-

PLANTS. Six stove and greenhouse plants, Joseph Fox, Lidget Green; 2. Mr. Cuthbert, gardener to Mr. Joseph Craven, Ashfield. Three fuchsias, Messrs. Jennings & Broadhead; 2. Joseph Robinson. Three calceolarias, Joseph Robinson. Three geraniums, Mr. Cuthbert. Light and dark liliums, Jennings & Broadhead. Society's prize for best three cottager's plants, Joseph Robinson; 2. Jennings & Broadhead. Best rose, fuchsia, and verbena, Joseph Robinson. Best miniature garden, Joseph Hardy; 2. E. Harper; 3. Thomas Jennings. Best arranged cottage garden, Fred. Drake; 2. Wm. Butterfield; 3. James Drake.

CUT FLOWERS. Six dahlias, Mr. Cuthbert. Eight roses, Jonas Gawthorp; 2. E. Harper. Six pansies, J. Robinson; 2. Jennings & Broadhead. Hand bouquet, Joseph Robinson; 2. Mr. Cuthbert. Stocks, marigolds, asters and verbenas were successfully shown by John Hey, Miles Mitchell, and Joseph Robinson.

FRUIT. Dish of strawberries and raspberries, M. Mitchell. Dish of yellow and white gooseberries, black and red currants, Mr. Cuthbert. Dish of apples, gooseberries, red and white currants, Jonas Gawthorp. Two dishes of gooseberries, John Hey. Apples, John Hey. Black currants, Mr. Cuthbert. Red and white currants, Jonas Gawthorp. Raspberries and strawberries, M. Mitchell. Heaviest gooseberry, Thomas Bairstow, for Leveller, 17dwts, 20 grs.* Steward's prize, Jonas Gawthorp. Twins, A. Drake, 24 dwts, 4grs.*

VEGETABLES. Society's prize for tray of six varieties, Mr. Cuthbert; 2. J. Robinson; 3. M. Mitchell. Other prize-winners in vegetables were Joseph Robinson, Miles Mitchell, Jennings, Broadbent, and A. Drake.

* 1 Troy pennyweight (dwt) = 24 Troy grains (gr).

Black Dyke Quarry.

Bradford Observer, 19 August 1876

To the OVERSEERS of the Poor in the township of THORNTON in the parish of Bradford in the West Riding of Yorkshire, and to GEORGE BALL, Superintendent of the Police of the said Riding, and to all whom it may concern. I, JOSEPH ROBERTSHAW, of New Road, in the township of Thornton, in the said Riding, do hereby give notice that it is my intention to apply at the General Annual Licensing Meeting for the Licensing District of the East Morley Division, in the said West Riding, on the Twelfth day of September next ensuing, for a LICENCE TO KEEP A PUBLIC BILLIARD TABLE and BAGATELLE BOARD at the House, Shop, and Premises situate in New Road, in the township of Thornton, in the said Riding. Given under my hand this Twentieth day of July, 1876. JOSEPH ROBERTSHAW.

Chapter Twenty-One
1877-1879

Shoplifter steals beef — Mr Craven bankrupt again — Albert Street property owner ordered to construct new sewer — Thornton passenger railway station opens for business — Omnibus driver killed by own wagon

Bradford Observer, 2 January 1877
LOCAL POLICE INTELLIGENCE. WEST RIDING COURT – MONDAY
(Before Mr. JOSHUA POLLARD, Mr. J.V. GODWIN, and Mr. W. FOSTER.)
IMPUDENT ROBBERY FROM A BUTCHER'S SHOP
John Whitaker, labourer, Thornton, was charged with stealing 6lbs of beef, the property of James Pearson, butcher, Thornton, on Saturday night. From the evidence of the prosecutor, it seemed that on the night in question prisoner went into his shop and purchased half-a-pound of sausages. After he had left, prosecutor missed a piece of meat, weighing 6lbs, which had been bought by another person, and left till called for. Prosecutor went in pursuit of the prisoner, and found him at the Bull's Head Inn, with the meat in his possession. Prisoner, who pleaded guilty, was sent to prison for one month, with hard labour.

Bradford Observer, 6 January 1877

Great Northern Hotel, Lower Headley, Thornton.

By Mr. THOMAS SUNDERLAND, who has received instructions from Mr. Henry Hallam, Sub-Contractor on the Bradford and Thornton Railway, to Sell by Auction, on Monday, the *8th January 1877.*

THE Whole of the Valuable DRAUGHT HORSES, Carts, Pigs, Furniture, &c., comprising:-

One Grey Draught Horse, 'Charley,' 15 hands; a very good worker.

One Brown Draught Horse, 16 hands 1 inch; a very powerful animal, suitable for any draught purposes.

One Bay Mare, rising 6 years; suitable for any kind of work.

One Patent-armed Cart, nearly new; Broad-wheeled Cart, suitable for farm work; three full sets of Horse Gears, nearly new; bridles, reins, and other gears and chaining too numerous to mention.

Wood horse mangers and various stable requisites, comprising sundry horse sheets, collars, lick-tubs, shovels, and a large quantity of spades such as are used by railway contractors.

Also three Fat Pigs, and about twenty-five head of Poultry of various breeds.

The Furniture and beerhouse moveables include ale tables, chairs, benches, English timepiece, a quantity of carpeting, numerous glasses, goblets, pint and quart range, brass taps, spittoons, and ten iron bedsteads, with mattresses, blankets, sheets, quilts and counterpanes to same.

For particulars see bills.

Sale at 10.30 in the Forenoon.

The whole will be sold without reserve, as Mr. Hallam has finished his contracts, and is leaving the district.

Auctioneer's Office, Thornton.

Bradford Observer, 26 January 1877

FOUND, on Monday, in Denholme Clough, Black and Tan KING CHARLES or Cock Dog; white on breast, longish tail, weighs 12lbs. The Hedge House, Thornton.

Leeds Mercury, 18 May 1877

The Rev. F. Hall, who has been eight years pastor of Kipping Congregational Chapel, Thornton, near Bradford, and who has accepted the pastorate of Upper Chapel, Heckmondwike, has been presented by the congregation he is leaving with a pair of gold candelabra and a timepiece, purchased at a cost of fifty guineas. Advantage was taken of the event by the ministers of other communions to attend and express the regard they felt for Mr. Hall, in conjunction with the members of his own congregation. The rev. gentleman preached his last sermon as minister of Kipping Chapel on Sunday evening.

Leeds Mercury, 20 June 1877

THE FAILURE OF FRANCIS CRAVEN. At the London Bankruptcy Court, yesterday, an application was made to Mr. Registrar Brougham, sitting as Chief Judge, for the appointment of a receiver to the estate of Francis Craven, commission agent, of Bow-lane, Cheapside, who has failed for £1,400. The debtor failed in 1874 for £62,000, he then carrying on business at the Dole Mill, near Bradford, and under that petition the secured creditors obtained 20s in the pound. MR. T. MICKLEM now applied, on behalf of the debtor, for the appointment of a receiver to the estate of the debtor. He read from the debtor's affidavit the fact of the presentation of the petition, and that the assets consisted of household furniture at Clapham, £500; furniture at Kipping House, Bradford, £250; and also the remainder of the lease of the house. He proposed Mr. J. Pollard Lovering, accountant, Graham-street, as receiver to the estate. A creditor named Stephen Mattison, of Bread-street, Cheapside, had taken proceedings in the High Court of Justice to recover the sum of £280, and it was necessary, in the interests of the creditors, that he should be stayed from further proceedings for a week. His Honour granted the application.

Bradford Observer, 13 July 1877

LOCAL POLICE INTELLIGENCE. WEST RIDING COURT. AN OBSTINATE FARM SERVANT. Richard and Margaret Mattocks, man and wife, were summoned at the instance of Robert Cundell, farmer and corn merchant, Leaventhorpe, for loss sustained through breach of contract. Mr. Berry appeared for the complainant and Mr. Rennolls defended. It appeared that the defendants had been in the employ of the complainant. Richard Mattock's duties were to attend to the cows and fill up the rest of his time by doing his best on the farm, ploughing excepted; and his wife had to assist him in milking the cows, sixteen in number. For this service, the defendants, as agreed at the engagement, received 26s per week, a quart of new milk per day, a house, and leading of coals. A month's notice on either side was to be given to terminate the engagement. On the 2nd instant the female defendant had to attend the West Riding Court, to give evidence against a boy who had stolen her watch. Her husband told complainant that he would be obliged to go too, to swear to the watch. Complainant said the wife would do, but as Mattocks persisted, he said 'Well, you can go if you like.' The case was heard early in the day, and Mrs. Mattocks returned with Mrs. Cundell at

Thornton Viaduct from Alderscholes Lane.

James Street Primary School in the 1940s.

two o'clock in the afternoon. The male defendant, however, did not get back until dark. The complainant had seven acres of grass ready for leading, and he had given Mattocks orders to see it properly stacked in the barn. As he did not turn up, complainant had to supervise the hay leading, and was thus unable to attend the market at Leeds. Next morning he sent to the male defendant asking him to come to his work during that week, and he (complainant) would accept that in lieu of the month's notice which he ought properly to receive. Mr. Cundell had sustained considerable loss – probably £20, besides the loss of the market – but he would only ask the Bench to order payment of a sum equal to a month's wages of the defendants. Mr. Rennolls, for the defence, said the male defendant had been warned by the police to attend the Court. When he told the complainant that he must go, Mr. Cundell informed him that if he went he must consider himself as discharged. Next morning Mrs. Cundell asked him if he would come back to his work. Colonel Pollard said the Bench had no hesitation in giving a verdict for a month's wages, with costs, and they considered that the male defendant had acted in a most infamous way.

Bradford Observer, 17 July 1877

LOCAL BOARDS. THORNTON. This Board met on Friday, Mr. Fredk. Mossman presiding. The other members present were Messrs. Bunting, Townend, Carter, Northrop, Walton, and David Craven. The medical officer's report stated that 50 births and 24 deaths had been registered. The death-rate was hardly 15.6 per annum. One fatal case of zymotic disease was recorded from erysipelas. The Surveyor submitted plans and sections of that part of Albert Street which the owners refused to put into proper order. The clerk was directed to give the owners notice to sewer, form and make the street within one month, and on default the Board will do the work and recover the cost in a summary manner. A plan of a new bridge, intended to be made below the surface of the New Road at Thornton on the Bradford and Thornton Railway, submitted by Mr. Fraser, the engineer, was considered. The Board were unable to approve of it, as it was proposed to make the bridge 35ft wide only, the road being 40ft wide, and not being of sufficient depth under the surface of the road. Notice of motion was given by Mr. Northrop that he would at the next meeting propose a revision of the charges for the water supply, with a view to making the waterworks self-supporting.

Bradford Observer, 6 September 1877

THE LATE MR. JONAS CRAVEN, OF THORNTON

By the death of Mr. Jonas Craven, of Rose Cottage, Thornton, his entire village has been deprived of one of its most honoured inhabitants. Mr. Craven was one of the last representatives of the old race of master manufacturers who contributed in so great a degree to the development of the worsted trade in this district, and as far as the Thornton valley is concerned, the class may be said to have become extinct by his decease. During his long life – extending over eighty-four years –

Mr. Craven has witnessed the growth of the trade from its most primitive stages, and from the humblest beginnings had in his own active pursuit of it reaped the just reward of persevering industry and enterprise. Mr. Craven was born at Black Carr, in Thornton, in May, 1798. He commenced business in 1824, in partnership with Mr. Henry Harrop, and for thirty-three years the firm continued as 'Craven & Harrop.' As worsted manufacturers the firm were the first to use cotton warps in this district, and they were also the first to manufacture Orleans and Coburgs. Previous to that nothing but woollen warps prevailed, and bombazines, plainbacks, &c., formed the staple trade. As some indication of the extent to which the firm were engaged, it may be stated that from 1836 to 1844 they employed a thousand hand-loom weavers, throughout a district embracing places as far away as Haworth and Stanbury. In 1844 the firm built Dole Mill, Thornton, and from that period hand-loom labour gradually ceased and power-looms increased. At Dole Mill the firm employed on average 500 weavers, and also ran Waterloo and Prospect Mills, Bradford, altogether running over a thousand looms. In taking the principal management of (for that period) large manufacturing establishments, Mr. Craven displayed much energy and business aptitude, and was the means of adding considerably to the prosperity of his fellow villagers.

It is as a neighbour and friend, however, that the deceased gentleman will be most missed in his native village. As a dalesman he was fond of Thornton and of all that belonged to it. Latterly he never cared to leave it, except for occasional visits to inspect the growing wonders of Bradford and Leeds, in which latter town he took some interest, as it was there he sold his 'pieces' long before there was a merchant established in Bradford. He was never what is known as a public man, in the sense of taking the lead in township affairs. As one of the staunchest Nonconformists in this district, and as a Liberal of the most pronounced type, he dearly prized civil and religious liberty, and his means were ever forthcoming for any movement having for its object its perpetuation and extension. He had been a deacon at Kipping Chapel for many years, and upon its being rebuilt in 1845, he and his partner, Mr. Harrop, contributed the sum of £1000. On the erection of New Road Side Congregational Church, in 1866, he contributed largely towards the building fund, and up to the last was the principal supporter of the new Nonconformist interest. In both places he actively identified himself with the Sunday school, and almost up to the day of his death his delight was in teaching young people. Above either his fidelity to creed or party, however, he was pre-eminently a kind-hearted citizen.

His own mode of life was of the simplest and quietest, and that portion of his means not required to satisfy his modest wants he gave to others. It is said that for years he has given away two-thirds of his income. Mr. Craven was twice married, and had by his first wife a family of whom six children, three sons and three daughters, arrived at maturity. Mr. Joseph Craven, of Clapham, London, who died in June, 1873, was his oldest son, and the two still living are Mr. Francis and Mr. Edwin Craven, also of London. His wife, to whom he had been married thirty-eight years, still survives him. Mr. Craven's illness was of very short duration. He was in Bradford a week before his death, but succumbed to natural decay on Sunday morning last. His remains were yesterday deposited at Kipping Cemetery, Thornton, in the presence of a large concourse of his old neighbours and friends. Preceding the hearse were representatives of the New Road Church and congregation; the Sunday school; the Thornton Local Board, headed by its chairman, Mr. Frederick Mossman; the School Board; and gentlemen of Thornton and other places. Among the latter we noticed Mr. Henry Illingworth, Mr. Nathan Drake, Mr. Phineas Craven, Mr. John Glover, Mr. Thos. Baines, Mr. J. Waterhouse, Rev. J. Gregory (Leeds), Rev. Thomas Roberts (Bradford), Mr. Joseph Craven (Ashfield), Dr. Rawson, Mr. W.L. Bunting, Mr. Jonathan Northrop, Mr. R.J. Walton, Mr. Joseph Shackleton, &c. From Rose Cottage the corpse was taken to the New Road Church, where the burial service was read by the Rev. John Stevenson, the minister, and an appropriate prayer offered by the Rev. Thomas Davis, of Wellington, Salop. Upon the coffin a beautiful wreath, sent from Ashfield by Miss Craven, was deposited. The service at the Cemetery was also conducted by the Rev. J. Stevenson, who, it is announced, will preach a special sermon upon the event on Sunday morning week.

Bradford Observer, 2 October 1878

OPENING OF THE BRADFORD AND THORNTON RAILWAY. The directors of the Great Northern Railway Company have at last made an official announcement to the effect that the Bradford and Thornton line will be opened for passenger traffic on Monday next, the 14th inst., and have issued time tables. There will be five trains a day despatched from Bradford to Thornton, viz. at 7.45, 9.5 a.m., 12.20, 5.5, and 6.10 p.m., and two trains to Thornton from Laisterdyke at 10.43 a.m. and 2.50 p.m.. The return trains to Bradford will be at 8.20, 11.50 a.m., 1.40, 4.27 and 6.45 p.m., and to Laisterdyke at 9.40 a.m. and 5.35 p.m.. There will be four trains each way on Sundays. The tariff of fares has not yet been communicated to the booking-clerks.

Bradford Observer, 7 October 1878

FATAL OMNIBUS ACCIDENT AT THORNTON. An omnibus driver named Albert Robertshaw, nineteen years of age, was killed on Saturday evening by being run over at Thornton. The deceased was driving an omnibus, drawn by two horses, from Bradford to Thornton, and when near School Green, Thornton, at half past ten, the deceased, who was then walking on the causeway, observed that another omnibus, driven by John Ackroyd, was about to pass his conveyance. He went across the road and took hold of the head of one of his horses, the horses of the conveyances then being close together. Robertshaw either fell or was knocked down by the horses, and the wheels of his own omnibus passed over him. He got up, but again fell to the ground, and some of the passengers went to his assistance. Drs. Bentham and Crosby were soon on the spot, but the young man died before their arrival. The body was conveyed in one of the omnibuses to the home of the deceased's mother, at Bottom Holes, Thornton.

Bradford Observer, 13 January 1879

DEATH OF MR. A. GETZ. We regret to announce the death of Mr. Adolphus Getz, of Manningham Lane, Bradford, which occurred very suddenly about eight o'clock on Saturday night, at the Bradford Club, Manor Row. Whilst playing a game of billiards he had an attack of coughing which increased in severity and compelled him to take a seat. After having sat down, he asked for a glass of water, but before it could be brought to him, a stream of blood began to issue from his mouth, and he expired almost immediately. His medical attendant, Dr. Bronner, and Mr. C.H. Taylor, surgeon, were at once sent for. The latter gentleman attended immediately, but medical aid was of no avail, death having resulted from a ruptured blood vessel. Mr. Getz, who was, we understand, a native of Frankfort, came to Bradford upwards of thirty years ago, and had for a long time carried on the business of a manufacturer. In addition to the mill in Bradford which he worked, he some years ago purchased from Mr. Craven a mill and business at Thornton, which he has since carried on. Deceased was a bachelor. Though he never entered public life, he was esteemed by a large number of persons in Bradford and the district, for his kindliness and unostentatious charity.

Bradford Observer, 20 January 1879

THORNTON MECHANICS' INSTITUTE.. The course of lectures and entertainments in connection with Thornton Mechanics' Institute, which was suspended during the Christmas festivities, was resumed on Tuesday evening, when Mrs. C.L. Balfour delivered a lecture on 'The Poets' Corner of Westminster Abbey.' Unfortunately, the weather was again unfavourable, but the number who faced the fog and rain must have thoroughly enjoyed the interesting, but too rapid, survey of the lives and writings of the illustrious dead who have found a last resting place in the ancient abbey. In responding to a vote of thanks proposed by the chairman, the Rev. Jas. Gregory, Mrs. Balfour said that when coming to deliver the lecture she had doubted her ability to accomplish the duty on account of the severe cold under which she had lately been suffering.

Bradford Observer, 14 July 1879

LOCAL BOARDS. THORNTON. This Board met on Friday, Mr. F. Mossman presiding; there were also present Messrs. D. Craven, W.L. Bunting, John Carter, J. Shackleton, B. Hill, John Walton, Richard Booth, Josh. Wood, and Midgley Priestley. The Medical Officer presented his report for the quarter ending June, showing a birth-rate of 26.6 per 1000, and a death-rate of 18.8 per 1000 annually. The births registered during the quarter were 41 and the deaths 29. The Board resolved to relay several causeways in the district, and it was resolved to ask for tenders for the same, and also the relaying of the crossings opposite the Reform Chapel, Wellington Inn, and Green Lane Head. The Board had under discussion the advisability of erecting additional lamps in the district, and finally the matter was referred to the Lighting Committee for further consideration. It was resolved to have an inspection of the roads within the district on Wednesday next.

Bradford Observer, 17 July 1879

THORNTON ENDOWED SCHOOL, Thornton, near Bradford. Wanted, a HEAD-MISTRESS for the Girls's School, established under the Scheme of the Endowed Schools Commission. The Mistress will receive a fixed Stipend of £40 per annum and Capitation Fees. Income guaranteed for first year, £100. Apply by letter, with testimonials, not later than the 25th instant, to JOHN R. JEFFERY, solicitor, 5 Piccadilly, Bradford, Secretary to the Governors. July 8th 1879

Bradford Observer, 18 July 1879

LOCAL POLICE INTELLIGENCE. DRUNK AND RIOTOUS. John Ogden Holdsworth, quarryman, of Denholme Clough, was fined 10s and costs for being drunk and riotous at Thornton on the 8th inst. He was also fined in the same amount for being drunk and riotous at the same place on the 12th inst. Squire Drake, forgeman, Wyke, was fined 10s and costs for being drunk and refusing to quit the Crown Inn, Wyke, on the 7th instant. Abraham Pearson, general dealer, Cleckheaton, for being drunk and refusing to leave the Commercial Hotel, Cleckheaton, was fined 20s and costs. John Jowett, labourer, Thornton, was fined 10s and costs for drunkenness.

Chapter Twenty-Two
1880-1889

Suicide in brewer's boiling vat – Black Edge Farm for sale – Two Thornton gentlemen elected MPs – Victoria's Jubilee celebrated with tea and a new shilling for sixty-five year olds – Billiard balls stolen by Thornton man

Bradford Observer, 8 April 1880

NOTICE IS HEREBY GIVEN that the partnership heretofore subsisting between us, the undersigned JOSEPH ROBERTSHAW and GREENWOOD BAIRSTOW, carrying on business as Stone Merchants, at Thornton, near Bradford, in the county of York, under the style or firm of 'Robertshaw & Bairstow,' has been this day Dissolved by mutual consent. Dated this 1st day of April 1880.

JOSEPH ROBERTSHAW GREENWOOD BAIRSTOW

Witness to all the Signatories – JNO. EDW. GAUNT, Solicitor, Bradford.

Bradford Weekly Telegraph, 27 May 1882

THORNTON: SERIOUS TRAP ACCIDENT. On Sunday afternoon, a serious accident occurred at Spring Head, near Thornton. Mr. B. Town, landlord of the Market Tavern, Bradford, who was driving with his daughter and a niece, Miss Duff, in a trap, stopped his horse at the Brown Cow, Ling Bob, Wilsden, and removed the bridle in order that the animal might drink. No sooner had he done this than the horse took fright at something, and bolted. When turning a corner at Spring Head the vehicle was overturned, and both ladies were thrown to the ground. Miss Town was severely shaken and cut, and Miss Duff received a bruise at the back of the head. Medical aid was called in, and the injured ladies were removed home.

Bradford *Weekly* Telegraph, 10 June 1882

THORNTON. CATTLE DISEASE ORDER. The 'London Gazette' of Tuesday night contained an Order in Council declaring the following area to be infected with foot-and-mouth disease from the 7th inst.:- 'An area comprising so much of the township of Thornton, in the West Riding of Yorkshire, as lies within the following boundaries: Long Causeway Side on the north, the footpath from Long Causeway Road to the Keighley and Halifax Road on the west, the Halifax and Keighley Road on the south, and the brook from the Halifax and Keighley Road to Long Causeway on the east.'

Bradford *Weekly* Telegraph, 1 July 1882

THORNTON. FATAL ACCIDENT TO A CHILD. A little boy fourteen months of age, named Albert Henry Lee, the son of Abraham Lee, labourer, of Thornton, was killed on Monday morning outside his parents' house, School Green, Thornton, by a miller's waggon from Bingley, which knocked the little fellow down and passing over his head caused instantaneous death.

Bradford *Weekly* Telegraph, 15 July 1882

West Riding Police Court, MONDAY. WORKING A BROKEN-KNEE'D HORSE. William Greenwood, a milk dealer at Thornton, was summoned for having cruelly worked a horse in an unfit condition. Sergt. Harman said that on the 29th June he saw a horse and cart belonging to the defendant standing at the door of the Denholme Gate Inn. He examined the horse, and found its knees covered with knee-caps. Underneath these were two large wounds, one on each knee, and they were suppurating from the knee joints, matter being hardened on the inside of the knee-caps. The animal appeared to be lame, and lifted first one foot and then the other to ease itself. The Bench fined the defendant 10s and costs, or 14 days' imprisonment in default of payment. ASSAULT ON THE POLICE. John Graham, a navvy living in the neighbourhood of Thornton, was charged with having been drunk and riotous, and having assaulted P.C. Jackson in the execution of his duty. It appears that the officer found the prosecutor [sic] drunk, and creating a disturbance, and when he apprehended him the prisoner seized him by the thumb, and remarking that he would break his thumb, pulled it until it was broken and severely injured. The prisoner was fined 10s and costs.

Bradford *Weekly* Telegraph, 2 January 1883

A YOUNG MAN DROWNED. A young man named James Crabtree, a mason, residing at Foresides, Thornton, met with his death on Monday under the following circumstances:- He was engaged at work on the reservoir of the Bradford Corporation at Thornton Moor, and left home to go to his work at half-past six. The morning was a dark one, and on turning round a corner on the bank of the large conduit he stumbled and fell in. Some of his companions who were near heard his cries, but as the water was about eight feet deep they were some time in getting the body out, and life was then quite extinct. Deceased was 18 years old.

Leeds Mercury, 20 January 1883

The Rev. A.S. Trotman, pastor of the Ripon Congregational Church, had this week presented to him a purse of gold and a service of plate, on the occasion of his leaving Ripon for Kipping Chapel, Thornton, near Bradford.

Bradford Weekly Telegraph, 21 April 1883

SHOCKING SUICIDE. On Wednesday an inquest was held at the Denholme Gate Inn, Thornton, by Mr. T.E. Hill, deputy-coroner, respecting the death of John Hey, aged 33 years, who was found dead in a steam-boiler at the Denholme Gate Brewery on Tuesday morning. Evidence was given to the effect that the deceased was employed as a night watchman by Messrs. Jonathan Knowles and Sons at the brewery in question. For some time past he had been in ill-health but was not depressed in spirits. About 6.30 p.m. on Monday last he left home to attend to his duties at the brewery, and was last seen alive about 7.15 p.m. the same date at the brewery by a drayman named Edward Hainsworth. On the following morning deceased could not be found, but his cap and vest were found on the top of the steam boiler used for heating water for cleaning purposes. This led to an examination of the boiler, and the remains of the deceased were then found in a horrible condition, and quite beyond recognition, having been literally boiled. The body was identified by the clothing. Deceased must have wishfully unfastened the man-hole lid of the boiler, and deliberately committed suicide by jumping inside among the boiling contents. The Jury returned a verdict of 'Suicide by drowning.'

Bradford Weekly Telegraph, 9 June 1883

ACCIDENT ON THE RAILWAY AT THORNTON. Last Friday afternoon a serious accident happened at Thornton to a coal agent called Joseph Cockcroft. Two children were picking up coal on the railway at the Great Northern coal wharf, whilst waggons were being shunted, and Cockcroft seeing their danger ran to them to rescue them from their position. He succeeded in accomplishing this object, but unfortunately paid a heavy penalty for his brave act, as he fell and one of the waggons passed over one of his legs. Dr. Jackson promptly attended the injured man and ordered his removal to the Infirmary where, unfortunately, it has since been found necessary to amputate the injured limb. Much sympathy is felt with Cockcroft, who is married and has six children, and it is stated that a subscription in their behalf will be raised by the inhabitants.

Bradford Weekly Telegraph, 30 June 1883

The construction of the new Great Northern Railway from Keighley to Thornton for Halifax and Bradford is being proceeded with rapidly, and I hear that every effort is being made so that one line at least may be clear right through from Keighley in the course of about three months. If this is accomplished the contractors will have much greater facilities for the completion of the second line of rails, and the time should not be very far distant when the railway may be expected to be opened for traffic. In view of this prospect rumours are already in circulation to the effect that when the line is opened the Great Northern Railway Company will grant passes available from Keighley to either Halifax or Bradford, via Thornton, this enabling business-men to travel to both towns from Keighley at one rate. If this arrangement should be carried into effect it will undoubtedly prove advantageous to many. It should be mentioned that the charge for these dual passes is likely to be the same only as that now charged by the Midland Railway Company from Keighley to Bradford.

Bradford Weekly Telegraph, 28 July 1883

OUTBREAK OF FIRE. A telegraphic message was received at the Bradford Town Hall shortly after five o'clock on Saturday morning requesting the attendance of the fire brigade at a fire which had broken out in Thornton. Supt. Hudson and a staff of his brigade were speedily at their posts, and proceeded with the steam fire engine to the scene of the fire. On arrival at Thornton they found that the fire had broken out in a draper's shop and dwelling-house situate in New Road, owned by Mr. Samuel S. Hirst, of Clayton Heights, and occupied by Mr. Abraham Illingworth, draper, and his family. By the time the brigade arrived the fire had been practically mastered by means of hose obtained from neighbouring factories. The fire was discovered about five o'clock by the inmates, who were aroused by the strong smell of burning and the smoke which filled the premises. Fortunately they succeeded in effecting their escape from the building, but the shop and dwelling-house, with their contents, were completely destroyed. Singular to state the top storey of the building, which is used as the rooms of the Liberal Club, was practically uninjured. The damage to the building is estimated at about £300, but this, it is said, is covered by insurance. The stock, fixtures, and furniture belonging to Mr. Illingworth have been rendered completely valueless, and being uninsured he has sustained a loss of £500 or £600.

Bradford Weekly Telegraph, 24 January 1885

FATAL FALL INTO A QUARRY

On Wednesday last an inquest was held at the Bull's Head Inn, Thornton, into the death of John Henry Calvert, 35 years of age, plasterer, of Havelock Street, Thornton, who fell into Egypt Quarry on Sunday night, and died the same night as the result of the injuries he sustained. Robertshaw Robinson, of Ball Street, Thornton, and deceased went about half-past three or four o'clock on Sunday afternoon to the Robin Hood Inn, Black Dyke Lane. They left the public-house about eight o'clock, and walked arm-in-arm along Black Dyke Lane. After walking along the lane as far as Messrs. Farrar's stable, Robertshaw suddenly noticed that they were walking on grass. He remarked to the deceased that they must have gone out of their way, and that he was going to get over a wall that was near. He then heard deceased falling down the quarry. He called to the deceased, but received no answer, and could not see anything of him. He then went to the Rock and Heifer Inn and gave an alarm. Returning to the quarry with other men, he found the deceased lying in an insensible condition at the bottom of the quarry. Neither he nor the deceased were sober. The deceased was insensible, and was carried home as soon as possible. He must have fallen a distance of fifty feet. The wall at the roadside near the quarry was only about two feet high. The jury returned a verdict of 'Accidental death whilst in a state of intoxication,' and recommended that the wall on the road near the quarry should be raised to a proper height and a suitable gateway made.

Bradford Observer, 10 October 1885

To be Let, A Good Farm, called Black Edge Farm, situate at Denholme Gate, in Thornton, in the parish of Bradford, together with the cottages, barns, outbuildings, &c., and also all those Closes of LAND, containing seventy-two acres, and now in the occupation of Jonathan Whitaker. The tenant will show the farm, and for further particulars as to rent, &c., apply at 41, Beverley Terrace, Akroyden, Halifax.

Leeds Mercury, 8 February 1886

LIBERAL DEMONSTRATION AT THORNTON. A very successful Liberal demonstration, to celebrate the election as Members of Parliament of two Thornton gentlemen – Mr. Joseph Craven, the Member for Shipley Division, and Mr. Briggs Priestley, the Member for the Pudsey Division – and the return of Mr. Isaac Holden as first Member of the Keighley Division, was held on Saturday. In the afternoon a knife-and-fork tea was provided in the Kipping Schoolroom, to which between three and four hundred persons partook. Subsequently a large public meeting was held in the Mechanics' Hall, under the presidency of Mr. GEORGE TOWNEND. Supporting the Chairman on the platform were Mr. Alfred Illingworth, M.P., Mr. Isaac Holden, M.P., Mr. Joseph Craven, M.P., Mr. John Brigg (Chairman of the Keighley Division Liberal Association), Mr. J. Clough, Mr. D. Craven, Rev. E.H. Steel, Mr. Pickles, and others. The

217

CHAIRMAN, after briefly opening the meeting, called upon Mr. Wm. Pickles to read a congratulatory address from the Thornton Liberal Club to Messrs. Craven, Priestley, and Holden. The address stated it was especially gratifying to Thornton Liberals to see Mr. Joseph Craven, who had laboured so faithfully and long to promote the spread of Liberal principles in their midst, elected by one of the largest constituencies in the kingdom to that position which he was so eminently fitted to fill, for it was with authority they said, 'He that is faithful in that which is least is faithful also in much.' It was with the very greatest pleasure and satisfaction that they hailed Mr. Priestley's attainment to the distinguished position he now held. Though no longer actively associated with Thornton, his public life reflected credit on his native town, and proved that his early Liberal principles were based upon intelligent convictions, and had won for him the esteem and confidence of others. To Mr. Holden they also offered their heartiest congratulations. They were proud to welcome as the first Member for Keighley Division one who had for so many years had laboured so earnestly for the good of the country. To all of them they could say they honoured their independence of character, and their genuine sympathy with all movements which were likely to promote the welfare and happiness of the whole people. Mr. CRAVEN and Mr. HOLDEN both responded. The latter, in referring to the Irish question, remarked that he hoped the people of this country would not have hard thoughts about the Irish people, but would exercise a large amount of sympathy with, and give to the Irish such a measure of liberty as would compensate them for the past generations of oppression which had ground down that country. He did not know what Mr. Gladstone's scheme was, but he hoped and trusted and prayed it would be a large and wide scheme of Home Rule. The landlords said we ought not to give Home Rule to Ireland, because they said it would deprive the landlords of their just rents. He thought the landlords could not be worse off than they were at present, because they get no rent at all. (Laughter.) When a whole people agree not to pay a rack-rent, it was very difficult for any Government to force them to pay that rent; in fact it was impossible. They might as well try to pluck the sun from the firmament as to try to make a whole people do what they were resolved not to do. Some way must be found out of this embroglio, and he trusted Mr. Gladstone would show them the way to do it. (Applause.) Mr. DAVID CRAVEN then moved, Mr. JOHN BRIGG seconded, and Mr. JOHN CLOUGH supported, the following resolution, which was carried with great cordiality:- 'That this meeting expresses its unabated confidence in Mr. Gladstone, and trusts that, along with the newly formed Administration, he may be able to bring the Irish question to a just and peaceful issue.' Mr. ALFRED ILLINGWORTH replied to the resolution at considerable length. He warned his audience not to be led away with mere sentiment on the Irish question. People talked about the unity of the empire and of it being a source of strength. In his opinion Ireland had always been the palsied limb, the sickly child of the family, the paralytic, and had never been a source of strength to the empire. Something must be done at once for Ireland; indeed, in his opinion, it would be infinitely better Ireland should be absolutely separated from this country than that we should have the same trouble with her during the next century as we had during the past. Votes of thanks concluded the meeting.

Leeds Mercury, 20 July 1886

KIPPING INDEPENDENT SUNDAY SCHOOL, THORNTON. On Saturday afternoon the memorial-stones of the new premises connected with Kipping Independent Sunday School, Thornton, near Bradford, were laid by Mr. Joseph Craven, M.P., and Mr. Briggs Priestley, M.P. The ceremony was witnessed by a large number of persons. There were present on the platform the Rev. A.S. Trotman, the Rev. E.H. Steel, Ald. John Hill (Bradford), Mr. D. Craven, and Mr. Bunting. After a short service, the Rev. A.S. Trotman said they were exceedingly glad to welcome amongst them the two gentlemen who were to take a prominent part in the day's proceedings. They regarded Mr. Craven as one of themselves; and in the building of the new school they had found in him – as Thornton had always found – a friend ever ready to put his shoulder to the wheel. Mr. Priestley and Ald. John Hill were old friends of Kipping, and as such they were glad to see them on such an occasion. It was his pleasure to co-operate on a committee of earnest and determined men in this enterprise; they felt it a great honour to be engaged in the great work of advancing the principles of the New Testament; and in order to promote more efficiently the religious education of the young they were erecting a new building. Mr. David Craven presented a trowel and mallet to Mr. Craven, who, after duly laying a stone, alluded to the successful work which had been carried on in the old school, and to the pleasant recollections he had in connection with it. He regarded the work of Sunday schools as of the highest value, and he was glad to find that they were preparing to carry it on under circumstances of greater convenience and comfort to both teachers and scholars. Mr. Bunting next presented a trowel and mallet to Mr. Briggs Priestley, who, having declared another stone well and truly laid, touchingly referred to his former connection with the village and with Kipping Sunday school. Speaking to the youths present, he urged them to make use of their opportunities for self-improvement, and remarked that personally he was much indebted to the Sunday school and the Mechanics' Institute for such success as he had attained. Ald. John Hill also addressed the assembly.

Leeds Mercury, 18 June 1887

THORNTON. In connection with the Queen's Jubilee celebrations, Mr. Joseph Craven, M.P., will provide a substantial tea for persons in the district over 65 years of age, and will also present to each person a new shilling. The choir of Kipping Chapel will entertain the party with music after the tea.

Illustrated Weekly Telegraph, 14 January 1888

Thornton Local Board met on Wednesday. The clerk was instructed to write to Mr. Joseph Thwaites, New Road Side, informing him that unless proper plans of the alterations and additions to the Old Skating Rink, now used as a spinning shed, be submitted to the Board within fourteen days, legal proceedings would be taken against him. The clerk was instructed to write to the gas company complaining of the quality of gas supplied to the Thornton district.

Illustrated Weekly Telegraph, 18 February 1888

CONCERT. On Saturday evening a concert was given in the Mechanics' Institute, Thornton, by Mr. Walter Holmes' Operatic Concert Party. There was a fair attendance, and the programme was very attractive. Mr. H. Ullathorne was the conductor, and Mr. W. Holmes ably acted as accompanist. The hunting song by Mr. C.W. Sykes and chorus 'Away, away' ('Don Quixote') was efficiently rendered, and the madrigal, 'Brightly dawns our wedding day' ('Mikado'), by Miss A. Saville, Miss Oates, Mr. J.E. Biggin, and Mr. S. Holmes, was well received. Mr. Williams sang the two humorous songs, 'My object all sublime' ('Mikado') and Sir Joseph Porter's patter song in 'Pinafore' in a very amusing manner; the latter won a well-deserved encore. Mr. W. Holmes showed his powers excellently in the two pianoforte solos, 'Zampa' and 'Isolee' (for left hand only); and Mr. Sykes gave a violin solo with much effect. 'Alas, those chimes', by Miss E. Rhodes, was tastefully rendered, and Mr. H. Biggin was heard at his best in the two songs 'Once upon a time' ('Nell Gwynne') and 'Silent Heroes' ('Les Cloches de Corneville'). Miss A. Saville and Mr. J.E. Biggin sang in 'The Miserere Scene' neatly, and the quintet 'She will tend him' ('Sorcerer') by Miss A. Saville, Miss Townend, Mr. J.E. Biggin, Mr. J. Coates, junr, and Mr. H. Biggin caused much amusement, and had to be repeated, as had also the song 'The Torpedo and the Whale' ('Oliverette') by Miss L. Saville. Miss A. Saville's 'Lullaby' ('Erminie') was sung with great expression, and the duet 'Why answer so demurely' was much appreciated. The chorus 'Now for the eggs and ham' ('Sorcerer') and the National Anthem brought an enjoyable concert to a close.

Illustrated Weekly Telegraph, 24 March 1888

PRESENTATION TO MR. H.E. FOSTER AT THORNTON. On Monday evening the National School-room, Thornton, was crowded, on the occasion of a presentation by the members of the Thornton Conservative Association to Mr. H. E. Foster, of Thornton Hall, of an illuminated address congratulating him on his marriage.

Illustrated Weekly Telegraph, 21 April 1888

FATAL ACCIDENT AT THORNTON. On Tuesday morning Mr. James Stoney, butcher, of Denholme, was found in a helpless condition on the railway line near the mouth of the Well Heads tunnel. It is conjectured that he had got over the wall at the point stated, intending to walk through the tunnel to Denholme, and had fallen down the slope and fractured his skull. He was conveyed to the

Great Northern Inn, Thornton, and attended by Dr. Nuttall, but died the same evening. He was apparently under thirty years of age, and was unmarried.

Illustrated Weekly Telegraph, 12 May 1888

Bradford Borough Police Court. SATURDAY. THEFT OF BILLIARD BALLS. George Dawns, a traveller, of Thornton, was charged in custody with stealing six billiard balls, of the value of 48s, the property of Edgar Sealey Jones, the proprietor of the County Restaurant, Bradford. On the 4th inst., the prisoner went into the billiard room at the County Restaurant, and after playing a game at billiards left. Soon after he had gone the marker missed the balls produced, and the prisoner was subsequently found dealing with them. He has now pleaded guilty, and was fined 10s and 10s costs, or 14 days to the House of Correction.

Illustrated Weekly Telegraph, 14 July 1888

FOUND DROWNED. Police-constable Redshaw, of the West Riding force, found the dead body of Wm. Pollard Robertshaw, a carter, aged fifteen years, of Allerton Lane, in Pitt [*sic*] Beck, Thornton, at ten minutes past three on Sunday afternoon. The body was removed to the house of Jeremiah Robertshaw, in Allerton Lane.

Illustrated Weekly Telegraph, 15 September 1888

The Thornton Local Board met on Wednesday. The lighting and waterworks committee recommended certain alterations at Hill Top water shaft. The Board wish to rely upon this source for 30,000 gallons of water per day. The Board will act upon the recommendation. A deputation was appointed to treat with Mr. Joseph Craven respecting land for the widening of Albert Street.

Illustrated Weekly Telegraph, 6 October 1888

The body of a labouring man named Jonathan Robinson, about forty years of age, and of no settled place of abode, was found at the bottom of the pit-shaft opposite the Albion Mill, Thornton, on Tuesday morning, when the pitmen went to their work. Robinson was seen in an intoxicated condition by several people on Monday night. It is presumed that he was in search of a sleeping place when he stumbled over the edge of the shaft, and fell a depth of 270 feet.

Illustrated Weekly Telegraph, 26 January 1889

Bradford West Riding Police Court. Monday. INDECENT ASSAULT AT CLAYTON. James Broughton, a chimney sweep, of Thornton, was charged with committing an indecent assault upon a girl named Clara Robinson, at Clayton, on Friday evening last, and was fined £3 and costs. Prisoner was defended by Mr. C. L. Atkinson.

Railway line over Thornton Viaduct towards Clayton.

Illustrated Weekly Telegraph, 10 August 1889

ACCIDENTAL DEATH AT THORNTON. On Saturday night last it was reported to the police that Joseph Saville, aged 60 years, of Hill Top, Thornton, had met with an accident which resulted fatally. It was stated that the deceased went home under the influence of drink, and at once proceeded up stairs to bed. On getting to the top of the stairs he last his balance, and fell to the bottom. Dr. Drake was at once called, but the man died before his arrival.

Illustrated Weekly Telegraph, 16 November 1889

At Thornton on Wednesday evening Mr. George Hill Smith, the Unionist lecturer, delivered his lecture on 'Home Rule: What is it and how will it work?' in the National Schools.

Chapter Twenty-Three
1890–1894

Dr Rawson dies – Iron mission church opens – Smallpox at Thornton Isolation Hospital – Little Pete becomes jilted suicide – Minister preaches sermon against football

Bradford Observer, 26 September 1890

DEATH OF DR. RAWSON OF THORNTON. We regret to announce the death of Mr. Edwin Elsworth Rawson, which event took place at his residence, Brooklands, yesterday morning after a very short illness. The deceased gentleman, who had only returned from Scarborough on Wednesday afternoon, had a fit about eleven o'clock the same evening and died shortly before eight o'clock the next morning. Dr. Rawson had resided in Thornton for thirty years, and was a very popular man. He had been medical officer of health and medical inspector of factories for a great many years in the village. He married a Miss Foster, of Denholme, who survives him, with a family of seven children.

Leeds Mercury, 15 April 1891

BEERHOUSE for SALE, situate at Thornton Back Heights. Address, W 199, Observer-office, Bradford.

Bradford Observer, 23 April 1892

THE LATE MR. JONATHAN NORTHROP. Mr. Jonathan Northrop, formerly of Thornton, but latterly residing at Fern Hill, Moorhead, Shipley, a successful man of business, whose figure was familiar to Bradfordians, died on Tuesday last.

The funeral took place yesterday in the cemetery attached to the ancient Kipping Chapel at Thornton. In accordance with the desire of the deceased, expressed shortly before his death, the funeral was of a very quiet nature, only relatives and a few close personal friends being present. A short service was conducted by the Rev. J.A. Hamilton, pastor of the Saltaire Congregational Church, and the funeral party afterwards proceeded to the cemetery, where the service was conducted by the Rev. A.S. Trotman. The chief mourners were the two surviving sons of the deceased, Mr. Alfred and Mr. Arthur Northrop, and amongst those who were present at the funeral were Mr. Joseph Craven, M.P. (who was unable to leave his carriage), Alderman John Hill, Mr. Isaac Smith, Mr. Henry Illingworth, Mr. William Bunting, and Mr. Marsland Tankard. Born at School Green, Thornton, in October 18-5, the deceased was sixty-six years of age. It was in 186- that he first entered into business on his own account, having formerly been in the employment of Messrs. Craven & Harrop, at Thornton. His first place of business was at Laisterdyke. He afterwards removed to Leeds Road, and in 1870 he built the Albion Mill, at Thornton, where the business of worsted manufacturing has since been carried on under the style of J. Northrop & Sons. Of the three sons who were taken into the business as partners one has died. Several years ago Mr. Jonathan Northrop retired, and left the management of the business to his sons. On retiring he went to live at Moorhead. For some time he had been in weak health, and the end came on Tuesday last. The deceased was closely associated with Kipping Chapel for many years as trustee and Sunday-school superintendent. He served for some years on the Thornton Local Board, and he was an active advocate of progressive Liberalism. Besides the two surviving sons already mentioned, Mr. Northrop leaves a widow and five daughters to mourn their loss.

Bradford Observer, 11 July 1892

NEW MISSION CHURCH AT THORNTON. On Saturday afternoon last a memorial stone was laid in the new mission church which has just been built in connection with St. James's Church, Thornton, by Mrs. Theo. Peel of Apperley Bridge. The church, which is of iron, and was built by Messrs. Humprius & Co., London, and is the gift of Mrs. Peel, cost over £200, and will accommodate over 200 people. Mr. Peel gave the ground for the site. The ceremony was witnessed by a large assembly. The Rev. J. Leighton (vicar) and the Rev. A.E. Dams (curate) went through a short service, assisted by the choir and a band of local instrumentalists. The vicar and Mr. Peel afterwards gave short addresses. A tea was provided in the church, and a large number sat down.

Bradford Observer, 13 July 1892

SUDDEN DEATH AT THORNTON. Yesterday afternoon, Peter Harker of Lane Side, Thornton, died very suddenly while engaged at his employment at Messrs. John Morton & Co.'s Fireclay Works. Deceased leaves a wife and four small children.

Leeds Mercury, 29 November 1892

THORNTON AND DISTRICT JOINT HOSPITAL. On Saturday a joint hospital for the treatment of infectious diseases which has been erected at Thornton was formally opened. The building has been erected at the cost of the three local sanitary authorities of Thornton, Clayton, and Wilsden, in accordance with the recent general orders of the Local Government Board. The hospital is situated at Thornton Heights, on the ridge separating the Thornton and Bell Dean valleys. There are four wards, in which accommodation is found for six beds and six cots. There are two nurses' kitchens, from which every bed and cot can be inspected, and there are verandahs for shelter and the use of convalescents. The administrative block contains living-rooms for the master and matron, a doctor's room, an ambulance room, and other conveniences. There is also a detached block of buildings containing washhouse, laundry, mortuary, and disinfecting-rooms. The latter contain a steam disinfecting apparatus, made by Messrs. Goddard, Massey, and Warner, of Nottingham. The sewage will be treated by precipitation in the lower portion of the ground. The total cost of the building, including fittings and furnishings, and site of three acres (which was purchased for £325) has been about £3,000. Messrs. W. and J. B. Bailey, of Bradford and Keighley, are the architects, and the works have been carried out by the following firms:- Masonry, Messrs. Balmforth and Reece; joinery, Mr. S. Benn; slating, Mr. T. Nelson; plumbing, Mr. F.W. Higginbotham; plastering, Messrs. Laycock and Son; painting, Messrs. Varley and Roebuck. The ventilators were supplied by Mr. Kershaw, of Lancaster; the gates and railings by Messrs. Longbottom Bros., of Bingley; the chimney-pieces by Messrs. Taylor and Parsons, Bradford; furniture and carpets by Thomas Simpson and Sons, Halifax; and beds and ironmongery by Mr. J.H. Barraclough. The inaugural proceedings took place at the hospital on Saturday afternoon. Invitations had been sent out by the chairman of the Hospital Board (Mr. William Pickles) to the members and officials of the three Local Boards named.

Illustrated Weekly Telegraph, 7 January 1893

STACK FIRE AT THORNTON. A large stack of good hay belonging to Mr. James Pearson, of Grandage Gate Farm, was completely destroyed by fire on Saturday night. The stack was worth about £100.

Illustrated Weekly Telegraph, 7 January 1893

THORNTON MUSICAL UNION. The third annual assembly was held in the Mechanics' Hall on Saturday evening. A varied selection of songs, part-songs, glees, &c, were rendered by members, and Mr. E. Tankard sang 'One More Polka' and 'Sister Mary.' Dancing was indulged in from 7 to 11.30.

Illustrated Weekly Telegraph, 14 January 1893

PRESENTATION TO THE LATE VICAR OF THORNTON. The annual tea and entertainment took place in connection with the St. James's Church Sunday School, Thornton, on Saturday last. The most interesting feature of the proceedings was the presentation of a cheque of fifteen guineas and a case of cutlery to the Rev. J. Leighton, the late vicar, who has been appointed vicar of Great Horton. The presentation was made by Mrs. Walton. Mr. Leighton, in returning his thanks, mentioned that during his ministry of two and a half years the debt on the church had been relieved to the amount of £750, a new mission church had been erected, through the generosity of Mr. and Mrs. Theo. Peel, and the affairs of the church seemed to be in a flourishing condition.

Illustrated Weekly Telegraph, 14 January 1893

SOCIAL AFFAIRS AT THORNTON. The annual ball of the Thornton Rangers Football Club was held on Saturday night in the Mechanics' Hall, and was very successful. The teachers under the Thornton School Board, which comprises Thornton, Keelham, and Denholme, held their annual assembly in the James Street Board School, Thornton, on Saturday, when a programme of songs, &c, was gone through, and dancing was indulged in. About 70 persons were present, including members of the Board and friends. The annual tea and meeting of St. James's Church Sunday School was held in the National School on Saturday, and was largely attended. The new vicar – Mr. Tolly – presided at the meeting, and gave an address.

Illustrated Weekly Telegraph, 11 February 1893

From the report of the Medical Officer to the Thornton Local Board it appears that a gradual improvement in the sanitary state of the district is taking place.

Illustrated Weekly Telegraph, 11 March 1893

A DESTITUTE LABOURER'S END AT THORNTON. On Thursday afternoon, Mr. W. Barstow, the district coroner, resumed his inquiry at the School Green Hotel, Thornton, relative to the death of Samuel Ambler, a middle-aged labourer of Thornton, who died suddenly near the School Green Hotel on Tuesday night last. The jury expressed the opinion that the case had been a little oversight or mistake through the case not being fully comprehended; but returned a verdict of 'Death from natural causes.'

Illustrated Weekly Telegraph, 15 April 1893

THORNTON LOCAL BOARD. The final meeting of the old Board was held in the Board Office in Kipping Lane on Wednesday afternoon, under the presidency of Mr. John Wilkinson, nine members being present. The plan for a house to be built at Spring Holes by Mr. Robert Birch was approved. Forty-four applications for the post of surveyor and nuisance inspector had been received, and the following four candidates will be requested to meet a special meeting of the Board on the 18th inst.: Messrs. Ezra Graham and Alfred Southwart, Thornton; Mr. Thomas Wade, Birmingham; and Mr. G.J. Clark, Brighouse.

Illustrated Weekly Telegraph, 22 April 1893

The marriage of Mr. Albert Wesley Priestley, son of Mr. Midgley Priestley, of Schooledge, Thornton, with Miss Jemima Bowick, daughter of the late Mr. Alexander Bowick, of St. Cyrus, Montrose, was celebrated at St. Mary's Church, Harrogate, on Tuesday.

Illustrated Weekly Telegraph, 22 April 1893

SMALL-POX AT THORNTON. A case of small-pox has been discovered at New Road End, Thornton. The patient is a married man named Clough, who had been working as an engine stoker with some travelling showmen in the neighbourhood of Halifax, where it is supposed he contracted the disease. The man has been removed to the joint hospital for infectious diseases at Storr Heights, Thornton, and the house in which he lived has been fumigated.

Illustrated Weekly Telegraph, 6 May 1893

The man Peter Foster, of Well Head, Thornton, better known as 'Little Pete,' who hanged himself on Monday, although about 70 years of age is said to have had some disappointment in a love affair. It is said that the banns had been published twice at the church, but that almost at the last moment his intended – who was some few years his junior – refused to marry him – hence the tragic finale.

Illustrated Weekly Telegraph, 15 May 1893

FATALITY AT THORNTON. On Monday forenoon an accident occurred, at the quarry belonging to Messrs. John Farrar & Sons, Thornton, resulting in the death of a young man, nineteen years of age, named Richard Swanston. Swanston, in trying to catch the runaway horse attached to the 'drug,' tripped and fell with his head across the line, under the wheels of the 'drug,' which passed over his head and neck, killing him instantly. At the inquest on Wednesday the jury returned a verdict of 'Accidental Death.'

Illustrated Weekly Telegraph, 17 June 1893

THORNTON LOCAL BOARD. The monthly meeting of the Thornton Local Board was held on Wednesday, Mr. J. Barraclough presiding. The receipts from all sources were reported to be £295 13s 10d, and the payments £506 11s 6d. Plans which have been prepared by Mr. John Drake, with reference to the new water scheme, included in the purchase of Hedge House Farm [sic], also of the new sewerage works, were accepted by the Board, subject to approval by the Local Government Board. It was decided to honour the Royal wedding by giving a tea to the aged and poor in the village, and the Board resolved itself into a committee (with power to add) to collect subscriptions, and carry out the project, Mr. Joseph Craven, of Ashfield, having promised £20 towards the fund.

Illustrated Weekly Telegraph, 24 June 1893

The members of the Thornton P.S.A. Association had their first annual excursion on Saturday afternoon, when above 300 persons journeyed to Morecambe. A very pleasant afternoon was spent, the party reaching Thornton again at 12 o'clock.

Illustrated Weekly Telegraph, 1 July 1893

SACRED CONCERT AT THORNTON. Under the auspices of the Thornton Philharmonic Society, a sacred concert was given yesterday afternoon by the Wyke Temperance Brass Band, in a field near to Messrs. Peel Bros. & Co.'s mill, lent by Mr. J.O. Wood. There was a good attendance, the receipts amounting to £9 11s 5½d.

Illustrated Weekly Telegraph, 15 July 1893

ROYAL WEDDING FESTIVITIES AT THORNTON. The Royal wedding was honoured at Thornton on Saturday, when about 250 aged and poor persons were provided with a substantial meat tea in the Mechanics' Hall, and about 800 children in the various day schools were treated to buns and tea, each child also being presented with a bag of sweets. The whole party – old and young – afterwards repaired to a field in James Street, when the Manningham Brass Band was in attendance, and played selections of music, a very pleasant evening being spent. The expenses were met by a public subscription, which realised about £27, the arrangements being carried out by the Thornton Local Board.

Illustrated Weekly Telegraph, 15 July 1893

The Thornton Local Board at their meeting on Wednesday decided to hand over the sum of £6 1s 2d to the Thornhill colliery disaster fund, being the balance in hand after paying the expenses in connection with the Royal wedding festivities last Saturday.

Illustrated Weekly Telegraph, 22 July 1893

SCALDING FATALITY AT THORNTON. On Sunday, the only child of Mr. T.P. Couldwell, New Road End, Thornton, died from scalds by falling into a bowl of hot water on Friday.

Mechanics Institute Billiards Team, 1913.

Mechanics Institute Chess Team, 1890s.

Illustrated Weekly Telegraph, 22 July 1893

THORNTON GRAMMAR SCHOOL. The following results have just come to hand in connection with the science and art examination. Photography – Pass: Charles Appleyard, John Shackleton, and Charles Roberts. Mathematics: – Charles Roberts and Herbert Waugh.

Illustrated Weekly Telegraph, 22 July 1893

THORNTON AND DISTRICT TEMPERANCE AND BAND OF HOPE UNION. The annual summer demonstration took place on Saturday in a field at the top of Ashfield Road. During the afternoon a procession was formed at the Mechanics' Institute, which proceeded round the village to the field, accompanied by the Dewsbury Old Prize Band. The attractions comprised a juvenile concert, when topical and other songs were sung, accompanied by the band, conductor Mr. Joseph Southwart; juvenile athletic festival; and an industrial and art exhibition, consisting of needlework, artwork, model and sloyd work, penmanship, etc. In the evening the band played selections of music for dancing. The affair was largely attended, and was a complete success.

Illustrated Weekly Telegraph, 29 July 1893

THORNTON GRAMMAR SCHOOL. The following results in connection with the Science and Art Department have just been received:- Model Drawing – First class: C. Appleyard and J. Shackleton. Second class: J. Jarrett, J. Sutcliffe, and A. Stocks. Freehand – Second class: C. Appleyard, J. Shackleton, J. Sutcliffe.

Illustrated Weekly Telegraph, 29 July 1893

THORNTON WESLEYAN CHOIR TRIP. This choir had their annual excursion on Monday, when a party of 35 persons journeyed to Worksop. The various places of interest at the Dukeries were visited, and the weather being all that could be desired, a most enjoyable day was spent.

Illustrated Weekly Telegraph, 12 August 1893

BRADFORD COUNTY COURT, TUESDAY, Before His Honour Judge Gates, Q.C. AN UNFORTUNATE YOUNG MAN.

Mr. E.H. Hill, solicitor, Halifax, made application for a bankrupt's discharge on behalf of R.J. Walton (23), formerly in business at Old Mill, Thornton. The Official Receiver's statement was to the effect that a receiving order was made on September 9th, 1892, on the bankrupt's petition. The public examination was concluded on 4th November, 1892. The liabilities to rank for dividend were £11,930, but the actual amount was £12,189. The assets were estimated to produce £3,893, but they were expected to realise £4,205. Since there had been a first dividend of 5*s* in the pound paid, and a further dividend of 6*d* was probable. Richard James Walton, grandfather of the bankrupt, commenced business as a worsted spinner at the Old Mill, Thornton, 30 years ago. He died in March, 1882, and his son John, the bankrupt's father, carried on the business until March, 1887, when he died. Afterwards, until September, 1891, it was continued by his widow (bankrupt's mother). At that time Mrs. Walton retired, and the business was then left entirely in the hands of the bankrupt. Figures showed at the time of the grandfather's death a surplus of liabilities over assets amounting to £8,873, and at the death of the son £11,889, and at the time when the bankrupt took over the estate from his mother, £4,006. The debtor's chances of succeeding in the business were, therefore, very frail. His Honour said with regard to the Official Receiver's report he was happy to think that there were none of the ordinary trading offences brought against the bankrupt, but on the other hand he had not been able to pay 10*s* in the £. There was no imputation upon the debtor in regard to the way he had carried on business or kept his books and accounts. Not having paid 10*s* in the £, the Court, by Act of Parliament, had power to suspend the discharge for at least two years, unless the debtor could not justly be held responsible for what had taken place. The bankrupt had been placed in an unfortunate position. His discharge was suspended for two years.

Illustrated Weekly Telegraph, 26 August 1893

SUDDEN DEATH AT THORNTON. The death took place on Wednesday afternoon of the six-year-old daughter of Mr. D. Robinson, Sowden Field, Thornton, from English cholera. On Tuesday evening she ate some plums, and was soon afterwards taken very ill, being seized with fits almost continually, expiring about four o'clock on the following afternoon.

Illustrated Weekly Telegraph, 2 December 1893

PROPERTY SALE AT THORNTON. The Alderscholes pit, Thornton, containing three beds of coal and one of fire-clay, was offered for sale last Friday at the Wellington Inn by Mr. John Tillotson, and was disposed of for £312 to Mr. Julius Whitehead, of the Clayton Fire-clay Works.

Illustrated Weekly Telegraph, 13 January 1894

CHARGES AT THORNTON JOINT FEVER HOSPITAL. The monthly meeting of the Thornton Local Board was held on Wednesday, Mr. Wm. Bunting presiding. An account, amounting to £83, for the maintenance of patients from the Thornton district at the joint hospital for infectious diseases at Thornton, had been received from the joint Hospital Board. Mr. Barraclough moved that in all cases families having had members treated in the hospital be asked to contribute towards the cost of maintenance while in the hospital. Mr. Pickles seconded the motion which was carried. The account was brought before the medical officer, and Mr. Pickles asked whether such ailments as scarletina might not be treated at home. Dr. Drake asked, what was the use of the hospital if it was not for the treatment of infectious disease? Mr. Pickles: But the expenses amount to a serious sum. Dr. Drake: Then you'll get very few cases in the hospital. Some families, he said, expect to have to contribute towards the cost of maintenance, say, about one-half, and that was what he understood the Board expected them to pay.

Illustrated Weekly Telegraph, 24 March 1894

HOIST ACCIDENT AT THORNTON. A somewhat serious accident happened on Friday afternoon at Messrs. Mark Dawson & Sons, Prospect Mill, Thornton. A lad, aged 13, named J.J. Armstrong, of Sapgate Lane, Thornton, was looking over the guard of the hoist when the descending cage caught him, seriously tearing the flesh off his face and head. Dr. Tunstall attended him, and ordered his removal to the Bradford Infirmary, where he is making satisfactory progress.

Leeds Mercury, 21 April 1894

COUNTY COUNCIL INQUIRY AT THORNTON. An inquiry was held on Tuesday at Thornton by Mr. J. Lister, Mr. John Hutton, and Mr. J.J. Carter, members of the West Riding County Council, and Mr. W. Vibart Dixon, Deputy-Clerk of the Council, as to the changes occasioned by the new Local Government Act. Mr. Dixon explained that in the parish of Thornton there were two local government districts – and under the Act these would become separate parishes unless the County Council should see fit to order differently. The inquiry was held for the purpose of ascertaining the wishes of the people of these districts.

Illustrated Weekly Telegraph, 28 April 1894

A WESLEYAN MINISTER ON FOOTBALL. The Rev. Albert Clayton, superintendent of the Great Horton Wesleyan Circuit, preaching at Thornton on Sunday, referred to the game of football. He said the game did not come under the term physical exercise, and he must protest against 10,000 to 15,000 men standing in all sorts of weather to witness 30 men engage in a struggle, also against the drinking before and after the game, and against the gambling associated with it. He said that it was in so many cases ruining the morning Sunday School, absorbing sadly too much time in factories, and the time of employers generally on the part of the employes and that it tended to juvenile gambling.

Illustrated Weekly Telegraph, 2 June 1894

On Saturday an alarm of fire was received at the Bradford Town Hall requesting assistance for a fire which had broken out in the boiler house of Messrs. David Craven & Co., shawls manufacturers, Thornton. The small engine was at once despatched, and subsequently a message was received stating that the brigade need not be sent as the fire had been got under. The engine was, however, then on the way. The boiler-house and mechanics' shop were completely gutted. A quantity of wood had been stored in the boiler-house, and this is supposed to have overheated and taken fire. The fire was prevented from spreading to other parts by an iron door. The damage will probably be two hundred pounds.

Illustrated Weekly Telegraph, 14 July 1894

From Thornton on Saturday afternoon a party of about 100 members of the P.S.A. Society and the Foresters' Club went to Ingleton. A violent thunderstorm and heavy rain prevailed, precluding any visit to the falls. About 60 persons from the adult classes of the Methodist Free Church Sunday School Thornton, went to Kirkstall Abbey.

Bradford Observer, 9 August 1894

LOCAL AFFAIRS AT THORNTON. The monthly meeting of the Local Board of Thornton was held yesterday, Mr. John Wilkinson presiding. From the report of the Buildings and Sanitary Committee it appeared that the clerk, Mr. Raywood Stansfeld, had been instructed to write to Mr. William Brown drawing his attention to a nuisance in Thompson's Square, arising from defective drainage belonging to his property, and requiring him to remedy the same without delay, and also to Mr. Fielding's trustees drawing their attention to a nuisance arising from the cart-shed at the Wellington Inn. The clerk was also instructed to write to Messrs. Stocks & Co. in reply to their letter complaining of damage suffered by their tenant at Raggalds Inn by water running from the road in to his land, and to point out that the water only discharged itself on the lane as it had done beyond living memory, and that the Board denied any liability. Mr. Drake, medical officer, reported that the birth-rate in Thornton had been equal, during the month, to 12.1 per thousand per annum and the rate of mortality to 19.0 per thousand. Eight deaths had occurred from whooping-cough since February last. A case of typhoid fever had also been notified in a house in Sapgate Lane, of which complaints had been made as to the prevalence of bad smells. All necessary steps, however, had been taken by the medical and sanitary authorities in regard thereto. Several applications were made for the renewal of licences for slaughtering purposes in the Local Board district, and the medical officer (Dr. Drake), the sanitary inspector (Mr. Wade), and Messrs. Tom Jarratt and T. Craven (two members of the Board) were nominated to view the various premises before the licences were granted. The seal of the Board was affixed to loan mortgages for waterworks and recreation ground purposes, at 3¼ per cent per annum, and also to other loans at the same rate of interest for works of sewage disposal.

Market Street looking east from the top of Bridge Street.

Illustrated Weekly Telegraph, 8 September 1894

DEATH OF AN OLD THORNTONIAN. The death took place on Tuesday morning at his residence, Carbine House, Thornton, of Mr. Daniel Ackroyd, formerly a butcher, at the age of 71 years. He visited Morecambe in the early part of the summer, and since then has been far from robust, and succumbed to dropsy. Mr. Ackroyd was a well-known figure in Thornton and district.

Chapter Twenty-Four
1895-1898

New Thornton Urban District Council formed – Salt Pie Farm for sale – Horses and carts collide in West Lane – Bradford postmen's band plays at gala – Annual holidays from Thornton to east and west coasts

Bradford Observer, 1 January 1895

THORNTON. A TIE FOR THE CHAIRMANSHIP. The first meeting of the newly-elected Urban District Council for Thornton was held last night, at the offices of the former Local Board, Kipping Lane, Thornton. Mr. R.M. Stansfeld, clerk of the old Local Board and returning officer at the recent election for the Urban District Council, presented a return showing the election of the following members of the Council, all of whom were present, viz:- Messrs. John Hey, Joseph Wood, Thomas Craven, John Morton, Abraham Hardy, Richardson Jennings, Richard Hollingsworth, Richard Johnson, William Pickles, Robert Fisher, James Barraclough, and Jonas Illingworth. As returning officer, Mr. STANSFELD also presided during the initial stages of the proceedings, and invited propositions for the election of the chairman and Council for the ensuing year. Mr. RICHARDSON JENNINGS proposed, and Mr. JOHN MORTON seconded, a motion that Mr. Joseph Wood should be the first chairman of the new District Council. As an amendment, Mr. JOHN HEY proposed the name of Mr. William Pickles. In so doing, Mr. Hey drew attention to the long and good service rendered to Thornton in many ways by Mr. Pickles. At the same time, he said, he had not a word to say against Mr. Wood, who was, as all recognised, qualified for the position by long and faithful service. Mr. James BARRACLOUGH said he would no doubt be in the position of many other members of the Council, inasmuch as he would have wished to be able to give his vote for both the gentlemen named. Both had rendered long service to the interests of Thornton, but probably Mr. Pickles had given the closer attention to the matters of sanitation and one or two other subjects of immediate interest to the people of the district. On a vote being taken six votes were given for Mr. Pickles and six for Mr. Wood. The CHAIRMAN, being appealed to, stated that as returning officer he had no power to give a casting vote. The matter was solely in the hands of the councillors present. Someone thereupon suggested that the names of the two gentlemen, Mr. Pickles and Mr. Wood, should be placed in a hat and drawn by lot. Mr. Pickles's name being the first drawn it was agreed to unanimously, on the motion of Mr. JOHN HEY, seconded by Mr. ILLINGWORTH. Mr. Pickles, on taking the position of chairman of the District Council, which carries with it that of justice of the peace for the county, was received with applause. He said, whether he had been elected or not, his desire for the welfare of Thornton and its interests would have prompted him from a sense of duty to do all that lay in his power to further those interests as a member of the District Council. He was elected chairman of the first School Board and now he found himself in the position of being the first elected chairman of the District Council. He tendered his heartiest thanks for the honour conferred upon him (applause). Mr. John Hey and Mr. Joseph Wood were elected to serve on the Joint Hospital Board. The members of the Council then divided themselves into four committees for carrying on the work of the Council during the ensuing term of office.

Illustrated Weekly Telegraph, 5 January 1895

Mr. Wm. Pickles, who was on Monday elected chairman of the Thornton District Council, is well qualified for the position of a J.P., and his election is popular in the village. He was born in Thornton, and is a life-long resident, and has served the public in various capacities for a generation. He is a prominent member of the Liberal Association, and an ardent worker in connection with the Methodist Free Church.

Illustrated Weekly Telegraph, 9 March 1895

The business of Messrs. C. Weatherall and Co., worsted spinners, Old Mill, Thornton, has been taken over by Messrs. Harker and Weatherall, the gentlemen now constituting the firm being Mr. F.W. Harker and Mr. Charles Weatherall. Mr. Weatherall has severed his connection with Ira Ickringill and Co. Ltd., Keighley, by a dissolution of partnership dated December 31st last.

Illustrated Weekly Telegraph, 13 April 1895

HAYSTACK FIRE AT THORNTON. A stack of hay owned by Mr. R. Hollingsworth was consumed by fire on Saturday morning, when damage to the extent of £50 was done. The stack was stored in a field near Dole Mills.

Illustrated Weekly Telegraph, 8 June 1895

Mrs. Joshua Craven, of Westfield House, Thornton, died somewhat suddenly at her residence on Monday morning from paralysis. Mrs. Craven was forty-five years of age, and was the daughter of Mr. Henry Foster, of Denholme.

Illustrated Weekly Telegraph, 9 November 1895

THORNTON FAIR. The annual cattle fair was held on Tuesday adjoining the Great Northern Hotel, when there was a moderate attendance of farmers, dealers, etc.

Bradford Observer, 8 January 1896

HEALTH LECTURES AT THORNTON. The committee of the Thornton Mechanics' Institute have arranged for a course of lectures on 'Health and Sanitation' by well-known local doctors. The first lecture was given last night by Dr. Meredith Young, of Brighouse, on 'The Management of the Sickroom.' There was a very large audience, over which Mr. R. Fisher presided. The next lecture is to be on 'Infection and Prevention,' by Dr. Rabagliati, of Bradford.

Bradford Observer, 28 January 1896

ODDFELLOWS GATHERING AT THORNTON. On Saturday last the annual tea and meeting of the Rock of Hope Lodge of the Independent Order of Oddfellows were held in the Mechanics' Hall, Thornton. There were 350 persons present at tea, after which Mr. Robinson Kershaw, P.P.G.M., presided. The report showed an increase of 20 members during the year, the total being 263 with an average age of 38 years. The worth of the society is £2855, securely invested at good interest, and average per member of £10 9s 11d, which is a slight decrease on previous years owing to the large increase in members. The juvenile tent is also flourishing, with a total membership of 113 – an increase of 22; the average age being 9 years 6 months, and the worth per member, 7s 11d. Addresses were delivered by Mr. B.T. Copley, P.P.G.M., Mr. I.D. Sloane, P.P.G.M., Mr. T. Craven, P.P.G.M., of Bradford, and Dr. Tunstall of Thornton, medical officer to the lodge. During the evening a long and varied programme of songs, duets, and glees was efficiently rendered by Misses Lee, Waddington, Tapp, and Crossley, and Messrs. J. Laycock, J. Ball, F. Cockcroft, F. Robertshaw, and Milton Atkinson, of Keighley (humorist). Mr. F. Bairstow was an able accompanist. There was a crowded and enthusiastic audience.

Leeds Mercury, 9 April 1896

THORNTON DISTRICT COUNCIL. Mr. William Pickles presided at the monthly meeting last night, when Mr. Wm. Pickles and Mr. Abraham Rhodes were appointed Overseers. The medical officer reported a death rate equal to 21.1, and birth rate to 29.5. Plans of new offices and chambers, to be built in New-road by the Mechanics' Institute, were sanctioned. It was also decided to accept the offer of £40 a year for rent of rooms for the Council in their new building.

Illustrated Weekly Telegraph, 20 June 1896

THORNTON CHURCH. A very interesting description and picture of the Brontë memorial organ, which will shortly be erected in Thornton Church, appears in the current issue of 'The Sketch.' The organ will be 23ft. high, 11ft. 6in, across the front, and 8ft. along the sides. It contains 46 stops, consisting of the most modern combination, and will be one of the largest organs in the West Riding. Messrs. Harrison and Harrison, of Durham, are the builders.

Illustrated Weekly Telegraph, 26 July 1896

FARM SALE AT THORNTON. At the Great Northern Hotel, Thornton, on Friday, Salt Pie Farm, situate in Small Lane, Thornton, and containing 7a 0r 6p of freehold land with farm buildings, was offered by auction. Mr. J.O. Wood became the purchaser for £450.

Illustrated Weekly Telegraph, 8 June 1897

ST JAMES'S CHURCH, THORNTON. The Thornton Parochial Magazine for June announces that Mr. A.B. Foster, who some years ago gave the site on which the church stands, has now promised an adjoining site on which to build a vicarage, on condition that the work will be undertaken. Other gentlemen are promising help towards the cost of the building, amongst whom may be named Mr. J. Foster and Mr. E. Wheatley Balme, each of whom has promised £100.

Illustrated Weekly Telegraph, 22 January 1898

TRAP ACCIDENT. Mr. Isaac Wood, of Headley Hall, had a narrow escape from being seriously injured on Friday. Whilst driving along West Lane his horse bolted and dashed into a cart belonging to Mr. Jonas Leach, butcher, Thornton. Mr. Wood was thrown heavily to the ground, and his trap was completely smashed, whilst the shafts of Mr. Leach's cart were broken. Mr. Wood received rather severe injuries to the head and face, but after these had been dressed by Dr. Yeoman, he was then able to proceed home.

Illustrated Weekly Telegraph, 12 February 1898

The second of a course of four lectures on 'Alcohol in Health and Disease' was delivered in the Methodist Free Church Sunday School, Thornton, on Tuesday, by Mr. John Cryer, of Bradford.

Illustrated Weekly Telegraph, 12 February 1898

DEATH OF MR. JOHN WILKINSON, THORNTON. The death took place on Sunday afternoon of Mr. John Wilkinson, of Ashfield Road, Thornton, in his fifty-eighth year. He had suffered for some years from an affection of the stomach, but had been out within the past few days in pretty much his usual health, and only on the 1st inst. presided at the monthly meeting of the Thornton School Board, of which he was chairman. He became worse on Saturday, and Dr, Yeoman was called in, but death took place from exhaustion of the system. He retired from business several years ago, having been for a long period in the employment of Messrs. Joshua Craven and Sons, Prospect Mills, and subsequently as manager for Messrs. H.E. Foster and Co. He was one of the past presidents of the Mechanics' Institute, and held the chairmanship of the Local Board in 1894, and had been a consistent Liberal throughout his life. Religiously he has a life-long connection with the church and congregation at Kipping Chapel, and had taken an active part in the management of the church. He leaves a widow, but no family. The funeral took place on Wednesday at Kipping Cemetery. The coffin, which was of pitch-pine, with brass fittings, bore the following inscription:- 'In loving memory of John Wilkinson; born March 29th, 1840; died February 6th, 1898.' The cortege left his late residence, Ashfield Road, Thornton, at 2.15, and proceeded to the Kipping Independent Chapel, where a brief service was conducted by the Revs. J. Gregory, B.A. (Manningham) and A.S. Trottman (Thornton). Amongst the many beautiful wreaths sent was one from the members of the Board School 'As a token of sincere respect.' The chief mourners were Mrs. Wilkinson, widow; Mr. and Mrs. Edwin Speight, Mr. and Mrs. Waddington, and Mr. and Mrs. J. Varley. The following public bodies were represented:- Thornton School Board: Dr. Yeoman, Rev. A. Brown, Messrs. J. Sugden, B. Pickles, G. Nicholson, and Mr. Ashby; Thornton District Council: Messrs. W. Pickles, J. Bartle, and A. Hardy; Board of Guardians: Mr. J. Marsden. Other friends present included Mr. A. Booth, rate collector; Mr. T. Laycock, of Harrogate; Mr. W. Robinson, and Mr. J. Firth. At a special meeting of the Thornton School Board, on Wednesday, a vote of condolence was ordered to be sent to the relations of the deceased in their sad bereavement.

Illustrated Weekly Telegraph, 12 March 1898

PROPOSED MEMORIAL TO THE LATE VICAR OF THORNTON. A public meeting took place in the National Schools, Thornton, on Monday, to consider a proposal to erect a memorial to the memory of the late Rev. Richard Henry Heap, who died last year, and who was vicar of Thornton for 35 years, from 1855 to 1890. There was a somewhat small attendance, over which the vicar, the Rev. J.

Jolly presided. After several suggestions had been made, it was decided unanimously that the memorial should take the form of the provision of a prayer desk for the clergy and two choir stalls for the choir, and that a brass plate suitably inscribed should be affixed thereto. It was decided to open a 'Heap Memorial Fund,' and the following officers were appointed to carry out the scheme: Mr. C. Norton, secretary; Mr. J.O. Rouse, treasurer; and Messrs. C. Norton, J. Tordoff, and Mrs. Alfred Robertshaw, collectors.

Illustrated Weekly Telegraph, 29 April 1898

THE ROADS OF THORNTON. The members of the Thornton Local Board, after inspecting the roads in their district on Tuesday, were entertained to dinner at the Great Northern Hotel by their newly-appointed chairman, Mr. John Wilkinson, and to tea by Mr, W.L Bunting.

Illustrated Weekly Telegraph, 30 April 1898

A stained glass window was unveiled in Thornton Parish Church on Saturday by Dr. Robertson, Vicar of Bradford, who also preached a sermon. The window has been presented by Mr. Wilman, of Kenilworth, Cape Colony, to the memory of various members of his family, and has been executed by Messrs. Mayes and Co., of London.

Illustrated Weekly Telegraph, 15 July 1898

On Saturday the annual demonstration of the Thornton and District Temperance and Band of Hope Union was held, the procession being led by the Bradford Postmen's Brass Band, in a field in Ashfield Road, and a varied programme of entertainments was gone through, including a juvenile concert, under the leadership of Mr. Eli Barker, athletic sports, maypole dancing, etc., and terminating with a display of fireworks.

Illustrated Weekly Telegraph, 13 August 1898

WORKMEN'S PRESENTATION. On Saturday, at the Albion Mill, Thornton, the employees of J. Northrop and Sons presented Mr. Samuel Bardsley with a pipe and pouch as a token of respect on his leaving the village, after working for the firm ever since it began 28 years ago, in the capacity of carrier.

Illustrated Weekly Telegraph, 13 August 1898

LOCAL TIDES. The mills and workshops generally closed on Friday last at Thornton until Tuesday morning for the usual feast, on account of the general quietness of trade. The week-end and ten-day bookings have been as follows:- Blackpool 100, Morecambe 70, Brighton 4, Filey 3, Bridlington 6, and Scarborough 13. On Monday about 300 persons journeyed to Blackpool by a day excursion promoted by the Oddfellows, and the bookings to Liverpool were 97, Morecambe 70, and to Skegness 40. The annual tides at Denholme, Clayton, and Allerton are also being celebrated.

Bradford Observer, 15 September 1898

TO-MORROW. New Inn, Thornton, near Bradford. By Mr. J. ACKROYD, on the premises of Mr. Hezekiah Duckett (who is declining the bottling business), on the above premises, on Friday, September 16th, 1898. THE WHOLE of his BOTTLING PLANT, &c., comprising 4 h.p. vertical engine and boiler, 6ft. by 2ft. 6in.; patent bottle-washer, with cistern and piping and patent syringe; corking machine, three-bottle siphon, about 100 gross half-pint bottles, sixty (six dozen) bottle crates; 110 (two dozen) bottle boxes; three bags of corks; about twenty-five gross Bass ale and bottles; and items too numerous to mention in connection with the business of a bottler. Also Whitechapel Dogcart and Flat Cart; Wheelbarrow; set of Harness; Hay-chopper; walnut Pianoforte, by Samuel Thomas; large wood Bottling shed and Engine-house, &c., &c. For further particulars see posters. Sale at Two o'clock. Auctioneer's Offices, Keighley and Haworth; and at Grand Junction Hotel, Halifax, on Saturdays, from Three to Five.

Illustrated Weekly Telegraph, 24 December 1898

THORNTON PUBLIC AFFAIRS. On Wednesday a meeting of the Urban District Council was held under the presidency of Mr. J. Barraclough. It was resolved to make application to the Local Government Board for an extension of five years within which to repay the loan of £750 borrowed on surplus land account. The surveyor was instructed to prepare an estimate of the cost of conducting the sewage from the Albion Mills down to the new road by a sewer, and to submit the same to the Sanitary Committee for consideration. The Medical Officer's report showed that during the month of November 17 births and 8 deaths had been registered. Two cases of erysipelas and one case of typhoid had been notified. The report also stated that there was not as much general sickness in the district at present as there was a month ago.

Illustrated Weekly Telegraph, 31 December 1898

It is announced that the curacy of St. James's church, Thornton, has been accepted by Mr. Downer, B.A., of Cambridge, and of Wickliffe Hall, Oxford, and that he expects to be ordained in February. He will succeed the Rev. F.C. Scott, who removed to Harrogate last July. Mr. Downer is the son of a former vicar of Ilkley.

Chapter Twenty-Five
1901-1909

New trams affecting rail traffic – Downs, Coulter buy Thornton Mills –Denholme furniture works destroyed by fire – Blind man falls out of train at Cullingworth – Rabbits and pigeons stolen

Bradford Weekly Telegraph, 5 January 1901

The new tramway from Four Lane Ends to Thornton has already had a very appreciable effect on the passenger traffic by the Great Northern Railway, and naturally this is likely to continue as long as the railway company persist in their present fares for ordinary and season tickets.

Bradford Weekly Telegraph, 12 January 1901

THORNTON. Mr. J. Harold Barraclough, who has held the position of organist at the Wesleyan Chapel, Thornton, for twenty years, was on Wednesday presented with a handsome revolving walnut book-case, with suitable brass inscription plate, by the present and a few past members of the choir. Mr. J. Booth made the presentation.

Bradford Weekly Telegraph, 16 February 1901

Thornton Mills, which up to July of last year were run by Messrs. Peel Bros., have been purchased by Messrs. Downs, Coulter, and Co., of Pudsey and Dudley Hill. It is expected that the restarting of the mills will find employment for some four hundred hands. Messrs. Downs, Coulter, and Co. will remove their entire business from Pudsey and Dudley Hill.

Bradford Weekly Telegraph, 16 February 1901

Thornton Mechanics' Institute Orchestral Society. This recently formed society gave their first concert in the Mechanics' Hall, Thornton, on Saturday, before a large and appreciative audience. The band, under the leadership of Mr. Barnard Langdale, has made satisfactory progress, and their rendering of the four selections was eminently satisfactory. The two vocalists were Miss Linda Robinson, of Guiseley, soprano, and Miss Mary Tapp, of Thornton, contralto, while Miss Marion Webster, solo violin, and Mr. Arthur Robinson, solo violoncello, each contributed to the enjoyment of the audience. Another big attraction was the engagement of Mr. John Paley, the cornet player, who was in good form, his selection including 'My Pretty Jane,' 'Killarney,' 'The Lost Chord,' etc. The pianoforte accompaniments were shared by Mr. Langdale and Mr. Wilfred Spencer.

Bradford Weekly Telegraph, 16 February 1901
LOCAL MILLS ABLAZE
BRADFORD BRIGADE'S SMART WORK

A serious outbreak of fire occurred at an early hour on Saturday at Denholme Gate, just outside the city boundary. It appeared that shortly before two o'clock, Police Sergeant Parker, of the West Riding Constabulary, stationed at Clayton, observed smoke and flames issuing from the works of Messrs. Raywood & Co., Cabinet-makers, Foreside Mills. He at once gave the alarm, and in the meantime despatched a messenger to Thornton to communicate with the Bradford Fire Brigade. Some little delay was caused by the fact that the Telephone Exchange was closed, but the messenger made for the Thornton Police Station, and from there

THE ALARM WAS TELEPHONED

To the Central Fire Office, where it was received at thirty-five minutes past two. Chief Officer Scott left immediately in charge of the tender, and a full complement of firemen. The roads beyond the tram terminus at Thornton were deeply covered with snow and ice, and greatly interfered with the progress of the Fire Brigade, yet they arrived at the scene of the outbreak within fifty minutes of the receipt of the alarm. It was at once seen that the main building, which is about forty-five yards long by thirty-five yards deep, was doomed. The fire appeared to have first occurred at the end nearest the road, and had spread from there rapidly backwards towards the boiler house, over which is the polishing shop. The building is divided into two sections, one half being three and the other two storeys high. The efforts of the Fire Brigade were principally devoted to the boiler house, with a view to

CUTTING-OFF THE FIRE

From that place, and in this they were successful, the damage to that end of the mill being trifling, but the main building was practically gutted. With the assistance of onlookers a large quantity of furniture was removed from the building, and much valuable wood taken to a place of safety. The origin of the fire is at present unknown. The damage is estimated at £1000, and is fully covered by policies placed with the Guardian and North British & Mercantile Fire Offices. The works were partially destroyed by fire about five years ago.

Bradford Weekly Telegraph, 9 March 1901

An inquest was held on Monday at the Boar's Head Hotel, Thornton, by the Bradford City Coroner (Mr. J.G. Hutchinson) relative to the death of John Ramsden, 60 years of age, basket and skep maker, of 11, West Lane, Thornton. From the evidence it appeared that the deceased was travelling by the 6 a.m. train from Thornton to Cullingworth on Friday Jan. 4th. The train was stopped by a signal about 100 yards from Cullingworth Station and the deceased, who was blind, and alone in the compartment, thought that he had arrived at the platform, and stepped out. He fell down the embankment, and received a severe shock from which he died on Friday last. Inspector Joseph, of the Great Northern Railway Co., attended the inquest. Dr. Tunstall said in his opinion the cause of death was exhaustion following nervous prostration, consequent upon the shock received, and the jury returned a verdict of 'Accidental Death.'

Bradford Weekly Telegraph, 23 March 1901

THORNTON SPINNER'S DEATH. The Bradford City Coroner (Mr. J.G. Hutchinson) held an inquest at the Great Northern Hotel, Thornton, on Thursday, relative to the death of Mr. Riley Farnell, 56 years of age, of 2, Vine Terrace, Thornton. The evidence was to the effect that the deceased was owner and occupier of Ash Tree Shed, Thornton, where he had carried on business as a worsted spinner for about 13 years. Mr. Farnell was well known in the Bradford trade. Of late he had been very much depressed owing to business worries. On Tuesday morning the deceased rose earlier than usual, and went out. Not returning some fears were advanced, and his nephew went out in search of him, eventually finding his body floating in the dam adjoining the deceased's mill. The deceased was unmarried, and lived with a sister. Selina Farnell, sister of the deceased, said her brother went out early on Tuesday morning, presumably to go to his sister's, who lived in the next street. It was not unusual for him to go out so early in the morning. Some two month ago deceased had some difficulty with his creditors, and she was informed that he had made a deed of assignment in favour of them. The first instalment was payable in May. The matter had played upon deceased's mind to a considerable extent. He had been very low spirited, and had slept badly. He had, however, never threatened to do away with himself. Eli Barker, a nephew of deceased, said that on his aunt telling him that deceased was missing, he went down to the mill to look for him. Not finding him there he went to the pond, and saw a jacket floating about. He then fetched police assistance. Deceased had to climb a fence to get to the water. Witness further said that the deceased had been troubled by his creditors. One of them would not accept the terms of the deed of assignment, and had sent him writs, which had troubled him yet more. On Monday night witness had informed the deceased that some gentlemen who had promised to help him free himself from his financial difficulties stated that they were not now able to do so, and this overcame deceased entirely. A policeman who took deceased from the water having given evidence, the jury returned a verdict of 'suicide whilst of unsound mind.'

Bradford Weekly Telegraph, 4 May 1901

A pile of waste paper caught fire in the boiler room at Ashtree Mill, Thornton, on Monday afternoon, but the flames were extinguished with a few bucketsful of water before any damage was done.

Bradford Weekly Telegraph, 4 May 1901

Walter Craven (15), a son of Jonas Craven, farmer, of School Green, was on Saturday kicked on the forehead and chin by a horse while he was unyoking the animal from a milk-cart. Dr. Stuart, of Thornton, who attended the lad, was able to report that his injuries were not serious.

Bradford Weekly Telegraph, 27 July 1901

The annual summer demonstration promised by the Thornton Temperance Union took place on Saturday in brilliant weather, and was, perhaps, the most successful even for a number of years. A procession was formed at Wensley Bank of the various temperance societies and bands of hope, together with the members of the Rechabites' lodge. A new venture, in the shape of a horse parade, also added to the interest of the procession, and in this event substantial prizes are offered by the Union for the best groomed horses and cleanest harness, and a large number of entries were made. After proceeding down the main road and up Market Street, headed by the Denholme Brass Band, a halt was made at the top of Market Street, where two hymns were sung. The procession then went to a field in West Lane, where tea was served, and in the evening a number of athletic events were down to take place.

Bradford Weekly Telegraph, 24 January 1903

THORNTON. Robertshaw Craven, a weaver, 15 years of age, of 22, Well Heads, Thornton, was going to his work at Albion Mills shortly after eight on Tuesday morning, when he slipped on the pavement and broke his right leg. He was taken to the residence of his sister, No. 2, Albion Place, and Dr. Tunstall was called in. The injuries were dressed and the doctor ordered the lad's removal to the Bradford Royal Infirmary.

Bradford Weekly Telegraph, 14 February 1903

THORNTON. Mary Ibbotson (60), 14, Providence Terrace, Thornton, fell on Saturday and fractured her right leg. Dr. Stuart was called in, and on seeing her condition on Monday ordered her removal to the Bradford Royal Infirmary. On Tuesday a retired gentleman named Jonas Jennings, residing at Stream Head, Thornton, had occasion to call at the Black Horse Inn, Thornton, at about 5 o'clock. He had scarcely got inside the doorway when he fell backwards and expired almost immediately. He was afterwards conveyed to the Bradford Mortuary. It is stated that the deceased had previously enjoyed good health.

Bradford Weekly Telegraph, 11 April 1903

THORNTON. At noon on Saturday, Rebecca Driver (57), of 30, Back Field, Thornton, met with a serious accident as she was crossing New Road, opposite James Street, at Thornton. A tram car was standing at the terminus, and in passing behind it, she was knocked down by a horse and trap driven by Mr. Fred Dalby of the Craven Heifer Inn, Four Lane Ends. The woman was rendered unconscious, and after being attended to at the Police Station, was removed to the Bradford Royal Infirmary. There she was found to be suffering from cuts and bruises on the face and head. Enquiring as to her condition this morning, we learn that although she had passed a very good night, she was still in a serious condition. The woman, it is stated, was intending sailing to America next week.

Illustrated Weekly Telegraph, 22 April 1905

At the Parish Church, Thornton, on Sunday afternoon, the choir gave a good rendering of Maunder's Lenten cantata 'Penitence, Pardon, and Peace.' Solos were sung by Miss Agnes Baines (Queensbury) and Mr. J.A. Robertshaw (Thornton).

Illustrated Weekly Telegraph, 6 May 1905

WHAT A CONSTABLE OVERHEARD. A Thornton man appeared to be the principal character in a strange little scene in Ingleby Road on Tuesday night. The parties concerned were a young man and his sweetheart (!) and another woman. The following conversation was overheard by a constable, who was standing on one of the side streets abutting the road in question.
Young man (embracing the girl): Kiss me, and I'll tell you where I live.
Young woman: I know where you live; you live at Manningham.
Young man: No, I don't.
Another female (recognizing the young man): 'No, he doesn't; he lives at Thornton and (with emphasis) he's a married man.'
The first young woman thereupon 'rounded on' the man from Thornton to some tune.

Illustrated Weekly Telegraph, 22 December 1905
THE DISMANTLING OF A MILL
COUNTY COURT ACTION
A KEIGHLEY-THORNTON CASE

At Bradford Bankruptcy Court on Tuesday, Judge Bompas, K.C., was occupied for some time in hearing an action brought by John Hugill, secretary to the Keighley Building Society, and the owner in fee simple of the Old Mill, Thornton, against Seth Ormondroyd, iron broker, West Holme Mills, Bradford, for £75 15s as damages for certain mill fittings removed by the defendant from the Old Mill. Mr. Richard Watson (instructed by Messrs. W.G. Burr and Co., Keighley) appeared for the plaintiff and Mr. Harold Newell (instructed by Mr. A.V. Hammond, Bradford) represented the defendant.

The plaintiff stated that for some time the mill had not been running, and in November 1904 he entered into negotiations for the sale of the premises and all they contained to a man called Mawson. These negotiations ultimately fell through, but during the time they were in progress Mawson, under the impression that he had already acquired the premises, had entered into an agreement to sell an engine, boiler, and some upright shafting to a man named Bentley for £140. Plaintiff confirmed the sale of these things, and received £120 from Mawson, the remaining £20 being kept by Mawson for expenses.

Harry Hardaker, consulting engineer and general manager to the Fleece Mills Company, Keighley, said he bought all the line shafting and part of the pulleys at the Old Mill, Thornton, in May 1903, and in the Spring of 1904 he introduced Mr. Bentley to Mr. Mawson, when the former purchased the boiler, engine, and upright shafting and accessories.

Jabez Bancroft, machinery repairer, Keighley, stated that he met the defendant in August last, and asked him if he wanted to buy any machinery at the Old Mill, Thornton. Defendant offered 46s a ton for certain machinery as scrap iron, but the offer was not accepted, and a bargain was ultimately made to sell the stuff to Messrs. Summerscales and Co., Ltd, Keighley, at 50s a ton. Some days later witness visited Old Mill and found Bentley and two of the defendant's men removing certain stuff. Defendant afterwards told witness that he had bought the stuff from Bentley, and at a subsequent interview refused either to return the material or pay for it.

Seth Ormondroyd, West Holme Mills, Keighley, said he had purchased certain fittings in the Old Mill, and also some scrap iron from Mr. Bentley, and that he had removed nothing but what he had a right to. Such things as he had removed he had bought about May, 1904, from Bentley, who produced an invoice showing that he purchased them from Howard Hodgson, who was then the tenant of the Old Mill.

His Honour gave judgement for the plaintiff for £35.

Bradford *Weekly Telegraph*, 9 March 1906

A THORNTON ROBBERY. At Bradford Police Court on Tuesday – before the Stipendiary Magistrate (Mr. Skidmore), Mr. George Harley, and Mr. James Burnley – Jos. Robertshaw, 9, Kipping Court, Thornton, pleaded guilty to stealing £9 belonging to Thos. Hindle. Mr. N.L. Fleming stated that the prosecutor was a grocer carrying on business in Thornton. On the 6th February the defendant, who was a joiner's apprentice, was engaged to do certain repairs for the prosecutor, and he took the money from a drawer. £3 15s had been returned by the defendant, and the prosecutor did not wish to press the case. Defendant was ordered to come up for judgement in a month.

Bradford *Weekly Telegraph*, 30 March 1906

ALLEGED THEFT OF PIGEONS. Yesterday at the Bradford Police Court, Wm. Mark Lister (20), woolcomber, 318, Thornton Road, was remanded for a week, charged with stealing six pigeons and ten rabbits, valued at £20 15s, on March 16th, belonging to Alfred Clayton, a well-known local fancier.

Bradford *Weekly Telegraph*, 13 April 1906

THORNTON GENTLEMAN FINED. At the Bradford Police Court on Monday – before the Stipendiary Magistrate (Mr. Skidmore), Mr. S.P. Myers, Mr. J. Popplewell, Mr. C. Beverley, and Mr. R. Johnson – John Ed. Shackleton, woollen merchant, residing at New Road, Thornton, was summoned by the Excise Authorities for employing a male servant without a licence, and with keeping a carriage without a licence. Mr. Jas. Flynn, who appeared for the Inland Revenue, said that Mr. Shackleton had employed a servant to drive his carriage and pair, and neither the servant or the carriage were licensed. The declaration was served in December last, but Mr. Shackleton did not take out licences until the 6th of this month, two months after it was due. The defendant did not appear, and Warrant Officer Flood said he had served the summons on Mr. Shackleton, who had gone to Southport for the Easter holidays. Fines and costs amounting to £2 14s were imposed, with the alternative of 20 days' hard labour.

Bradford *Weekly Telegraph*, 22 January 1909

Miss Grace Downs, of Cote Gap, Thornton, one of the old-age pensioners, has only lived to receive two payments, her death taking place on Friday last, when the third instalment was due.

Bradford *Weekly Telegraph*, 25 January 1907

Herbert Arnold, driller, of Alderscholes Lane, was admitted to the Bradford Royal Infirmary on Wednesday suffering from concussion of the brain. Whilst he was at work at Thwaites Bros., Limited, engineers, of Thornton Road, Bradford, his head was struck by a falling piece of wood.

On Wednesday Herbert Arnold (26), 36, Alderscholes Lane, was following his employment at Messrs. Thwaites Bros., iron founders, when a piece of wood that had been used for packing the crane chain fell on his head, rendering him unconscious. He was conveyed to the Royal Infirmary in the horse ambulance.

Yorkshire Observer, 29 January 1909

Death of the Rev. J. Jolly, of Thornton.

The death took place yesterday morning at Thornton Vicarage, Bradford, of the Rev. John Jolly, for sixteen years vicar of Thornton. Mr. Jolly preached his last sermon in his church on Christmas morning. He was suffering at the time from a cold, and though somewhat feverish, he left his bed to attend the early Communion on Christmas morning. He received a severe chill, but he persisted in taking the service later in the morning, with the result that he was seriously ill in the afternoon, and complications afterwards set in. For three weeks his situation had been realised to be of the deepest gravity.

Mr. Jolly was born in April, 1845, at the little village of Oving, in Buckinghamshire. In early life he was associated with the Baptist Church, and he was for a considerable number of years minister of a Baptist chapel at Boston, Lincolnshire. Subsequently, owing to a modification of his doctrinal views, he determined to enter the Church of England. He then studied at Trinity College, Dublin, where he graduated in 1882. He was ordained by the Bishop of Ripon, and he served for a considerable time as curate at Kirkby Wiske, under the present Bishop of Richmond. After a short curacy at Wakefield, he was in 1888 appointed as a curate at Bradford Parish Church under the Rev. Canon Bardsley. His duty gave him special charge of a small mission-room in Bolton Road, where he worked assiduously until largely through his efforts, aided by many good friends of the parish, funds were raised for the erection of St. Chrysostom's Church. He was then appointed the first vicar of the church.

After four and a half years' labour in the parish Mr. Jolly was preferred by Canon Bardsley to the vicarage of Thornton, then vacant by the removal of the Rev. J. Leighton to Great Horton. In Thornton Mr. Jolly had worked with the utmost energy, and there is much reason to fear that his untimely death is in large measure due to his having overtaxed his strength in the discharge of his parochial duties. He was an acceptable preacher and a good organiser and business manager. Through his exertions the debt of £1000 which, largely consequent upon the building of the spire of the church, still existed when he became vicar has been cleared off, and funds have been raised to carry out a restoration of the church, to erect a new organ – one of the best in the Bradford district – and in conjunction with his fellow-foundation managers he was instrumental in procuring two extensions of St. James's Day Schools, Thornton. But what is of still greater importance, he won the confidence and regard of his flock, and had been successful in effecting excellent work in the parish.

Mr. Jolly married Miss Hardy, of Leicester, whom he leaves a widow, with four sons and one daughter. One of the sons, the Rev. Harold H. Jolly, is curate at Lancaster Parish Church, and the second son, who has done well at Oxford, is about also to be ordained into the Church. The funeral is fixed for to-morrow afternoon at Thornton.

Bradford Weekly Telegraph, 29 January 1909

It has transpired that the late Rev. J. Jolly, M.A., vicar of Thornton, was in his early manhood – that is, until the year 1887 – associated with the Baptist denomination, being appointed pastor of a large church in Boston in 1871. There his congregation was so large that the building was twice enlarged, and he was popularly known as 'the Spurgeon of Lincolnshire,' so renowned was he for his skill and power in preaching. In 1887, however, he returned to the church of his youth, being ordained deacon and priest in the same year.

Yorkshire Observer, 1 February 1909

Funeral of the Vicar of Thornton.

The interment of the late Vicar of Thornton, the Rev. John Jolly, took place on Saturday afternoon amid many signs of regret. That the deceased gentleman was held in high esteem was shown by the large attendance of clergymen and parishioners. Among the former were Canon Maguinness, the Rev. J.E. Perkins (vicar of St. Michael's, Bradford), the Rev. R.B. McKee (vicar of Christ Church, Bradford), the Rev. G. Pedley (vicar of Girlington), the Rev. R. Pulleine (vicar of Queensbury), the Rev. W.E. Laidman (Clayton), the Rev. J. Bentley, the Rev. T. Lewthwaite (Halifax), and others. Prior to the arrival of the body at the church, which was crowded, the organist (Mr. R.H. Broughton) played 'I know that my Redeemer liveth,' and the choir sang special hymns, one of which was the deceased vicar's favourite, 'Jesu, Lover of my soul.' Here the service was conducted by the Vicar of Bradford (the Rev. H. Gresford Jones) and the Rev. H. Kendall (vicar of St. John's, Bowling). As the coffin was borne out of the church, Mr, Broughton played the Dead March. The service at the graveside was conducted by the Rev. J.E. Perkins.

The principal mourners were Mrs. Jolly, Messrs. N.H.H. Jolly, R. B. Jolly, C. Jolly and N. Jolly and Miss Elsie Jolly. Others in attendance were Messrs. W.M. Brookes and T. Bilsborough (representing the lay elders), J.C. Langton (lay reader), J.O. Rouse (vicar's warden), and Walter Briggs (people's warden), Dr. A.E. Tunstall, Dr. Hamilton Stewart, Messrs. John Lawson, E.W. Margerison, Jonas Drake, J. Cockcroft, J.R. Knowles, Abraham Hardy, and A.W. Ward (Bradford), Miss Gladwin, and the Rev. Leonard Hills. The Rev. W.M. Waton, minister of Kipping Chapel, was prevented from attending by his having to officiate at the interment of one of his own congregation at the same hour.

Yesterday the Vicar of Bradford occupied the pulpit at the morning service at Thornton Church, and in his sermon referred in sympathetic terms to the death of the late vicar.

Bradford Weekly Telegraph, 26 February 1909

DEATH OF MR. W.L. BUNTING

Great regret will be caused throughout Bradford and district by the announcement of the death of Mr. William L. Bunting, which took place at his residence at Prospect House, Thornton, on Monday afternoon.

Mr. Bunting, who had reached his eighty-fourth year, was one of the old school of Liberals once so numerous in Bradford. Although he never took an active or prominent part in public affairs he was an ardent politician, and until quite recently a constant habitué of the Bradford Liberal Club. Here he was one of the select few who formed what was known as the 'Deacons' Corner.'

Among his numerous acquaintances he was in some demand as a raconteur, for he had a great store of good stories and a pretty wit. For many years he was frequently a member of the shooting party comprising Mr. Joseph Craven, of Thornton, the late Mr. Briggs Priestley, the late Mr. William Harker, of Pateley Bridge, the late Mr. George Hodgson, and others, who rented the shooting in Upper Nidderdale, and used to assemble for the Twelfth at Middlesmoor. His personality was exceedingly genial and kindly, and his death will cause a gap which it will be difficult to fill.

A native of Northamptonshire he came to Bradford over sixty years ago when he was a young man of 21. Entering the service of Mr. Thos. Clayton, woolstapler, of Thornton Road, he quickly acquired an intimate knowledge of the wool trade. After some years he found himself in a position to set up in business for himself as a spinner and manufacturer. He was keen and possessed much insight, soon becoming successful. His business ability was never better exhibited than in 1857, the year of the panic in the Bradford trade, when so many well-known firms were driven on the rocks. The price of Bradford's staple commodity went down to astoundingly low prices, the city was nearly bankrupt, everyone was selling, few dared to buy. But Mr. Bunting, risking much, purchased at panic prices, and in the end made large profits. After that he took into partnership Ald. Henry Sowden, who at one time was a well known and active member of the Town Council. Mr. Bunting has now been retired from business for some twenty-five years.

Always a deeply religious man, he early joined Horton Lane Church, later becoming a member at Listerhills Congregational Church when that cause was commenced as an off-shoot. On taking up his residence in Thornton he attached himself to the congregation at Kipping, though he never took a prominent part in the work.

Mr. Bunting's wife, who was a sister of Mr. Joseph Craven, died many years ago. He had two children, who survive him – a daughter who resided with him at Thornton, and a son, who is in business at Melbourne, in Australia.

Bradford Weekly Telegraph, 9 April 1909

The Rev. Arthur H. Tollitt will commence his duties as vicar of Thornton Parish Church on Monday, April 19th, and the institution and induction to the parish will be conducted at the church on that date by the Lord Bishop of

Richmond. The curacy of Thornton has been accepted by the Rev. W.W. McKew, of Eccleshill, who was formerly curate of St. Augustine's, Bradford.

Bradford Weekly Telegraph, 23 April 1909

The Rev. Arthur Henry Tollitt was inducted into St. James's Parish, Thornton, on Monday. The Bishop of Richmond, who conducted the ceremony, made sympathetic reference to the death of the late vicar, the Rev. J. Jolly, and spoke with deep feeling of the deceased gentleman's religious convictions. Dr. Pulleine had also many encouraging things to say of the new vicar, and impressed upon the congregation the necessity of assisting him in his work if the change was to be a blessing to the church. It was responsible and difficult work, and he hoped they would not assume that everything depended on the vicar.

Bradford Weekly Telegraph, 7 May 1909
YORKSHIRE WILLS

Mr. William Lansbury Bunting, of Prospect House, Thornton, Bradford, woollen manufacturer, formerly of the firm of Bunting and Snowden, and a member of the Bradford Liberal Club, who died on the 22nd Feb. last, left estate valued at £40,744 gross, and sworn at £40,648 net. Probate of his will has been granted to Mr. William Edwin Briggs Priestley, of Rosemount House, Bradford, worsted manufacturer, Mr. William Horsfall Maynard, of Haselmere, Shipley, Yorks., stuff merchant, and the deceased's son Mr. Nathan Craven Bunting, of 3 Prospect House, mechanical engineer.

Bradford Weekly Telegraph, 14 May 1909
A THORNTON STREET IMPROVEMENT DISPUTE

On Monday, at the Bradford County Court, before his Honour Judge Graham, K.C., an action was brought by Solomon Robinson, of Well Heads, Thornton, Bradford, quarry-owner, against Abraham Illingworth and John Sugden, both of Thornton, claiming £5 for work done in connection with the paving and repairing of Henry Street, Thornton, in the latter part of the year 1907.

It was stated that on receiving notices from the local authority for the work to be done a meeting of the property owners was called, and at that meeting the defendants were appointed secretary and chairman respectively of the property owners. For the plaintiff it was contended that the defendants on behalf of all the property owners engaged the plaintiff to act for them in the supervision and carrying out of the work, but the

Terminus for first tram service from Bradford.

defendants contended that the plaintiff had no instructions from them or from the property owners, except Miss S.A. Broadhead, for whom he acted.

His Honour, after hearing the defendant Sugden and without calling any witnesses, dismissed the plaintiff's case. He expressed the opinion that the plaintiff was not authorised to do any work on behalf of the defendants or the committee of the property owners, and gave judgement for the defendants with costs. Messrs. J. Wickstead Perkins and Hind appeared for the plaintiff, and Messrs. Moore and Shepherd for the defendants.

Chapter Twenty-Six
1911-1913

Housebreakers rampant near Thornton reservoir – Holiday money stolen by Havelock Street man – Thornton Tide attendances hit by exodus to seaside – New sanatorium planned for Maggot Farm – Girl falls into sewage tank near golf course

Bradford Observer Budget, 4 February 1911
Mr. J.H. Whitley, M.P., was the principal speaker at the annual meeting of the Thornton Liberal Association and Club, held in the Mechanics' Hall, Thornton, on Saturday. Mr. Alfred Farrar presided over a crowded gathering.

Bradford Observer Budget, 4 February 1911
SERIOUS FALL INTO A QUARRY. The danger attached to walking near quarries at night was brought to light at Thornton on Sunday morning, when a police officer found Mr. John Robbins (50), South Street, Denholme, in an exhausted condition in a disused quarry at Hill Top. Mr. Robbins missed the 11.35 p.m. train from Thornton to Denholme, and made his way up the fields to walk home. He took his path through Thornton cricket field, and climbed the wall in mistake and fell into the quarry. After having been there nearly seven hours he was found as stated, and taken to the Thornton Police-station, whence Dr. Stewart ordered his removal to the Bradford Royal Infirmary. Mr. Robbins had received injuries to the head, a fractured collar-bone, and fractured ribs.

Bradford Observer Budget, 25 March 1911

PRESENTATION TO A LOCAL MUSICIAN. A large number of friends assembled at the Exchange Station, Bradford, on Friday of last week to bid farewell to the vocalists from this district who are included in Dr. Coward's choir, whilst several went as far as Liverpool to see them safely embark. Prior to their departure an interesting presentation was made by Mrs. Waugh to Mr. J.W. Horsfall, who has conducted the local contingent at their rehearsals during the past twelve months. Mr. Horsfall was the recipient of a large and handsome picture containing the whole of the West Riding contingent. Mr. Horsfall also received a written testimonial, and he accepted an invitation to accompany the singers to Liverpool, where he saw the choir set sail.

Bradford Observer Budget, 19 April 1911

WINDOW-BOX COMPETITION. The window-boxes in the Lord Mayor's competition for the Thornton Ward were judged on Thursday last, and the judges made the following awards: Class A: Wright Driver; 2, J.M. Procter; 3, W.L. Emmett. Class B: Greenwood Butterfield; 2, S. Hainsworth; 3, Dale Slater. Class C: T.C. Emmott; 2, A.E. Smith. Class D: J. Robertshaw; 2, Exley Barker; 3, Percy Hollingworth. Class E, for clubs, shops, hotels, &c.: R.W. Illingworth; 2, Miss Robinson; 3, Mrs. Burnand. The local councillors, Messrs. Joseph Briggs, Jonas Drake, and J.H. Barraclough, have given some excellent prizes, and Mr. F.W. Hill gave a special silver cup.

Bradford Observer Budget, 17 June 1911

The members of the Kipping Brotherhood had a most enjoyable ramble to Harden Beck on Saturday. A cricket match, Married v. Single, resulted in an absurdly easy win for the benedicts.

Bradford Observer Budget, 8 July 1911

CORONATION FESTIVITIES. The Coronation festivities were continued on Saturday last when all those over sixty years of age living in the Thornton Ward were entertained to a substantial repast in the United Methodist School. After tea they were entertained with selections on the gramophone. Later a concert took place in the Mechanics' Hall, the contributors to the programme being Mr. Henry Hibbert, of Bradford, who gave some exhibitions of the London Coronation procession. The United Methodist Church Prize Choir rendered part-songs, &c., solos being given by Miss E.A. Butterfield and Mr. W.H. Barker. Mr. Robinson Feather gave recitals. Mr. James Barraclough made an appropriate speech, referring to the customs which obtained in the village about seventy years ago, many of which were remembered by the old folk. Through the kindness of Mr. Joseph Craven, of Ashfield, the guests were permitted free access to his grounds. Mr. J.H. Barraclough presided at the meeting.

Bradford Observer Budget, 15 July 1911

The choir boys of St. James' Church, Thornton, had their annual trip to Morecambe last Saturday. The members of the Thornton Vocal Union spent a pleasant afternoon at Ogden on Saturday last. The juvenile members of the 'Goodwill Tent' Independent Order of Rechabites, Thornton, had their annual outing last Saturday, visiting the Zoo at Halifax.

Bradford Observer Budget, 29 July 1911

During the past few weeks there have been several cases of housebreaking in Thornton. Four houses close to the reservoir were entered last week, and on Saturday evening one of the largest houses in Thornton was visited, but fortunately one of the daughters happened to be about, and the thieves made good their escape.

Bradford Observer Budget, 19 August 1911

LANTERN LECTURE. In connection with the Thornton Temperance and Band of Hope Union, an open-air lecture, illustrated by lantern slides, was given on Sunday in Firth Street. The president, Mr. Thomas Barnard, took the chair. The lantern was manipulated by Mr. Orlando Knapton.

Bradford Observer Budget, 19 August 1911

THORNTON MAN'S DISAPPEARANCE. A warrant was issued on Monday last for the arrest of Edwin Wallbank, of Havelock Street, Thornton, who is charged with misappropriating funds contributed by the workpeople of Messrs. Thomas Ambler & Sons, worsted spinners, of Longside Lane, Thornton Road, Bradford, for the purpose of holidays. On Friday of last week, when the workpeople wished to withdraw their deposits, the treasurer was stated to have left home.

Bradford Observer Budget, 19 August 1911

LOCAL FEAST. During this week most of the mills and quarries have been closed down, and on Saturday last there was a large exodus of residents, the bookings to Morecambe, Blackpool, and other seaside places exceeding that of many previous years. Sunday last being 'Thornton Tide Sunday' the tramcars were busy all day, and many visitors walked as far as Ogden Moors. The Feast proper, which is held in a field, or rather on a 'tip' behind the New Inn, was almost without music, the joy wheel alone having an organ. The old folks expressed the opinion that it is a long time since Thornton had such a poor 'tide.' There were plenty of people, and it was very difficult to get about in the fairground, but the attractions were very poor indeed. This is accounted for by the fact that a suitable field cannot be obtained for this yearly event, and, of course, the caterers go where there is more scope.

Bradford Observer Budget, 19 August 1911

HOMING SOCIETY RACE. The Thornton Homing Society had a race on Saturday last from Ashchurch, the distance being 125 miles, with the following results: J. Stow, with a velocity of 777 yards; 2, J. Stow, 655; 3, J. Kitson, 638; 4, J. Stow, 622; 5, W. Sutcliffe. 607; 6, J. Stow, 601.

Bradford Daily Telegraph, 26 September 1911
THE MAGGOTORIUM
NEW THORNTON SANATORIUM
PLANS SENT TO DISTRICT COUNCIL

The new sanatorium at the maggotorium farm at Thornton is likely soon to be in actual evidence. Plans have been sent in and came before a committee of the Denholme District Council last night. These show a building capable of providing 100 shelters, of an up-to-date pattern, with perfect drainage, water from the Bradford Corporation mains, and a verandah five feet wide on each side of the perforated floor. The whole sewage is to be dealt with in a detritus tank, and percolating filters, and on the whole the sanitary arrangements are such that it is confidently believed the plans will receive the Council's approval at their ordinary meeting next Tuesday. There have been quite a number of patients undergoing treatment lately. One gentleman, Mr. Bryant says, has gained 6lbs of weight in ten days, after having come from a sanatorium in which his health showed no improvement. He has also, he says, a lad in for treatment who was rejected by the medical officer of the Bradford Sanatorium as too far advanced in consumption for treatment there, but he is improving at the Thornton establishment in a wonderful manner.

Bradford Daily Telegraph, 3 October 1911
THE MAGGOTORIUM
EXTENSION SCHEME DISCUSSED
DISTRICT COUNCIL GIVE SANCTION

The conflict between Mr. A. Bryant, the maggot king, and the Sanitary Authority of Denholme, with respect to the extension of the now famous maggotorium, reached a further stage this afternoon, when Mr. Bryant submitted new plans to the Denholme District Council. These showed a building capable of providing 100 shelters with proper arrangement, water from the Bradford Corporation mains, and a verandah five feet wide on each side of the perforated floor. It was arranged that the sewage should be dealt with in a detritus tank and percolating filters.

Mr. Jonathan Bairstow presided, and other members present were Messrs. Jonas Foster, Jacob Foster, Holden, Rushworth, W. Garnett Foster and Jowett.

The Deputy Clerk read a letter from Mr. Keywood the architect for Mr. Bryant, stating that the plans recently deposited were disapproved by the Council because they did not comply with their bye-laws relating to air space, ventilation, drainage and water supply. 'Your bye-laws' he added 'do not regulate air space, floor space or water supply, and therefore they could not be complied with. Adequate ventilation was shown and a written undertaking was given to comply with all the requirements of your surveyor with regard to drainage. Further, the disapproval was not given within one month as required by the Public Health Act, 1875.' What really happened, he continued, was that the Council had disapproved the plans under a misapprehension of their powers, and in consequence they were now submitting fresh plans for the approval of the Council. These plans, he ventured to say, were now in full compliance with the building bye-laws, but the question was a much wider one than that of mere approval of the plans.

Mr. Keywood added, 'Our proposals are two in number; (a) the adding of an upper storey to the existing building now used for breeding maggots, so as to enable the people who are inhaling the gases by sitting in the same room and at the side of the trough in which the maggots are actually breeding to inhale the gases in more wholesome surroundings and in better, cleaner and more hygienic conditions. It is not intended that the patients shall sleep there, and we will give a written undertaking as to this. We are not proposing to increase our plant for maggot breeding, and as a matter of fact there will be less nuisance, if any at present exists, because of the gases being inhaled by the patient instead of being diffused into the atmosphere. We should further be prepared to take such protective measures as may be considered necessary by your medical adviser to help prevent the escape of flies and to render the surplus gases innocuous. We do not intend to create another offensive trade, but by utilising the fumes or gases given off to reduce the objections to the existing trade; (b) the plans also propose sanitori for open-air treatment. They show a minimum floor space of 144 square feet and fulfil the other requirements of the Local Government Board as to air space, floor space, windows, aspect, water supply, and drainage. As a matter of fact, the plans have been designed from a hospital designed by me and approved by the Local Government Board.' He asked the Council to look at the matter in a sympathetic light and not to put difficulties in the way. The Clerk (Mr. W.A. Brigg) wrote to say that the Council could not now refuse to pass the plans, and suggested bye-laws to deal with the offensive trade. Dr. Jackson (Medical Officer) said the plans were now satisfactory, and they were passed on the proposition of Mr. Holden seconded by Mr. W. Garnett Foster.

Bradford Daily Telegraph, 9 October 1911

St. Peter's Mission Church, Thornton. In connection with the above mission church, on Saturday a social gathering was held on the occasion of the presentation to Mr. Herbert Walker. The present was in the form of a silver-mounted ebony walking stick and a silver-mounted silk umbrella, both articles being suitably inscribed. Mr. Walker has been connected with the mission for the last ten years as lay reader, organist and choir master, and in recognition of his services the presentation was made. Mrs. Hainsworth, one of the oldest workers, made the presentation and remarked on Mr. Walker's long and faithful services. He has now handed over the position to Mr. P.P. Fawcett, the blind organist, and hopes in the future to devote more of his time to more important work of the mission. After the presentation Mr. Walker suitably responded. The Rev. W.G. McNeice (curate of Thornton) presided, and also spoke of the good and faithful work at Hill Top of Mr. Walker. Songs, recitations, and readings were given at intervals by the Misses Hardcastle, Cummings, West, and Heap.

Yorkshire Observer Budget, 3 August 1912

EMPLOYEES OUTING. The overlookers, manager, and engineers of Messrs. Mark Dawson & Son, Limited, Prospect Mills, Thornton, spent a very enjoyable day at Southport on Saturday last. Messrs. Dale Slater, Arthur Jowett, and H. Hill spoke in a very appreciative manner of the firm's generosity, to which Mr. Mark Dawson, jun., briefly responded. The weather was moderately fine.

Yorkshire Observer Budget, 5 October 1912

CONSERVATIVE CLUB. The new Conservative Club in Thornton, which was formerly the Friendly Inn, has now been opened. The building has been reconstructed, renovated, and furnished at a cost of about £500. The membership this year has been increased by 21. The old premises in Kipping Lane had been occupied by the club for the past thirty-three years.

Yorkshire Observer Budget, 23 November 1912

Mr. Thomas Hindle, of Cliffe Cottage, Thornton, left estate of the value of £7,187.

Yorkshire Observer Budget, 23 November 1912

ACCIDENT IN A STATION GOODS YARD. A man named James Pearson (57) of Back Field, Thornton, while crossing the Great Northern Railway Company's goods yard at Thornton on Wednesday was caught between some tracks. His right arm was severely crushed near the shoulder and he sustained a lacerated wound over the right eye.

Yorkshire Observer Budget, 23 November 1912

THORNTON PEOPLE IN THE STATES

Mr. Fred Illingworth, an old Thornton man, now residing in Jamestown, New York, writes to notify the death of Mrs. Julia Illingworth Bush, of Main Street, Jamestown, after a week's illness. Mrs. Bush was born in Thornton, and went to the States

with her parents, Mr. and Mrs. John Holmes Illingworth, in 1885. She is survived by two brothers and a sister – Franklin and Fred Illingworth and Mrs. W. Hazeltine. Mr. Illingworth continues:-
The 'Observer Budget' was our regular weekly paper when we lived in England, and I remember we always looked forward with great pleasure to its appearance, and I know we could not find a better means of notifying our relatives and friends of our loss. Although only thirteen years of age when I left Thornton I remember very distinctly all the old-fashioned nooks and corners there, such as Coffin End, Pig Throat, Pinch Beck, Ben Ting, and others, and the old walled-in wells around Market Street – one across from the Shuttle shop, one across from the Kipping Church, and one up Back Field. The Old Church was also standing at that time, and the parts of the stocks, near the old burial ground, where I have three brothers and one sister buried. I hope to return some day and see what changes have been wrought in the old home town since we left in 1885. I remember very well Caleb Tapp, who was the schoolmaster at the Board School. He made a great impression on me, both mentally and physically.

Yorkshire Observer Budget, 8 February 1913

UNITED METHODIST CHOIR CONCERT. The choir connected with the United Methodist Church, Thornton, had their sixth annual tea and concert in the schoolroom on Saturday, and the attendance at both the tea and the concert was very good. The choir, in gipsy costumes, gave several choruses and part songs in excellent style, and solos were very well rendered by Misses E.A. Butterfield, Edith Butterfield, Cissie Letham and Lilian Pickles. The following represented the various characters in a humorous sketch entitled 'Mixem's Matrimonial Mart':- Messrs. E. Leach, W.H. Pickles, F.H. Barker, and E. Robinson, and Misses G. Butterfield and N. Emmett. The Rev. Frank Keyworth occupied the chair. On Sunday afternoon Mr. Fred Jowett, of Bradford, gave an organ recital in the Wesleyan Chapel. Miss Winnie Tapp was the soloist.

Yorkshire Observer Budget, 8 March 1913

The position of organist at the United Methodist Church, Thornton, recently vacated by Mr. Walter Horsfall, has been taken up by Mr. Hartley Bancroft, A. R.C.O., of Denholme. Mr. Bancroft has until recently been organist at Egypt Chapel, which is a branch of the United Methodist Church, Thornton.

Yorkshire Observer Budget, 8 March 1913

Mr. Henry Pickersgill, who up to six or seven years ago held the position of stationmaster at Thornton station, died suddenly on Monday last at his residence, Scansby Hall, Bradshaw, near

Halifax, where he had lived in retirement since he left Thornton. Mr. Pickersgill was the first stationmaster at Thornton, having occupied that position since 1878, when the Great Northern line was first opened. He was closely associated with the Wesleyan Chapel, at which place of worship he was one of the trustees. In December last, Mr. Pickersgill, who was 71 years of age, had a seizure, and it was a repetition of heart trouble which caused his death.

Yorkshire Observer Budget, 29 March 1913

THORNTON. ACCIDENT IN THE FOOTBALL FIELD. A very unfortunate accident happened to Victor Barker, overlooker, Corrie Fold, Thornton, on Monday morning last whilst engaged in a practice match on the Hill Top football field, Thornton. It appeared that Kipping Brotherhood Reserves should have played a team from Idle on Monday morning last, and as the latter team failed to appear it was decided to have a game with players selected from the spectators. It was in this game that Barker broke his leg a little above the ankle. He was medically attended and taken home.

Yorkshire Observer Budget, 12 April 1913

A CHILD IN A SEWAGE FILTER. A little girl has had an alarming experience at the Bradford Corporation sewage filters, situated at the bottom of Green Lane, Thornton. The attention of a party of golfers was attracted by the cries of children, and on going to the filters they found that a girl had fallen into one of the tanks containing black sludge. She appeared to be sinking slowly into the sludge, but was promptly rescued by Mr. Horace Kitchen and Mr. Alfred Farrar, assisted by two other gentlemen. Beyond soiled clothing she was little the worse. The girl's name was not ascertained.

Yorkshire Observer Budget, 1 November 1913

QUARRY ACCIDENT. Whilst engaged at a quarry at Headley, Thornton, on Tuesday, George Farrar, Hill Top, Thornton, was caught by a fall of earth and stone and injured to such an extent that his medical attendant ordered his removal to the Infirmary, where he was detained.

Chapter Twenty-Seven
1924–1938

Fowl play at Moorcock Farm – Fresh air and cold baths for Thornton scholars – New swimming baths for Thornton – Bull's Head pub closes for good with a sing-song – Aminadab drowns after death wish – Sunday school attendances down

Yorkshire Observer Budget, 12 September 1924

WATER PROPOSAL. A proposal to borrow £21,500 for the erection of a filter house (and incidental works) at the Thornton pressure filters is recommended to the Bradford City Council by the Water Committee, and it is proposed to appropriate 3,000 square yards of the Thornton Cemetery lands for the building.

Yorkshire Observer Budget, 12 April 1929

MISSING FOWLS. William Arthur Mills, farm labourer, Moorcock Farm, Thornton, Bradford, was at Rotherham remanded in custody and handed over to the Bradford police on a charge of having stolen six fowls, valued at a guinea, the property of his employer, Robert Drake, farmer, of the same address. Police-sergeant Booth said he arrested defendant last night, and when charged he replied: 'Yes, I have had the fowls. I sold them and spent the money. The boss said he would see me later.'

Yorkshire Observer Budget, 24 May 1929

THORNTON. The St. James' Church choir held their annual trip on Monday. They went by train from Thornton to Bridlington, where they spent a very enjoyable day.

Yorkshire Observer Budget, 7 June 1929

'OPEN YOUR WINDOWS.' 'Keep your windows open. Get into your cold baths. Get back to the hardiness of Britain,' was the advice given to the scholars of the Thornton Grammar School by the Rev. David Railton (Vicar of Bolton) at a special Founders' Day service held at Thornton Parish Church yesterday.

'I dare say there are a great many of us to-day who know perfectly well that we saw God much better when we were younger,' he said. 'Remember that and don't forget you boys and girls of to-day are going to have a wonderful time. You are going to have a better opportunity than people in this country have ever had before in history.'

A procession from the school to the church was headed by the Lord Mayor of Bradford (Alderman H. Thornton Pullan) and the Lady Mayoress (Miss Dorothy Horne) who were followed by the governors, the staff, the scholars, and the old boys.

The Lord Mayor read the first lesson and the head master (Mr. H.A. Beaton) the second.

Members of the Bradford City Council present included Alderman Thomas Sowden, Mr. Walter Hodgson, Mr. George Muff, M.P., and Mr. Fred Spencer.

Yorkshire Observer Budget, 28 June 1929

THORNTON. The Mothers' Union, St. James' Church, held their annual outing which took the form of a chara trip to Blackpool.

Yorkshire Observer Budget, 12 July 1929

AN AMBITION REALISED. Thorntonians, who in the last 20 years or so have become a little sceptical about the prospect of securing public baths for their district, will have visible and official proof that their ambition is to be realized when the foundation stone of the new baths is laid on Monday. The ceremony will be performed by Mr. Tom Ashworth, the energetic chairman of the Baths Committee, who, since he was elected to the chair, has been indefatigable in his efforts to improve the services of his department.

The new baths will, of course, be much more than baths. As is usual in buildings of this kind nowadays the swimming pool will be covered in winter, and a fine hall will be available for dances and other social gatherings. There will even be a cinema operating room.

Yorkshire Observer Budget, 16 August 1929

The Thornton Church Lads' Brigade, under the leadership of the Rev. A.H. Tollit, are spending this week under canvas at Ingleton.

Yorkshire Observer Budget, 25 October 1929

LICENCE TRANSFERRED. The last night of the Bull's Head as a public house was marked by a sing-song. The premises are to be pulled down for street improvements, and the licence has been transferred to the Black Horse Hotel, West Lane. Mr. G.A. Phillips, landlord of the Bull's Head, has removed to the Black Horse, which was opened on Thursday with a concert and supper.

Yorkshire Observer Budget, 11 April 1930

DESIRE TO SLEEP. That he had said it would be 'good if he could sleep for ever' a few days before he was found drowned 100 yards from his home was the statement made by a witness at the inquest on Tuesday on Aminadab Wilkinson, aged 75, a former cloth weaver, of Albion Place, Thornton.

A verdict of 'Suicide, with insufficient evidence to show the state of the man's mind at the time' was returned.

Yorkshire Observer Budget, 11 April 1930

FARMER PROSECUTED. A dispute at Thornton between a farmer, Fred Greenwood, and a young husband, Basil Illingworth, out walking with his wife, led to Greenwood being summoned at the West Riding Police Court, Bradford, yesterday.

Illingworth said Greenwood hit him over the fingers with a heavy walking stick, as the result of which he had to seek medical attention. Greenwood declared that Illingworth hit him with a stone 'on top o' t' 'ead.'

Greenwood had to pay 40s and 10s costs.

Yorkshire Observer Budget, 31 October 1930

WATER PRESSURE. Gangs of workmen were busy from an early hour on Tuesday repairing the water main at the Thornton tram terminus which burst shortly before one o'clock. It is stated that the burst was caused by excessive water pressure. The main burst with a noise like a clap of thunder, and a gap several feet wide was torn in the pipe. Torrents of water rushed down the road, and 15 yards of pavement were damaged. Cellars in a house and a fried fish shop, occupied by Mr. F. Dewhirst, were flooded. Mr. Dewhirst showed a 'Budget' reporter his cellars, where buckets of potatoes and fish boxes, with other things, had been hurled about by the force of the water, which had burst through the top cellar window, taking the window frame in its course, and sweeping everything before it. In the road there was a deep subsidence in the setts with a hole in the centre from which the water shot like an immense fountain.

Yorkshire Observer Budget, 27 June 1936

NEWS FROM THORNTON. GRAMMAR SCHOOL SPORTS. The boys and girls of the Thornton Grammar School, Bradford, gave their annual gymnastic display in the grounds of Thornton Hall on Saturday afternoon. The programme included educational gymnastics, Scandinavian dancing, gymnastic games, primitive gymnastics, Greek dancing, skittle ball, and an exhibition of vaulting and agility.

Yorkshire Observer Budget, 4 July 1936

MEN'S OUTING. The members of the St. James's Church (Thornton) men's class had an outing on Saturday to Yeadon aerodrome. They spent an enjoyable afternoon inspecting the aerodrome machines guided by one of the officers.

Yorkshire Observer Budget, 16 January 1937

'Co-op' President. A quarter of a century of service to the Thornton Co-operative Society will shortly be completed by Mr. Spencer Hainsworth, of Prospect House, Thornton, who for the whole of that period has been president. It is a tribute to his ability and popularity that he has been their only president – he accepted the position when the society was founded nearly 25 years ago – and his long record of service is ample evidence of his interest in Co-operative matters. Mr. Hainsworth has served the district, of which he is a native, in several other capacities. He has been president of the Thornton Welfare Council for three years; he is today the oldest member of the Thornton Lodge of Foresters, for whom he has acted as president and also as sick steward; and at one period he was president of the Mechanics' Institute at Thornton. He is the only surviving member of the old Thornton Urban District Council Board.

Yorkshire Observer Budget, 6 August 1938

THORNTON. SCHOLARS' TREAT. The New Road Congregational Church on Saturday had arranged to hold their annual teachers' and scholars' walk to a field at Alderscholes Farm, kindly lent for the occasion by Mr. Harold Ambler. They met at the school, but on account of the inclement weather it was decided to have their buns and tea in the schoolroom. Games and competitions were then held in the schoolroom during the afternoon and evening.

Yorkshire Observer Budget, 20 August 1938

THORNTON. Over £400 raised by Sunday Schools. Although there is a decrease in the attendance of scholars at the Sunday Schools in Thornton, the parents and friends, along with the teachers and scholars, raised the sum of £444 12s 4d at the Sunday School anniversaries during the year. The amounts were as follows: Egypt Methodist Church, £46 5s 11d; Bethesda Methodist Church, £77 13s 11½d; New Road Congregational Church, £60; Thornton Road Methodist Church, £60 12s 5½d; Thornton Parish Church, £20; and Kipping Independent Church, £180.

Yorkshire Observer Budget, 20 August 1938

Bequest to Vicar. The Vicar of Thornton (the Rev. Arthur Henry Tollit) has been left £100 and the vicarage of Abbeydale, near Sheffield,, by his late friend, Mr. Charles Badcock, of Combe Road, Croydon, Surrey, who left £6,480 (net personalty £2,478).

Yorkshire Observer Budget, 3 September 1938

TENNIS CLUB FETE. The New Road Congregational Church tennis club held a garden party on their tennis ground. Tennis, games and competitions were held, and a picnic tea was served during the afternoon. The proceeds were in aid of the funds of the tennis club.

Yorkshire Observer Budget, 3 September 1938

Thornton Methodist Church Operatic Society's Garden Party. The Thornton Road Methodist Church Operatic Society on Saturday held a garden party in the grounds of Rosedean, the residence of Mr. and Mrs. Christopher Watkin. Games and competitions were played, and in the afternoon a picnic tea was held on the lawn. The proceeds were in aid of the society's funds.

Yorkshire Observer Budget, 17 September 1938

THORNTON FESTIVAL. The harvest festival services were held at the Kipping (Thornton) Independent Congregational Chapel on Sunday. The preacher morning and evening was the Rev. H.M. Davies. There was special singing by the choir, under the leadership of Mr. H.V. Ashton, who presided at the organ. At the close of the evening service flowers and fruit were distributed to the sick and aged people of the village.

Yorkshire Observer Budget, 17 September 1938

OUTING TO LONDON. The St. James' Church, Thornton, Men's Class had an outing to London on Saturday. They left Thornton at noon and arrived back at 5.30 a.m. on Sunday morning, after having had an enjoyable outing. Tea was served on the train, and they were shown around London by the Polytechnic representative, who, along with Mr. Jack Hainsworth, secretary of the class, made all the arrangements.

Yorkshire Observer Budget, 24 September 1938

FORCED LANDING. While instructing an air guard on Saturday Mr. Angus Dunlop lost his bearings in a cloud. His petrol was running low and he made a forced landing in a field behind the Thornton Fireclay Works. After having tea in a neighbouring house, both returned home by car. The machine was dismantled and taken back to Yeadon aerodrome on Sunday.

Bull's Head Inn, Market Street.

Thornton Grammar School gymnasts.

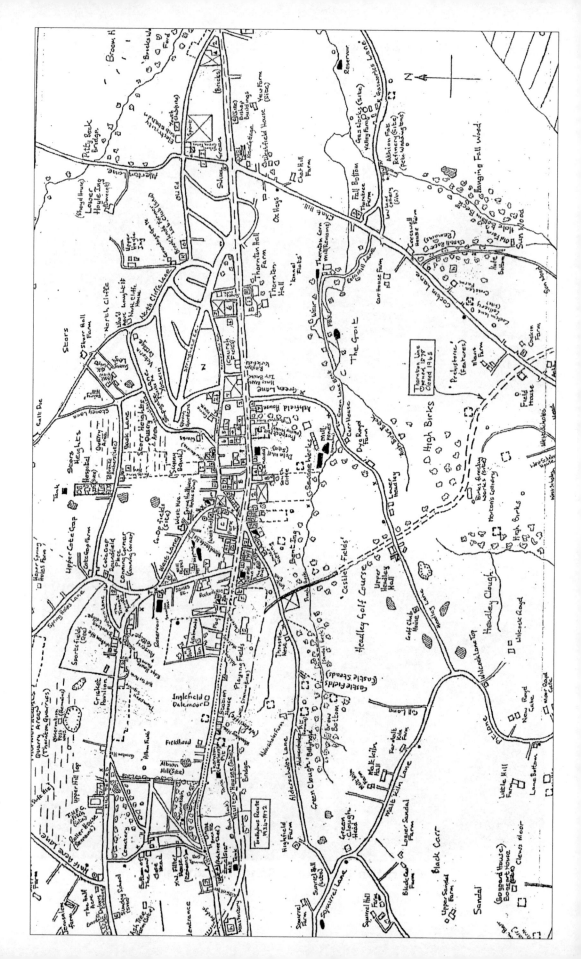

Yorkshire Observer Budget, 1 October 1938

MILITARY WHIST DRIVE. A military whist drive was held on Saturday in the St. James' Church (Thornton) Sunday School. The M.C. was Mr. Henry Kitching, and the prize-winners were Mr. and Mrs. Thomas Coulson.

Yorkshire Observer Budget, 1 October 1938

NEW ROAD CHURCH. The New Road Methodist Church, Thornton, held their harvest festival services on Sunday. The preacher morning and evening was the Rev. W.E. Stockley, of Bradford. In the afternoon a musical service was held, and the soloists were Miss Nellie Priestley and Master Eric Whalley. At the close of the evening service flowers and fruit were distributed to the sick and aged people of the village. On Monday evening, in the schoolroom, the Rev. W.E. Stockley delivered a lecture on 'Wonders of Earth, Sea, and Sky.' At the conclusion of the lecture a fruit banquet was held. The proceeds were in aid of the church funds.

Yorkshire Observer Budget, 8 October 1938

PARISH CHURCH. The harvest festival services were held at Thornton Parish Church on Sunday. The preacher in the morning was the Vicar (Rev. A.H. Tollit). In the afternoon the Rev. C. Hindle (Vicar of Cullingworth) and in the evening the Rev. L.D. Talbot (of Leeds) were the preachers. There was special singing by the choir under the conductorship of Mr. Harry Kitching, and Mr. Horace Platt played the organ. At the conclusion of the evening service, flowers and fruit were distributed to the aged and sick people in the village.

Yorkshire Observer Budget, 8 October 1938

COOKERY DEMONSTRATIONS. Cookery demonstrations were given in the Thornton New Road Methodist Sunday school on Tuesday and Wednesday by Mrs. George Waddington, of Thornton. The proceeds were in aid of the funds of the Thornton District Nursing Association.

Yorkshire Observer Budget, 5 November 1938

THORNTON 'FAIR.' Openers in Picturesque Costumes. Children in picturesque 'Dutch' costumes opened a 'Dutch Fair' at Thornton Church Schools on Saturday afternoon. They presented appropriate songs and dances. Miss Nora Moulds performed the opening ceremony on their behalf with Master Brian Sydes in the chair, and expressions of thanks were given by Roy Jennings, Agnes Pickles, Alan Whitaker, and Vera Newton. In the evening Mrs. G. Drake was the opener and Mr. Fred Spencer presided. On the previous day Mrs. Fred Walton (Bradford Moor) was the opener in the afternoon, and the Lord Mayor and Lady Mayoress (Alderman and Mrs. H. Hudson) officiated in the evening, the chairman being the Rev. W.G. McNeice (Bowling) and the Rev. A.H. Tollit (Vicar of Thornton). The choir gave entertainments in the evenings of both days. The decorations and dresses were features of the fair, which was a most successful event. Thanks must go to all workers, and especially is great praise due to members of the efforts committee, the secretary for which is Mr. G. Bairstow, and the treasurer, Mr. J. Hardy. The principal stall attendants were: Mrs. J.R. Hainsworth, Mrs. C. Hainsworth, Miss E. Nichol, Miss L. Ingham, Mrs. H. Hainsworth, Mrs. J. Hardy, Mrs. J. Pearce, Mrs. G. Bairstow, Miss E. Jackson, Mrs. A. Jackson, Scouts under the direction of Mr. F. Tiltson, Mrs. R. Smith, Miss E. Allen, Miss M. Robinson, Mr. F.J. Bairstow and Miss M. Binns.

Yorkshire Observer Budget, 12 November 1938

'PLOT' SUPPER. The members of the New Road Congregational Sunday School held a 'Plot' fire on their tennis court adjoining the Sunday School on Saturday. It was followed by a mashed potato and sausage supper, and social evening. There was a good attendance, and an enjoyable evening was spent.

Lightning Source UK Ltd.
Milton Keynes UK
09 December 2009

147267UK00001B/15/P